THE APOTHECARY CHEF

NATASHA MACALLER
PHOTOGRAPHY BY
MANJA WACHSMUTH

KYLE BOOKS

**To Michael,
With my love, joy and edible gifts
from the garden XX**

First published in Great Britain in 2026 by Kyle Books,
an imprint of Octopus Publishing Group Ltd
Carmelite House, 50 Victoria Embankment
London EC4Y 0DZ
www.octopusbooks.co.uk

An Hachette UK Company
www.hachette.co.uk

The authorised representative in the EEA is Hachette Ireland,
8 Castlecourt Centre, Dublin 15, D15 XTP3, Ireland
(email: info@hbgi.ie)

Text copyright (except for guest recipes)
© Natasha MacAller 2026
Photography copyright © Manja Wachsmuth 2026
Design and layout copyright
© Octopus Publishing Group 2026
Photo on page 133 © Julia Komp and Anne Kerne 2026

Aloha Pineapple Kimchi with Teriyaki Salmon (page 28)
adapted with permission from *Spicebox Kitchen: Eat Well and
Be Healthy with Globally Inspired, Vegetable-Forward Recipes* by
Linda Shiue MD (Balance/Hachette Book Group, 2021)
Dushpra, Cherries, Lamb & Sweet Spice Dumplings (page 14)
reproduced with permission from *Honey & Co: Food from the
Middle East* by Sarit Packer and Itamar Srulovich (Saltyard, 2014)

Distributed in the US by Hachette Book Group
1290 Avenue of the Americas, 4th and 5th Floors
New York, NY 10104

Distributed in Canada by Canadian Manda Group
664 Annette St., Toronto, Ontario, Canada M6S 2C8

All rights reserved. No part of this work may be reproduced
or utilized in any form or by any means, electronic or
mechanical, including photocopying, recording or by any
information storage and retrieval system, without the prior
written permission of the publisher.

Natasha MacAller asserts the moral right to be identified
as the author of this work.

ISBN 978-1-80419-280-1

A CIP catalogue record for this book is available from the
British Library.

Printed and bound in Dubai.

10 9 8 7 6 5 4 3 2 1

Publisher: Joanna Copestick
Art director: Yasia Williams
Senior developmental editor: Pauline Bache
Copyeditors: Vicky Orchard, Caroline West
and Corinne Colvin
Designer: Rachel Cross
Assistant production manager: Allison Gonsalves

CONTENTS

Introduction	4
GOOD FOR THE GUT	6
EVERYDAY JOY	42
A SENSE OF CALM	70
IMMUNITY BOOSTERS	94
LONGEVITY & RESILIENCE	126
BREATH & BALANCE	156
Beneficial Edible Plants	182
Beneficial Edible Plants References	226
Glossary	228
The Chefs & Experts	229
Useful Resources	236
Index	237
Acknowledgements	240

INTRODUCTION

The Apothecary Chef is a celebration of the fragrance and flavour of herbs, flowers, leaves, seeds, fruit, roots and pollens, all containing beneficial nutrients, whether harvested from faraway fields and waters, gathered at the local farmers' market, pulled from a garden bed, or pinched from the kitchen window box. These pages contain over 75 recipes starring more than 60 plant-based ingredients that are mixed, matched and blended for ultimate flavour, nutritional value and deliciousness!

My Father's veggie garden was planted into my memory from the age of six. He taught me how to make thumb-sized holes in the soil so many inches apart then drop two tiny seeds into the earth and cover just so. As the plants and flowers flourished, I was mesmerized by the rich colours, inspiring me to sketch rainbows into my childish signature; fully and joyfully aware of the gift to see colours.

Into adulthood, and as a chef, I also discovered how to smell and taste colour, through the use of these fragrant herbs, plants and flowers. Inspiration came from an array of softly scented pink English pea petals – their shocking bright green pods, stems and windy tendrils wrapped around the garden fence stretching to the sun. The addictive scent of sun-ripened backyard tomato vines as you reach for that heavy, bright red, homegrown tomato, will have you craving a flavoursome 'no recipe' seasonal plate of sliced rounds, topped with a handful of petite yellow, red, purple and green tomatoes, sprinkled with a few grains of mineral-rich sea salt flakes, bright green bruised basil leaves, a splash of balsamic vinegar, drops of Spanish cold-pressed olive oil, then finished with a few tiny white basil flowers floating on the shiny oil surface, all working in harmony to create an unforgettable warm summer's garden taste. Here is a little bit of heaven.

This delicious dive into the *Apothecary Chef* world features six chapters presenting recipes such as: Root, Rice Leek & Nettle Soup, Sticky Chicken Meatballs with homemade Ketjap Manis or Crispy Peach Amandine Dumplings with Pickled Rhubarb & a Coconut-Yuzu Whipped Posset. In addition, forty guest chef contributions include Ben Shewry's Shiitake Broth with aromatic Herbs, David Lebovitz's Tarragon Vinaigrette spooned over an Heirloom Tomato & Mozzarella Salad and Elizabeth Falkner's Out of this World Vegan Tacos.

Plant folklore and medicinal benefits are vetted with the assistance of my generous culinary medical team to verify the nutritional and beneficial secrets of these harvested ingredients. Along with my worldwide team of rockstar chefs, my medical experts have all contributed their own recipes too.

In addition, there are tricks and tips for shopping seasonally, harvesting and storing (or 'putting by'), plus handy preserving recipes to make your own hard-to-find ingredients. These recipes, showcasing beneficial herbs and plants, come from a worldwide array of cuisines, chefs and fresh ingredients.

Included within is advice for growing many of these advantageous edibles in your garden: be it in a plant pot, cozy window box, garden bed or even a freshwater stream or pond.

Or imagine the idea of nibbling on beneficial herbs and leaves grown in space? Or even harvesting nutrient-dense vegetables on the moon? According to the brilliant team of nutritionist chefs from the Canadian Space Agency (CSA), ongoing trials growing and eating densely nutritious greens from watercress to spinach, kale and chilies in sunless microgravity are showing promising results within the confines of the International Space Station. It is a beginning to the future.

In the meantime, let's go explore!

Chapter 1

GOOD FOR THE GUT

Jim Dodge

Overnight Oat Berries
with Avocado & Maple Syrup

avocado | maple syrup

SERVES 1

60g (2¼oz) oat berries
200ml (7fl oz) water
½ avocado
1 tablespoon pure maple syrup
70ml (2½fl oz) Greek yogurt or cottage cheese (optional)

'Whole oat berries, or groats, are the least processed form of oats. They are the whole kernels of the oats that have had the outer husk removed but still retain their bran, germ and endosperm layers. They have a nuttier flavour and more distinct texture compared to rolled, steel-cut or crushed oats and, combined with avocado, form a beneficial blood-sugar lowering meal.'

1. The night before, put the oat berries into a small saucepan with a lid and add the measured water. Place over a medium-high heat and bring to the boil. Turn off the heat and cover the pot with a lid. Let it stand on the stove overnight.

2. In the morning, cut the avocado into bite-sized chunks and set aside. Remove the lid; the oats should have swollen in size, be tender, and have absorbed most of the water. Tilt the pan to its side and, if no water remains, add an extra tablespoon of water. Reheat the oats over a medium heat until hot, then remove from the heat and stir in the avocado chunks.

3. Spoon into a bowl and pour the maple syrup over the top. For additional protein, garnish with plain Greek yogurt or cottage cheese, if liked.

Natasha MacAller

My Garden Ratatouille

artichoke | garlic | tulsi (holybasil)

A family favourite comfort dish, with the addition of artichoke hearts, this was inspired by a simple boquet garni of basil from Alice Waters's 'Chez Panisse Vegetables'. A hearty French vegetarian meal, it can be enjoyed as a starter with a chunk of warm bread smeared with extra virgin olive oil or as a main. Ratatouille is at its best when your garden tomatoes are at their juiciest peak, but it is truly appetizing in any season. It can be made a day ahead, as it tastes delicious the next day, too!

SERVES 4 AS A MAIN OR 8 AS A SIDE DISH

1 aubergine, about 300g (10½oz), cut into 1cm (½ inch) cubes
2 teaspoons sea salt
200g (7oz) artichoke hearts, frozen and thawed, or fresh and steamed, or canned in water and drained
olive oil, for frying and drizzling
10 garlic cloves, about 50g (1¾oz), chopped
1 carrot, about 100g (3½oz), peeled and grated
2 small jalapeños, deseeded and thinly sliced
1 large bunch of basil** and 1 small bunch of tulsi (holy basil), tied with twine
2 onions, about 600g (1lb 5oz), chopped
3 peppers, 2 red and 1 green, about 250g (9oz), cut into 1cm (½ inch) cubes
3 courgettes, about 300g (10½oz), cut into 1cm (½ inch) cubes
2–3 large tomatoes, about 500g (1lb 2oz), peeled and cored, or whole peeled canned tomatoes, or a little of each to equal about 500g (1lb 2oz)*, cut into 1cm (½ inch) cubes
sea salt and freshly ground black pepper

To serve
lemon juice, to taste
3 tablespoons capers, plus 1 teaspoon brine
small handful of flat leaf parsley, chopped
thinly sliced preserved lemon peel (optional)

1. Put the aubergine into a colander with a plate underneath. Scatter with the salt and toss to distribute evenly. Cover with a towel and leave to drain while you prepare the other ingredients.

2. Quarter the artichoke hearts, then spread them on a kitchen paper-lined tray to drain any excess liquid. Set aside.

3. Squeeze handfuls of the aubergine to extract any excess liquid, then squeeze dry the cubes with kitchen paper and transfer them to a small bowl. Discard the excess liquid.

4. In a heavy pan or large straight-sided frying pan with a lid, heat a few tablespoonfuls of olive oil over a medium heat until the oil begins to shimmer. Add the aubergine cubes in a single layer and cook, stirring occasionally, until golden brown on all sides. Using a slotted spoon, transfer the aubergine to a plate.

5. In the same pan, add 3 more tablespoons of oil, then the onions and cook for 6–8 minutes until translucent and tender. Stir in the garlic, carrot and jalapeños and lay the bouquet of basil on top, reserving a handful of leaves for garnish. Cover and let it steam for a few minutes. Remove the lid, adding a dash of oil if needed, then stir in the peppers and cook for a few minutes. Add the courgette, artichokes and tomatoes, cover and let it steam for 5 minutes.

6. Lastly, stir in the aubergine and cook for 15–20 minutes until the vegetables are just fork tender, gently stirring now and again to meld the flavours together.

7. Remove the basil bouquet, squeezing the basil juices into the pan, then season to taste with lemon juice, salt and black pepper. Finish with a good drizzle of oil, a scattering of the capers, the reserved fresh basil leaves, chopped parsley and preserved lemon peel, if using. Ladle into bowls and serve hot or cold.

*Feel free to substitute ingredients – if the tomatoes are good looking but tasteless, substitute 3 large tomatoes and add a 400g (14oz) can of whole peeled plum tomatoes.

**If fresh basil is unavailable, substitute 3 tablespoons basil paste.

Maria Kalenska

Spring Borsch
with Nettles

nettles | onion | dill

SERVES 8–10

50ml (2fl oz) sunflower or vegetable oil
2 onions, 1 roughly chopped and 1 finely chopped
1 carrot, peeled and roughly chopped
3 litres (5¼ pints) water
1kg (2lb 4oz) shin of beef with bone
2 bay leaves
3–4 black peppercorns
300g (10½oz) potatoes, peeled and cubed
4 eggs
150g (5½oz) nettles, finely chopped
300g (10½oz) spinach, finely chopped
100g (3½oz) flat leaf parsley, finely chopped
100g (3½oz) dill, finely chopped
50g (1¾oz) green onions, finely chopped
salt
soured cream, to serve

'Traditionally in Odessa, green borsch is served with a side of soured cream. It gives the slightly sour soup a more delicate and creamy taste, creating the perfect balance of flavour, and also adds a fresh note to the dish and makes the borsch thicker. Greek yogurt works just as well: one tablespoon per serving and you're good to go.'

1. For the broth, heat half the oil in a large pan over a medium heat. Add the roughly chopped onion and carrot and fry for 3 minutes. Pour the measured water into the pan. Add the beef, bay leaves, black peppercorns and season with salt. Bring to the boil, then skim the white residue off the top. Reduce the heat to low and simmer for 40 minutes. Remove the meat from the broth, transfer to a separate bowl, cut into large cubes and set aside. Discard the onion, carrot and bay leaves from the broth.

2. Add the potatoes to the broth and simmer for a further 15 minutes, until the potatoes are cooked. Heat the remaining oil in a frying pan over a medium heat. Add the finely chopped onion and fry for 10–15 minutes until golden brown. Remove from the heat.

3. In a bowl beat the eggs with 2 tablespoons of water until smooth. Stirring the broth slowly, pour in the egg mixture. Remove from the heat. Add the beef, fried onions, nettles, spinach, parsley, dill and green onions and season with salt. Cover with a lid and leave the borsch to rest for 5 minutes. Serve the green borsch hot with soured cream.

Itamar Srulovich & Sarit Packer

Dushpra
Cherries, Lamb & Sweet Spice Dumplings

alliums | mint | tarragon

MAKES 16

For the dumpling dough
200g (7oz) '00' flour
½ teaspoon salt
1 egg
40g (1½oz) butter, softened
about 60ml (4 tablespoons) water

For the sweet spice mix
6 cloves
½ a nutmeg, grated
10 cardamom pods
1 teaspoon whole fennel seeds
2 teaspoons whole mahleb seeds
3 teaspoons ground ginger
4 teaspoons ground cinnamon

For the braised shank
1 large lamb shank, at least 550g (1lb 4oz)
½ onion, skin and all
2 garlic cloves, unpeeled
2 star anise
1 cinnamon stick
2 teaspoons sweet spice mix (see below)
½ teaspoon salt
2 tablespoons sour cherry jam

For the filling
the cooked lamb, about 190g (6½oz)
30g (1oz) dried sour cherries, roughly chopped
½ teaspoon sweet spice mix (see above)
3 mint sprigs, leaves picked and chopped

For the sauce
100g (3½oz) cooked chickpeas, roughly 40g (1½oz) if starting from dried, or use canned
12 cherries, halved and pitted
fresh mint or tarragon leaves, to serve

'Original dushpra is a soup flavoured with cherries and lamb, with tiny dumplings floating in it. We loved the flavours but making the little dumplings would take up all our time. We decided to super-size the dumplings and turn this into a main course. It is still heinously time-consuming and fiddly, but it is a true stunner, and is the only dish we know that will stretch one lamb shank to feed four, and do it with incredible style.'

1. Start by making the dough. Mix the flour with the salt, egg and soft butter, then add a teaspoon of water at a time until it all comes together into a nice smooth dough. Cover it with clingfilm and keep in the refrigerator until needed.

2. Make the sweet spice mix. Toast the first 5 spices in a dry pan over a medium heat. Allow to cool, finely grind, and then mix in the remaining spices. Store in a sealed container until needed.

3. Place the lamb shank in a large pan with all the other braising ingredients and cover with water. Bring to the boil and skim any foam that comes to the top. Reduce the heat to a constant simmer, cover and cook for about 1½ hours until the meat comes away from the bone easily.

4. Strain and retain all the cooking liquid, pick out all the meat and discard the rest. Pour the cooking liquid back in the pan, add the chickpeas and set on the hob to simmer uncovered until reduced by half. This will be the sauce for your dumplings later on.

5. Shred the meat and mix it with the other filling ingredients. Taste and check for salt – you may want to add a pinch.

6. Roll out the dough as thinly as you can. If you have a pasta machine it would work well for this, but we usually just do it by hand as then we can roll the whole amount at once. Try to keep the dough in a square, so that you have no trimmings or waste. Cut the dough into a 4 × 4 grid of squares, each about the size of a drinks coaster (about 6cm/2½inches square). Divide the lamb filling evenly between them, so that you have a little heap in the centre of each one.

7. Brush the edges of the dough with a little water (to help them stick), fold each square corner-to-corner into a triangle to cover the filling and press down the edges to seal. I like to then take the two outer corners, fold them around my finger and pinch together, so that they look like little tortellini. Boil a large pot of salted water and drop the dumplings in for 3 minutes. Then transfer them to the reduced stock and add the cherries. Heat together for a minute or two to warm through, then serve with fresh mint or tarragon leaves on top.

Elmo Agatep

Tinolang Manok
Chicken Tinola

moringa

SERVES 6–8

2–3 tablespoons vegetable oil
4–6 garlic cloves, peeled and minced
1 onion, chopped
2 thumb-sized pieces of fresh root ginger, peeled and julienned
1 large whole chicken, about 1.8kg (4lb), quartered
1.5–2 litres (2¾–3½ pints) water
1–2 chicken stock cubes
1 large green (unripe) papaya, about 900g (2lb), seeded and cubed
30–60g (1–2¼oz) moringa (malunggay) leaves
50–100g (1¾–3½oz) siling labuyo, or spinach or hot pepper leaves if you can't find siling labuyo
2–3 tablespoons fish sauce, to taste
freshly ground black pepper
cooked long grain or basmati rice, to serve

'Malunggay, or moringa, was ubiquitous in many of the meals my family prepared for me growing up in the Philippines, but it is only recently that I have begun to appreciate the health-promoting benefits of this humble plant. It's rich in many essential nutrients like vitamins A, B1, B2, B3, C, calcium, potassium, iron, zinc and phosphorus. Packed with antioxidants and phytochemicals, Moringa is thought to have anti-inflammatory, antibacterial and antifungal properties.'

1. Heat the oil in a large saucepan or casserole dish over a medium-low heat. Add the garlic, onion and ginger and sauté for 5–7 minutes. When the onion starts to become transparent or lightly caramelizes, add the chicken. Lightly brown the chicken over a medium heat for about 10 minutes, then add about 5 grinds of freshly ground black pepper, or to taste.

2. Pour in enough of the water to cover the chicken and bring to a simmer. Reduce the heat to low-medium, crumble in the stock cubes, cover and gently simmer for about 30 minutes.

3. Add the papaya and stir together. Continue to let it simmer, covered, for another 5–7 minutes.

4. Add the moringa and siling labuyo or spinach and pour in the fish sauce. Simmer briefly, for 2–3 minutes, to gently cook the moringa and siling labuyo or spinach leaves.

5. Ladle the Tinolang Manok into individual serving bowls and serve aside platefuls of steamy white rice. Growing up I would take small spoonfuls of chicken pieces and moringa-packed juices as they soaked into the rice, and savour each small bite of the flavourful family meal – nourishing our bodies and souls.

Olia Hercules

Salted Herbs for Winter

dill | parsley | wild garlic

MAKES 1 × 350ML (12FL OZ) JAR

200g (7oz) washed herbs and greens, such as dill, curly leaf or flat leaf parsley, spring onions, sorrel and wild garlic, finely chopped
25g (1oz) sea salt

'There is so much talk around fermentation, it has become the buzzword of our age. But my interest in fermentation processes began long before it became the norm today. My grandmother used to preserve fresh herbs in salt because, in Ukraine, fresh herbs were unavailable during the winter months. And Ukrainians always cook with herbs, it would be incomprehensible to not, so she found a way to be able to keep them throughout the cold season.

'These mixtures of salt and herbs would ferment and although they lost their vibrancy, they were delicious. I make these herby salts often but the flavour can become a bit intense. If that happens, just rinse them off before you add them to any soups or stews.'

1. Mix all the herbs together. Put a layer of herbs in the base of a sterilized 350ml (12fl oz) jar with a lid and sprinkle over some of the salt. Now add another layer of herbs and more salt, pressing the herbs down with your hand. Keep alternating these layers until you run out of herbs and salt, packing them in tightly as you go.

2. Cover with a lid and leave at room temperature for 2–3 days (you might want to push the herbs down a little further on the second day). Once a layer of liquid has formed at the top, move the jar to the cellar or refrigerator, where the salted herbs will keep for several months.

Allium & Wild Mushroom
Spinach Galette

alliums | lovage | oregano

Allium. This silky-smooth sounding word is the family name for all things onion, including shallots, leeks, chives and garlic. The firmer alliums such as onions, shallots and garlic are ideal for confit; garlic confit being the most popular. The low and slow process of confit uses two ingredients: olive oil and peeled alliums. The alliums keep meltingly soft and sweet for two weeks refrigerated and submerged in the olive oil. Here is a sublime sharing dish highlighting the onion.

SERVES 4–6

20g (¾oz) Parmesan or Parmigiano Reggiano cheese, grated
80g (2¾oz) waxy baby potatoes, red rose, Desiree or similar, unpeeled, thinly sliced and poached
80g (2¾oz) mixed mushrooms, such as shiitake, chestnut, portobello and chanterelle, brushed clean
zest of 1 lemon
1 tablespoon fresh oregano leaves or 1 teaspoon dried oregano
1 egg
1 teaspoon whole or semi-skimmed milk or water
2 teaspoons poppy seeds
1 teaspoon flaky sea salt

For the allium confit
60g (2¼oz) shallots, peeled and halved if large
60g (2¼oz) baby onions, blanched in boiling water 10 seconds, then peeled and shocked in an ice bath
olive or grapeseed oil (or a combination), to cover
20g (¾oz) garlic cloves, peeled
2 thyme sprigs

For the dough
200g (7oz) plain flour, plus extra for dusting
1 teaspoon ground cumin
1 teaspoon granulated sugar
big pinch flaky sea salt
115g (4oz) unsalted butter or shortening
25–50ml (1–2fl oz) ice-cold water

For the creamy spinach
45ml (3 tablespoons) whole milk
60ml (4 tablespoons) double cream
½ onion, minced
1 tablespoon olive oil
1 tablespoon plain flour
40g (1½oz) full fat cream cheese
300g (10½oz) spinach leaves and tender stems, washed and dried
½ teaspoon minced garlic
¼ teaspoon pimentón
freshly grated nutmeg
white pepper and flaky sea salt

To garnish
20g (¾oz) pickled lovage or celery (use the same quantities and method as the quick pickled coriander on page 100)
3–4 halved or 2–3 sliced tiny cherry tomatoes
baby salad or spinach leaves

1. First, make the allium confit. Place the prepared shallots and baby onions in a small pan and pour in oil to cover. Bring to a simmer, then reduce the heat and poach for 15 minutes. Add the garlic and thyme and poach low and slow creating a shimmer on the surface with a minimal amount of bubbles for 1½–2 hours until the alliums are falling apart and light golden in colour.

2. To make the dough, whisk together the flour, cumin and sugar with a big pinch of salt in a mixing bowl. Rub in the butter with your fingertips or a pastry cutter until pea-sized. Drizzle in the ice-cold water, tossing gently with a fork or your fingers to combine. If the dough does not hold together, add a bit more water but don't overwork it. Turn the dough out on to a lightly dusted surface and gather it into a ball. Pat out and fold over twice. Wrap tightly in clingfilm and chill for 1 hour.

3. Meanwhile, make the creamy spinach. Heat the milk and cream in a small saucepan over a medium heat until scalding hot. Remove

continued overleaf

from the heat and set aside. In another pan, sauté the onion in the oil for about 4 minutes, then add the flour and a big pinch of salt to make a roux. Cook, whisking constantly, for about 3 minutes. Add the cream mixture in a quick stream, whisking to prevent any lumps from forming. Stir in the cream cheese, spinach, garlic and spices and season with salt and white pepper. Reduce until slightly thickened, then remove from the heat and set aside.

4. Preheat the oven to 190ºC (375ºF), Gas Mark 5.

5. Wrap the dough in a piece of baking paper, then roll or pat out into a free-form rectangular tart about 30 × 20cm (8 × 12 inch) and 5mm (¼ inch) thick. Lift it on to a baking tray, letting the paper edges hang over.

6. Making sure the creamy spinach is not too wet, spread a thin layer, about 40g (1½oz) over the dough, then scatter the grated cheese on top. Add a layer of thinly sliced potatoes, then the mushrooms and drizzle generously with oil from the allium confit.

7. Tuck the confit alliums around the top, then sprinkle with the lemon zest and oregano.

8. Fold over the edges of the dough to create a 2.5cm (1 inch) border around the galette. Beat the egg and milk together and use the mixture to glaze the crust. Sprinkle the poppy seeds and salt over the edges. Bake for 25–30 minutes until the crust is a medium golden brown.

9. Remove from oven and leave to stand for 5 minutes to set. Transfer to a serving platter and garnish with the pickled lovage, tiny cherry tomatoes and baby leaves. Slice and serve.

Natasha MacAller

Reyes Blue Cheese Caramelized Onion Tart
with Poached Pears & Pickled Beetroot

allium | beetroot | pear

A make-ahead starter to assemble at the last minute, full of slow-cooked caramelized onions, punchy Reyes blue cheese from the breezy Northern California Coast, is topped with garden-grown pickled beetroot, slivers of poached pear and chive flowers. These tarts pair beautifully with bubbles.

MAKES 4–6

225g (8oz) plain flour
pinch of sea salt
¼ teaspoon ground white pepper
140g (5oz) butter
1 teaspoon wholegrain mustard
1 tablespoon granulated sugar
1 large egg, beaten
50g (1¾oz) blue cheese, crumbled
chopped chives and chive flowers, to garnish
seasonal greens (optional), to garnish

For the pickled spiced baby beets
200g (7oz) small red beetroots, scrubbed
½ cinnamon stick
3 allspice berries
1 bay leaf
1½cm (⅝ inch), about 5g (⅛oz), fresh ginger, sliced
¼ teaspoon coriander seeds
¼ teaspoon fennel seeds
235ml (8fl oz) apple cider vinegar
1 tablespoon balsamic vinegar
120ml (4fl oz) water
2 tablespoons honey
pinch of salt
1 sterilized 500ml (18fl oz) canning jar with tight-fitting lid

For the prosecco poached pears
175g (6oz) white granulated sugar
juice of ½ a lemon, about 2 tablespoons, plus about 5cm (2 inch) piece of lemon peel
1½cm (⅝ inch) piece ginger, about 5g (⅛oz), sliced
2 allspice berries, toasted for 1–2 minutes in a dry pan
4 lemon thyme sprigs
about 5cm (2 inch) piece of orange peel
pinch of salt
2 firm ripe pears, such as Bosc or Concorde, about 175g (6oz) each, peeled with stems intact
120ml (4fl oz) prosecco (classic or alcohol-free)
1 sterilized 500ml (18fl oz) canning jar with tight-fitting lid

For the filling
60ml (4 tablespoons) sunflower or other light oil
100g (3½oz) butter
1kg (2lb 4oz) firm brown onions, thinly sliced
1 tablespoon runny honey
1 tablespoon apple cider vinegar
2 tablespoons wholegrain mustard

1. To make the pickled spiced baby beets, trim the beetroots, leaving 1cm (½ inch) of stems. Place them in a small saucepan, cover with water and bring to a boil. Turn down heat to medium and simmer. After 10–12 minutes, remove from the heat, cover the pan and let stand for about 30 minutes, after which the beetroot should be firm but with a little give when squeezed. Drain off water then, with a peeler, remove and discard the skin. Slice the beetroot into 6 or 8 wedges, depending on size, then place into the canning jar and set aside. Rinse the saucepan then add the remaining pickling ingredients. Bring to a boil, then reduce the heat to medium and simmer for 10 minutes. Pour the pickling liquid into the beet jar nearly to the top and seal tightly with the lid. Let stand for an hour then refrigerate. These will keep in a chilled, sealed container for 2–3 weeks.

2. To make the prosecco poached pears, select a medium-sized heavy-based metal pan – it should allow the pears to fit in snugly but also for them to be fully submerged during poaching. Add the sugar and 120ml (4fl oz) water to the pan and bring to a simmer over a medium-high

continued overleaf

heat, gently swirling the liquid occasionally. Reduce until syrupy and dark amber in colour, about 20 minutes. Place a metal strainer or splatter screen that covers the top of the pan, then pour a further 450ml (16fl oz) of water into the pan (the strainer will keep the water from splattering). Remove the strainer and add the lemon juice, ginger, allspice, thyme, citrus peels and salt to the pan. Return the mixture to a simmer, then add the pears and prosecco. Place a piece of damp muslin, or a circle of baking paper with a small cut in the middle, over the pears inside the pan to keep them gently submerged. Gently poach until the pears are tender but still retain their shape, about 18 minutes. Remove the pears from the liquid to cool, then pour the poaching caramel into a glass jar and chill in an ice bath. Halve and core the pears then cut them into quarters. Gently add the pears to the cooled liquid caramel, cover and chill until needed. (Once chilled, if the caramel is too thin, return it to the heat to reduce. If it's too thick add a bit more water.)

3. To make the tart shells, whisk together the flour, salt and pepper in a small bowl.

4. In a stand mixer or by hand, beat the butter and mustard on medium speed until smooth. Reduce the speed to low and add the sugar until well combined. Add the egg and beat until mixed. Add the flour mixture in 3 stages until just incorporated; don't overwork the dough. Turn out the dough on to a board dusted with flour and work the dough with a plastic dough scraper until smooth – it should feel like playdough. Shape into 2 discs, wrap tightly in clingfilm or beeswax wrap and chill until you're ready to bake.

5. When you are ready to bake, remove the dough from the wrap and divide the halves between four 12cm (4½ inch) wide tart tins, smoothing the dough with your hands. If the dough becomes too soft, place in the refrigerator, chill until firm, then rework the dough. You can also roll the chilled dough between 2 pieces of nonstick baking paper. Peel off the bottom layer and set the dough into tart tins, shaping the sides to fit snugly. Chill until firm.

6. Preheat the oven to 190°C (375°F), Gas Mark 5

7. Peel then replace the top layer of baking paper before filling the tarts with pie weights, such as rice, dried beans or metal spoons, before baking. Bake for about 14–16 minutes (a few minutes less if using a fan oven) until the edges are browned. Carefully remove the pie weights and paper and continue baking for another 10–12 minutes (a few minutes less if using a fan oven) until golden brown and dry. Set aside to cool on a baking tray.

8. To make the filling, add the oil and butter to a 2-litre (3½-pint) pan and warm over a medium-low heat until the butter sizzles. Add the onions and sweat for 8–10 minutes until translucent, stirring occasionally. Continue cooking low and slow, stirring occasionally until the onions are fragrant and caramel-coloured. Stir in the remaining filling ingredients, then remove from the heat, cool, cover and chill until needed. The filling can be frozen, tightly sealed, for up to 3 months.

9. To finish and serve, preheat the grill to medium-low. Spoon the caramelized onions into the tart shells, top with poached pear slices and beetroot pieces. Crumble the cheese on top, then place under the grill for about 10 minutes, to lightly brown the cheese. Once golden, gently unmould the tarts from the tins on to plates and sprinkle chives, chive flowers and seasonal greens, if using, on top. Serve warm.

Natasha MacAller

Fuyu Persimmon & Red Pear Wild Greens Salad
with Liquorice Mint Vinaigrette

persimmon | liquorice | mint | pear

A wild combination of garden-grown and foraged tender baby greens, edible flowers and herbs with an autumnal flair of persimmons and pears tucked in amongst the greens.

SERVES 4

160–200g (5¾–7oz) garden and foraged greens, such as mizuna, speckled radicchio, dandelion, chicory, frisée, baby spinach, lamb's lettuce, purslane, watercress, sorrel, little gem or chrysanthemum greens
1–2 small red pears, halved, cored and thinly sliced lengthways
2 firm, shiny fuyu persimmons, about 100g (3½oz), sliced horizontally into thin circles, then cut into triangles and deseeded
30g (1oz) pecans, broken and toasted
60g (2¼oz) feta cheese, crumbled
½ a small red onion, peeled and diced
4 generous handfuls of herbs, such as basil, orange mint leaves, pea shoots, fennel fronds, tarragon and chives
2 tablespoons pomegranate seeds
a small handful of edible flowers, such as violas, calendula petals, nasturtiums, borage, basil flowers and cornflowers
sea salt and freshly ground black pepper

For the liquorice mint vinaigrette
50ml (2fl oz) sunflower oil
50ml (2fl oz) extra virgin olive oil
4 tablespoons rice wine vinegar
1 heaped teaspoon Dijon mustard (or freshly grated wasabi root)
2 tablespoons yuzu juice or 4 teaspoons lime juice
50g (1¾oz) honey
1½ teaspoons liquorice root powder
6g (⅛oz) liquorice mint or anise hyssop leaves, plus extra to garnish
pinch of flaky sea salt

1. In a bullet blender, blitz all the vinaigrette ingredients together, or combine in a bowl and mix well with a whisk.

2. Divide the leaves between 4 flat-bottomed bowls, then add and arrange the pears, persimmons, pecans, feta and small cubed red onion. Add the herbs around the bowl, followed by a scattering of pomegranate seeds and edible flowers.

3. Delicately drizzle over the vinaigrette, then season lightly with salt and pepper and add extra liquorice mint or anise hyssop leaves to garnish. Serve immediately.

Linda Shiue

Aloha Pineapple Kimchi
with Teriyaki Salmon

pineapple | alliums

SERVES 4

500g (1lb 2oz) salmon fillet, skin on, cut into 4 pieces
pinch of salt
1 tablespoon rapeseed oil
3 small garlic cloves, mashed
1 teaspoon honey
1 tablespoon tamari or light soy sauce
2 spring onions, cut on diagonal into 5cm (2 inch) lengths

For the kimchi
2 tablespoons grated garlic (about 6–9 cloves)
1 tablespoon peeled and grated fresh ginger
1 teaspoon granulated sugar
4 tablespoons gochugaru (Korean red pepper flakes) or Aleppo chilli flakes, or 2 tablespoons crushed chilli flakes, smashed in a mortar and pestle or ground in a spice grinder into finer flakes
2 tablespoons finely chopped coriander leaves
2 tablespoons fish sauce
3 tablespoons water
1 ripe pineapple, peeled and cut into 2.5cm (1 inch) cubes (core included)

'I first made pineapple kimchi when we were celebrating Thanksgiving in Hawaii. I wanted side dishes to make our turkey dinner taste more "local" and came up with the idea of combining chunks of sweet local pineapple with kimchi, to use in place of cranberry sauce. This recipe gets straight to the pineapple for a refreshing, savoury-sweet side dish or this super accompaniment to teriyaki salmon.'

1. To make the kimchi, place the garlic, ginger, sugar, gochugaru, coriander leaves, fish sauce and water in a blender or food processor and blend until smooth. Combine the spice mixture with the pineapple in a bowl and allow to sit at room temperature for 30 minutes then refrigerate, unless you're using it right away. It makes around 1 litre (1¾ pints).

2. While the kimchi rests, prepare the salmon. Pat the skin dry with kitchen paper. Season both sides with the salt. Heat a medium non-stick frying pan over a medium-high heat, then add the oil, swirling to coat the pan. Add the garlic, then the salmon, skin-side down. Cook for about 4 minutes, then sprinkle with the sugar before flipping over. Pour the tamari on top and allow it to swirl under the salmon. Add the spring onions and reduce the heat to medium-low. Continue to cook for another 1–2 minutes, or until both sides are glazed and browned and flesh begins to flake apart when pierced with fork or tip of knife.

3. Spoon the kimchi over the top of the salmon and garnish with the microgreens. Serve immediately. Refrigerate the remaining kimchi in a tightly sealed container for up to 3 months.

Chris Cosentino

Hanger Steak, Charred Onions
with Dandelion Green Salsa

dandelion | alliums | chillies

SERVES 4

900g (2lb) hanger steak* (ask your butcher to clean, trim and remove inedible central sinew)
olive oil, for frying
½ white onion, cut into 2 thick rings
4 garlic cloves, peeled
1 bunch of thyme
115g (4oz) butter
2 bunches of spring onions, roots sliced off
sea salt and freshly ground black pepper

For the dandelion green salsa
350g (12oz) dandelion greens (tiny, tender leaves)
15g (½oz) flat leaf parsley
10g (¼oz) mint leaves
1 shallot, sliced
2 garlic cloves, crushed
1 tablespoon fresh lemon juice
2 serrano chillies, stems removed and deseeded

'It's important to get a great char on the onions to develop the flavour. Sweet charred onions, rich minerally hanger steak and the balanced bitter spiciness of the salsa makes each bite so well rounded. If you don't like your salsa to be too bitter pick younger dandelion greens; the larger they get the more bitter they become.'

1. To make the dandelion green salsa, blanch the dandelion greens, parsley and mint leaves in boiling salted water for 1–2 minutes, then shock in salted ice-cold water and drain.

2. Add all the salsa ingredients to a blender and blend until smooth. Adjust the seasoning with salt and lemon juice. Store in a non-reactive container in the refrigerator, for up to 2 days, until ready to use.

3. Pat the steak dry with kitchen paper. Line a plate with kitchen paper, place the steak on top and set aside to dry further and come to cool room temperature (30 minutes–1 hour, depending on the weather). Turn occasionally; replacing the kitchen paper as needed. Season the steak with salt and pepper.

4. Place a heavy-based frying pan, preferably cast-iron, on the hob and drizzle with olive oil. Turn the heat to high. Pat both sides of the steak dry again. When the pan is smoking hot, after about 5–8 minutes, place the steak in the pan. Add the white onions to the pan, next to the steak. Let the steak sear for 1 minute, then use tongs to flip it over. Press down gently to ensure even contact between the steak and the pan. Keep cooking over a very high heat, flipping the steak every 30 seconds. Flip over the onions, too – it's fine if they start to come apart.

5. Add the garlic cloves, thyme and butter to the pan. Once the butter has melted, use it to baste, stacking the aromatics and onions on top of the meat and drizzling butter over the top (in this order: steak, thyme, garlic, onions). Don't be afraid to add even more butter! Baste continuously, tipping the pan to scoop melted butter with a spoon and drizzle over your stack.

6. When the steak has contracted in size and developed a dark-brown crust, about 4 minutes in total, check for doneness – the meat should feel softly springy but not squishy to the touch. If using a thermometer, insert into the side of the steak. For medium-rare meat, 49–52°C (120–125°F) is ideal; steak will continue cooking after being removed from heat.

7. Remove the steak to a cutting board and tent lightly with foil. Leave to rest for 5 minutes. Add the spring onions to the pan and let them char slightly.

8. Serve the steak in uncut pieces, or thickly slice on the diagonal away from your body and with the top edge of the knife leaning toward your body. When cooking hanger or skirt steak, make sure to slice across the grain of the meat. Drape the onions and spring onions over the meat, then drizzle with the dandelion green salsa.

*Prized for its tenderness, hanger steak is also known as butcher's steak, hanging tenderloin or onglet.

Natasha MacAller

Old-fashioned Plum, Apple & Rye Buckle

apple | ginger | fennel

A simple stir, spoon and bake fresh fruit pudding; this vintage 'Buckle' originated in New England in the 1700s. It is a quick no-fuss solution to use up a summer's over-abundance of fruit, for when your trees seem to ripen with everything everywhere all at once!

SERVES 6

135g (5oz) white wholewheat flour* or plain flour
60g (2¼oz) rye flour
40g (1½oz) masa harina or fine polenta
1 teaspoon baking powder
1 teaspoon ground cardamom, plus extra for sprinkling
¼ teaspoon sea salt
150g (5½oz) granulated sugar
1 tablespoon lemon zest
75g (2½oz) butter, at room temperature
3 large eggs
85ml extra virgin olive oil, plus extra for greasing
2 teaspoons vanilla bean paste or extract
30g (1oz) crystallized ginger, chopped
3 large juicy plums, about 425g (15oz) in total, halved cut into 1cm (½ inch) thick slices
2 small apples, about 425g (15oz) in total, peeled, cored and cut into 1cm (½ inch) thick slices
1 tablespoon demerara sugar mixed with ¾ teaspoon fennel seeds
Greek yogurt or thickened cream, to serve
edible flowers (optional), to garnish

1. Preheat the oven to 180°C (350°F), Gas Mark 4. Liberally coat a 23cm (9 inch) square or oval baking dish with oil.

2. Whisk the flours, polenta, baking powder, cardamom and salt together in a medium bowl and set aside.

3. In a small bowl, mix 2 tablespoons of the sugar with the lemon zest and rub the sugar with the zest to release the citrus oils.

4. In a large bowl with an electric hand whisk, or in the bowl of a stand mixer fitted with the paddle attachment, beat the butter, sugar and lemon sugar until well combined and fluffy, scraping down the sides of the bowl occasionally. Add the eggs, one at a time, and beat until well combined. Scrape down the sides of the bowl. Add the oil, vanilla and ginger, then beat for another 30 seconds. Fold in the flour mixture in 2 stages, beating on low speed until just combined.

5. Spoon the batter evenly into the prepared dish. Arrange the plums and apples slightly overlapping on top, pressing them gently into the batter to partially submerge them. Sprinkle the fennel sugar over the top. Bake for 28–32 minutes until golden brown and a skewer inserted into the centre comes out clean (check at 20 minutes to avoid overbaking). Leave to cool in the tin on a wire rack for at least 15 minutes then, using a serving spoon, scoop the warm buckle into bowls and top with a dollop of Greek yogurt or thickened cream sprinkled with a little ground cardamom. Garnish with edible flowers, if liked.

*White wholewheat flour is milled from hard white wheat and is lighter in texture and has a milder flavour than wholewheat flour ground from whole red wheat grains.

Natasha MacAller

Crispy Peach Amandine Dumplings
with Pickled Pink Rhubarb & Coconut Yuzu Whipped Posset

rhubarb | yuzu | ginger

SERVES 4

For the pickled rhubarb
2 firm pink or red rhubarb stalks, diagonally sliced into 2.5cm (1 inch) pieces
½ teaspoon pink peppercorns
1–2 teaspoons dried edible unsprayed rose petals
120ml (4fl oz) rice wine, raspberry or white wine vinegar
5g (⅛oz) fresh root ginger, peeled and thinly sliced
4 tablespoons granulated sugar
1 teaspoon flaky sea salt

For the posset
45ml (3 tablespoons) yuzu juice
2 teaspoons cornflour
1 × 400ml (14fl oz) can coconut milk, shaken, then divided in half and 200ml (7fl oz) very well chilled
70g (2½oz) caster sugar

For the peach dumplings
4 firm ripe peaches
70g (2½oz) coconut palm sugar
1 teaspoon ground ginger
¼ teaspoon white pepper
¼ teaspoon salt flakes, crumbled
1 tablespoon cornflour
100g (3½oz) almond paste (see below)
250–300g (9–10½oz) sheet vegan puff pastry, thawed but kept cold in the refrigerator
1–2 teaspoons plain flour, for dusting
1 tablespoon vegan egg wash or 1 egg, beaten

For the almond paste
150g (5½oz) ground almonds
170g (6oz) icing sugar
¾ tablespoon almond extract
1 large egg white, beaten until foamy

To serve
zest of 2 yuzu or limes
2 teaspoons sugar

What the heck is a posset? It is a simple dessert of Elizabethan origin and greatly favoured by Shakespeare as it is mentioned passionately in several of his works. Originally made of boiled milk and sugar, wine or beer was then whisked in to curdle, 'cook' and thicken the drink, then poured into a little serving pot coincidentally known as a 'posset'. This modern vegan posset is thickened with cornflour and whipped coconut cream then spooned on top of the piping hot peach dumpling. Make sure your oven is up to temperature and your pastry is super chilled before wrapping the peach or the edges won't stay sealed when baking. This whole dessert can be made vegan by using vegan puff pastry, non-dairy and egg substitutes.

1. To make pickled rhubarb, add the rhubarb, pink peppercorns and rose petals to a sterilized 568ml (1 pint) jar with a tight-fitting lid.

2. Add the vinegar, ginger and sugar to a small saucepan and bring to a rolling boil. Reduce the heat and add the salt, then pour the pickling liquid into the jar. Tightly seal and allow the jar to come to room temperature, then refrigerate. Your fragrant pink pickled rhubarb will last in the refrigerator for up to a month. For best results, make and chill a day ahead.

3. To make the posset, whisk the yuzu juice and cornflour together in a small bowl until the cornflour has dissolved. In a small pan over a medium heat, bring 200ml (7fl oz) of the coconut milk, the sugar and yuzu-cornflour mixture to a simmer, stirring slowly but continuously for about 6 minutes until the sugar dissolves and mixture thickens. Remove from the

continued overleaf

heat and stir occasionally for 10 minutes until cooled. Pour into a small shallow container, cover and chill the posset for at least 1½ hours until softly set.

4. Once the posset is set, pour the chilled 200ml (7fl oz) coconut milk into the bowl of a stand mixer fitted with the whisk attachment and beat on medium-high speed until soft peaks form. Fold in the posset mixture, then whisk on high until you have a light and fluffy whipped cream texture. Cover and keep cold until you are ready to serve the dumplings.

5. To make the almond paste, using a food processor, pulse the ground almonds and icing sugar a few times to break up any clumps. Add the almond extract (or to taste) and pulse to combine. Drizzle in the egg white and process for 2 minutes. The mixture should be smooth and form a ball. If dough is still sticky, add 1 tablespoon or more of almond flour. Pat into a disc, wrap tightly in clingfilm and store in refrigerator. This makes 340g (11¾oz) but the quantities can be doubled and it will keep in the refrigerator for up to 1 month. Alternatively, seal tightly and freeze for up to 3 months and defrost when ready to use.

6. To make the dumplings, place four 15cm (6 inch) squares of baking paper or a silicone mat on a baking tray.

7. Carefully halve each peach and remove the stone. Using a sharp vegetable peeler or a small knife, from the top of the peach, gently peel off the skin of each half and set aside.

8. Whisk together the sugar, ginger, pepper, salt and cornflour in a small bowl and set aside.

9. Pat or thinly roll out four 15g (½oz) almond paste circles and set aside on the work surface.

10. Dust the work surface with the flour. Unroll the puff pastry on the floured surface and lightly roll out into four 15cm (6 inch) squares. Transfer the pastry squares to the prepared baking tray. Place one of the almond paste circles on top of each pastry square. Brush the inside edges of each square with the vegan or egg wash and place in the refrigerator to keep cold until ready to top with the seasoned peaches.

11. When you're ready to bake, preheat the oven to 200°C (400°F), Gas Mark 6 and place a rack in the centre of the oven.

12. Roll the peach halves, a few at a time, in the spicy sugar mix to coat. Place a peach half, rounded-side down, in the middle of the almond paste, then top with the other half (flat-side down). Working quickly, gather the corners of the chilled pastry, pinch and seal together the top and sides to seal, creating an 'X' shape on the top. Repeat with the remaining dumplings.

13. Brush the dumplings with the egg wash and bake for 25–30 minutes until crisp and medium to dark golden brown with the peach juices bubbling. Remove from the oven and leave to cool for 5–7 minutes. To serve, transfer the dumplings to serving bowls, then swirl a large spoonful of the whipped posset on the side. Mix the 2 teaspoons of sugar with the yuzu zest in a small bowl. Sprinkle the posset with the yuzu sugar, then arrange a spoonful of pickled rhubarb on the side.

Lemon Myrtle Cheesecake
with Anzac Wattleseed Biscuit

lemon myrtle | honey

SERVES 6–8

For the Anzac wattleseed biscuits
90g (3¼oz) plain flour
1 teaspoon ground ginger
110g (4oz) toasted rolled oats, blitzed for 5 seconds in a coffee grinder
85g (3oz) desiccated coconut
4 teaspoons crushed wattleseeds or whole black sesame seeds
25g (1oz) demerara sugar
pinch of flaky sea salt
60g (2¼oz) salted butter
3 tablespoons golden or corn syrup, warmed
¼ teaspoon bicarbonate of soda
2 tablespoons water

For the lemon myrtle infusion
100ml (3½fl oz) vodka (40% proof) or other neutral alcohol
1 tablespoon dried lemon myrtle, crumbled

For the lemon myrtle drizzle
100g (3½oz) caster sugar
50ml (2fl oz) water
1 teaspoon liquid glucose
1 teaspoon dried lemon myrtle

For the cheesecake
400g (14oz) cream cheese, I use Philadelphia
20g (¾oz) cornflour
¼ teaspoon fine sea salt
170g (6oz) mascarpone cheese
80g (2½oz) mild runny manuka honey, or local mild honey
4 tablespoons lemon myrtle infusion (see above)
2 large eggs, beaten

For the topping
250g (9oz) soured cream or crème fraîche
1 tablespoon caster sugar
1 egg white, beaten until frothy
1½ teaspoon vanilla extract
pinch of salt

To serve
edible flowers (optional)

Smooth, creamy classic New York-style cheesecake scented with lemon myrtle and manuka honey, designed by the planet's heroes – our precious bees. Make a day ahead of serving and leave to cool overnight. Serve with a lemon myrtle drizzle and an Anzac wattleseed biscuit. If you cannot find lemon myrtle, substitute it for an equal amount of dried lemongrass. Make sure all your ingredients are at room temperature.

1. First make the Anzac wattleseed biscuits. Whisk all the dry ingredients in a large bowl. Prepare 2 pieces of baking paper or clingfilm about the size of your baking tin to help roll out the biscuits.

2. In a small pan over a low heat, melt the butter and golden syrup. Bring to a gentle simmer and cook for 4 minutes. Turn the heat to medium and let come it to the boil. Whisk in the bicarbonate of soda: it will foam up a bit. Using a spatula, add the butter mixture and water to the dry ingredients, stirring well. Gather in to a ball then transfer to the baking paper.

3. Preheat the oven to 160°C (325°F), Gas Mark 3.

4. Pat out, then top with the second piece of baking paper. Roll out the dough into a 3mm (⅛ inch) thick square. Cut out circles using a 8cm (3¼ inch) round cutter or use cheesecake baking rings and, using a flat spatula, arrange the biscuits on a baking tray a few centimetres apart. You may need to bake the biscuits in 2 batches. Bake in the middle of the oven

continued overleaf

for 12–15 minutes until set and immediately transfer to a wire rack to cool. Store in an airtight container until ready to serve. The biscuits can be reheated and cooled if they lose their crispness.

5. To make the lemon myrtle infusion, warm the vodka in a small pan to 65°C (149°F), then remove from heat and add the lemon myrtle, swirling the pan until submerged. Put the lid on and leave to infuse for 30–45 minutes. Strain the cooled mixture through a fine metal sieve or muslin into a small, clean, dry bottle.

6. Now make the lemon myrtle drizzle. In a small clean pan, combine the sugar and water, it should have the consistency of wet sand. Turn on the heat and warm the sugar water until the sugar crystals dissolve. Using a clean teaspoon, add the glucose and stir to incorporate. Continue cooking at a low simmer about 5 minutes until the liquid is clear. Remove from the heat and add the lemon myrtle, swirling the pan to incorporate. Cool, then decant into a small squeezy bottle. Store until ready to garnish the cheesecake.

7. Wrap the bottom and sides of 6–8 steel baking ring forms, about 8cm (3¼ inch), or a 20cm (8 inch) springform tin with a double layer of heavy foil to make them watertight. Preheat the oven to 160°C (325°F), Gas Mark 3 if cooking individual cheesecakes or 150°C (300°F), Gas Mark 2 if making one large cheesecake. Boil the kettle.

8. In a medium mixing bowl with an electric hand mixer, or the bowl of a stand mixer fitted with the whisk attachment, beat cream cheese on medium speed until smooth. Stop and scrape down the sides of the bowl using a spatula and continue to beat and scrape until velvety smooth. Sift in the cornflour and salt, whisking well to incorporate, then turn off the mixer and scrape down the sides. Add the mascarpone, whisking it well, then fold in the honey and the lemon myrtle infusion for about a minute. Lastly, add the beaten egg until well combined and batter is smooth with no streaks.

9. Scoop batter into the lined tin(s), filling them two-thirds of the way up. Arrange the cheesecakes in the baking dish at least 5cm (2 inch) apart. Place the baking dish in the oven and pour boiled water into the corner of the dish so it is a quarter of the way up the sides of the tin(s) to create a water bath. Bake the individual cheesecakes for 35–40 minutes or the large cheesecake for 45–50 minutes until the cheesecake is jiggly in the middle with just semi-set sides.

10. While the cheesecake is baking, make the topping. In a small bowl, whisk all the ingredients together until smooth and creamy. When the cheesecake is baked, carefully remove from oven. Spread the topping 1–2cm (½–¾ inch) thick, which should just about top the baking rings, if using. Gently level tops with a butter knife or offset spatula and return to the oven. Close the oven door, turn off the oven and leave to sit for 30 minutes for individual cheesecakes or 1 hour for a large cheesecake. (Do not open oven door during this time.)

11. Lift the cheesecake(s) out of water bath on to a wire rack to and leave to cool for 1 hour. Transfer to a flat baking tray, cover with a sheet of baking paper and refrigerate at least 8 hours or overnight.

12. If serving individual cheesecakes, place a biscuit in the centre of each plate. Carefully peel the foil off the bottom of ring, hold in your hand, then run a paring knife around inside of each ring mould from the top to release the cheesecake. Hold the cheesecake over the biscuit and give a little up and down shake to release the cheesecake, lowering on top of the biscuit. Drizzle the syrup on top, letting it run down the sides. Garnish with edible flowers if liked.

13. If serving one large cheesecake, release the ring from sides of cheesecake and slide on to a serving plate. Drizzle with syrup and serve with Anzac biscuits on the side.

Mette Flora Helbæk

Rødgrød Med Fløde

rhubarb

'This traditional Danish rhubarb and berry compote with cream is the taste of summer for anyone from Denmark.'

SERVES 8–10

500g (1lb 2oz) rhubarb, cut into 1cm (½ inch) pieces
250g (9oz) granulated cane sugar
100ml (3½fl oz) water
500g (1lb 2oz) strawberries, sliced, plus extra to serve
1–2 tablespoons potato starch mixed with water

To serve
400ml (14fl oz) extra thick double cream
edible flowers (optional)
fresh berries
cacao nibs (optional)

1. Add the rhubarb, sugar and measured water to a pan and gently bring to the boil. Reduce the heat and let the rhubarb simmer for 10 minutes.

2. Add the strawberries to the rhubarb and let them simmer together for another 10–15 minutes until the strawberries are very soft.

3. Remove the pan from the heat and add the potato starch mixture. It's important that the liquid is no longer simmering as this will give a strange texture to the compote. On the other hand, if the compote is too cold, the potato starch will not dissolve.

4. Serve with ice-cold cream and extra strawberry halves (or other fresh berries, if you have them). Garnished with edible flowers and sprinkle with cacao nibs, if you like.

Chapter 2

EVERYDAY JOY

Sherry Yard

Energize Flatbreads

fennel | pizza thyme | shallot

MAKES 14–18

300ml (10fl oz) water at 16°C (60°F)
1.5g instant espresso powder
25g (1oz) blackstrap molasses (I use Yellow Label Plantation)
10g (¼oz) honey
20g (¾oz) olive oil
230g (8oz) bread flour
100g (3½oz) rye flour (ideally medium), plus extra for dusting
60g (2¼oz) teff flour
50g (1¾oz) wholemeal flour
6g (⅛oz) black cocoa powder (also known as Dutch cocoa powder)
6g (⅛oz) brown sugar
7g (⅛oz) sea salt
2 egg whites, beaten, for brushing
olive oil, for brushing
flaky sea salt and freshly ground black pepper

For the seed topping
5g (⅛oz) fennel seeds
5g (⅛oz) caraway seeds
20g (¾oz) pumpkin seeds
20g (¾oz) sesame seeds
5g (⅛oz) poppy seeds
100g (3½oz) dried shallots
10g (¼oz) thyme, leaves picked

'A moreish crispy flatbread cracker created for Spago in Beverly Hills. Bake in a pizza oven or on a pizza stone or baking tray in a hot oven. The flatbreads are best eaten fresh from the oven but they can be stored in an airtight container in the freezer for 1 week, then defrosted and warmed lightly to serve.'

---

1. Start the recipe a day ahead for best results. In a large bowl, whisk together 100ml (3½fl oz) of the water, the instant espresso powder, molasses, honey and olive oil.

2. In a stand mixer fitted with the dough hook attachment, add all the dry ingredients, then pour in the molasses mixture. Mix on low speed for 2 minutes until it looks like seeded flour. Very slowly, stream in the remaining water – don't worry if it looks dry. Once all the water is added, continue to mix on low speed for 8 minutes. Using a thermometer, test the dough – it should read 32°C (90°F).

3. Divide the dough into 3 parcels (lots of arm work here!). Wrap tightly in clingflim and refrigerate for 12 hours or overnight. Remove from the refrigerator and leave at room temperature for 1 hour.

4. Place a dough parcel back in the bowl of the stand mixer fitted with the hook attachment. Run on low speed for 2 minutes to make the dough malleable and easier to work with. Remove the dough to the work surface dusted with flour and pound with rolling pin to a thickness that you can work through a pasta machine. Begin to work the dough through the pasta machine at the highest setting, passing through several times and dusting lightly with flour. Lower the setting each time until you have no.2 thickness sheets.

5. Place the dough on a piece of floured nonstick baking paper set on top of a baking tray that will fit in your refrigerator. Sprinkle the top of the dough with flour then put a piece of baking paper on top. Repeat with the remaining dough parcels, making sure not to stack dough sheets directly on top of each other – they will stick! Refrigerate until ready to bake. At this point, you can also store the dough on sheet trays tightly wrapped in clingfilm in the freezer for up to a month to bake fresh.

6. Heat a pizza oven to 316°C (600°F) or preheat the oven to 240°C (475°F) Gas Mark 9.

7. Dust a work surface with flour and place the dough sheets on top. Brush each sheet evenly with the beaten egg white. Dust generously with the seeds, dried shallots and thyme. With a French rolling pin wrapped in nonstick baking paper and clingfilm, roll and press in the seeds. Brush with olive oil. Dust with black pepper and flaky salt.

8. Cut the sheet into 6 × 20cm (2½ × 8 inches) flatbreads. Dust a pizza peel or baking sheet with flour, then add the flatbreads and slide into the oven. Bake in the pizza oven for 2 minutes (3 minutes for a regular oven), then flip over and bake for another minute (3 minutes for a regular oven) until dark golden brown and crispy. Enjoy fresh from the oven.

Nancy Silverton

Rosemary Calendula Polenta Cakes

rosemary | calendula | honey

'Moist and crumbly at the same time, these tasty aromatic polenta cakes sweetened with manuka honey are a sweet-savoury delight.'

MAKES 12

2 teaspoons minced rosemary, plus 24 tips to garnish
1 teaspoon finely chopped dried calendula petals
45g (1½oz) light brown sugar
400g (14oz) plain flour or pastry flour, plus extra for dusting
190g (6¾oz) stoneground yellow polenta
1 tablespoon plus 1 teaspoon baking powder
350g (12oz) unsalted butter, cut into 3mm (⅛ inch) cubes and frozen
1 large egg plus 1 large egg yolk
3 tablespoons manuka honey
125g (4½oz) crème fraîche

To serve

2 teaspoons double cream
24 rosemary tips with a bit of sprig
1 tablespoon dried or fresh calendula petals

1. Adjust the oven rack to the middle position and preheat the oven to 180°C (350°F), Gas Mark 4. Line a baking sheet with nonstick baking paper or a silicone mat.

2. Put the rosemary, calendula and sugar into a small bowl. Rub the herbs with your fingers to release the oils into the sugar, then set aside.

3. In the bowl of a food processor fitted with the steel 'S' blade, or in the bowl of a stand mixer fitted with the paddle attachment, combine the flour, polenta, baking powder and sugar mixture and process, or mix on low speed, to incorporate. Add the butter and pulse, or mix on low, until the mixture is pale yellow and the consistency of a fine meal.

4. Transfer the mixture to a large bowl and make a well in the centre. Pour in the egg, egg yolk, honey and crème fraîche and whisk together. Using one hand, draw in the dry ingredients, mixing until just combined.

5. Wash and dry your hands, then lightly dust them with flour. Turn the dough out on to a lightly floured work surface and gently knead a few times gathering the dough into a ball. Roll or pat the dough into a rectangle about 2cm (¾ inch) thick. Cut the polenta cakes into rectangles (or whatever shape you wish), cutting closely together and keeping the trimmings intact.

6. Gather the trimmings and gently push and press together, then cut out the remaining dough. Place the polenta cakes 2.5cm (1 inch) apart on the prepared baking sheet. Brush the tops with the cream, then press 2 rosemary sprigs and a scattering of chopped calendula petals on top of each.

7. Bake for 30 minutes until slightly browned and firm to the touch. Let sit until cool enough to eat, then serve immediately.

Hiro Sone

Suimono
with Samphire & Shrimp Shinjo

samphire | kombu | yuzu

'*Suimono is Japanese clear soup made with dashi base stock. Shinjo is like a fluffy dumpling, usually made with fish paste, eggs, mountain potato purée, dashi and sake.*'

SERVES 2

For the suimono
1.2 litres (2 pints) filtered water
1 dashi kombu, about 10cm (4 inches) square
50g (1¾oz) shaved dried bonito (katsuobushi)
1½ teaspoons light soy sauce (usukuchi soy)
sea salt

For the prawn shinjo
160g (5¾oz) prawn tails, shelled and deveined
¼ teaspoon minced fresh ginger
¼ teaspoon coarse salt
1 egg white, about 40g (1½oz)
2½ teaspoons mirin
½ teaspoon cornflour
60g (2¼oz) samphire (preferably young tender part)

To garnish
40g (1½oz) enoki mushrooms, bottom part removed
3 tablespoons very finely julienned leeks (white part only)
1 shiso leaf, or a few baby shiso leaves, finely sliced into ribbons
20 fine strips of yuzu, lemon or lime zest

1. First, make the suimono. Put the measured water and dashi kombu in a pot and soak the dashi kombu for 1–2 hours.

2. Put the pot over a low heat and heat the water to 60°C (140°F) then simmer for 1½ hours while maintaining the temperature. After 1½ hours, remove the kombu, increase the temperature to 85–90°C (185–194°F), add the shaved dried bonito and remove any scum that comes to the surface. Boil for 1–2 minutes, remove from the heat, then gently strain the stock through a kitchen paper-lined sieve.

3. Season the dashi with the soy sauce and salt, keep the seasoning light because the samphire will release some saltiness later. (Ideally the suimono should be ready when the shinjo base is ready.)

4. Meanwhile, make the shinjo. Cut 140g (5oz) of the prawn tails into about 1cm (½ inch) cubes, then place the prawns, the ginger and the salt into a food processor, and blend until very smooth. Scrape down the inside of the processor a few times and continue blend until the mixture becomes sticky.

5. While blending, add the egg white and the mirin and keep blending until smooth. Transfer the shinjo to a mixing bowl. Cut the remaining prawns into small dices about 5mm (¼ inch). Dust with the cornflour and mix. Add the diced prawns to the prawn paste and, using a spatula, mix well.

6. Cut the samphire into pieces about 5mm (¼ inch) long. Spread them on a small tray.

7. Divide the shinjo into 4 equal balls and shape them into rounds. Place them on the cut samphire on the tray, then gently roll so the shinjo is coated with samphire all the way around.

8. Gently place the shinjo in the simmering suimono, bring up to a gentle simmer and cover. Cook for about 3 minutes, then flip the shinjo over, cover and cook for another 3 minutes. Add the enoki mushrooms to the suimono, then bring back to a simmer.

9. Place the shinjo in 4 serving bowls. Pour about 200ml (7fl oz) of the suimono along with the enoki over the shinjo. (The amount of the soup depends on the size of the bowls you use; you want to keep the top of the shinjo above the surface of the broth.) Sprinkle the leeks on the broth, then mound the shiso on the top of the shinjo. Place the yuzu zest on the shiso. Serve immediately.

Christine Manfield

Saltbush Tempura

saltbush

SERVES 2

750ml (1⅓ pints) vegetable oil, for deep-frying
8 old man saltbush sprigs (with leaves)
1 tablespoon Davidson plum powder (Ooray) or sumac
sriracha (or chilli) mayonnaise, to serve

For the tempura batter
55g (2oz) rice flour
55g (2oz) plain flour
½ teaspoon baking powder
pinch of salt
1 egg
300ml (10fl oz) soda water, chilled

'These delicious and nutritious native Australian leaves are coated with a wispy tempura batter to great ethereal effect – crunchy and moreish all at once and my go-to snack as they are so easy to prepare. The dusting of Davidson plum powder (Ooray) brings a lovely tang and balance to the overall flavour. If you can't source the powder (although readily available from many online retailers), you can swap it with sumac for a similar effect.'

1. Add the batter ingredients to a bowl and mix until combined. I use a chopstick. It is important not to overmix and don't worry if it isn't completely smooth – a few small lumps is a good thing. Set aside.

2. Pour the vegetable oil into a deep saucepan and heat over a medium-high heat until a little drop of batter sizzles immediately when dropped in.

3. Dip the saltbush sprigs and leaves into the batter to coat and shake off any excess. Holding the stem, place each one into the hot oil and fry for 1–2 minutes, or until golden and crisp. They are quite delicate so don't need to cook for long at all. Deep-fry a few at a time to prevent overcrowding and lowering the temperature of the oil.

4. Once cooked, remove using a slotted spoon and place on kitchen paper to remove any excess oil.

5. Dust with the Davidson plum powder and serve with sriracha (or chilli) mayonnaise.

* Note: Saltbush is most prolific in Australia, but around 250 varieties of drought and flood-tolerant *Atriplex* (see page 187) thrive worldwide, primarliy in subtropical and temperate climates. They are often foraged in deserts and salty brackish shorelines. Saltbush can be ordered online or found in specality garden shops worldwide.

Sean Sherman & Mecca Bos

Sumac-Egusi Drizzle
with Charred Sweet Potatoes

sweet potato | sumac

SERVES 4

4 large sweet potatoes

For the egusi
1 small onion, diced
2 garlic cloves
palm oil or coconut oil, for sautéing
2 roasted red peppers
70g (2½oz) egusi (melon) seeds (or pumpkin seeds), toasted
sea salt

For the sumac oil
250ml (9fl oz) sunflower oil
50g (1¾oz) sumac

Mecca says: 'Sean is an avid gardener, and putting his money where his mouth is with his often repeated "lawns are stupid" mantra (he even has a T-shirt emblazoned with the phrase), he put a large vegetable garden in front of our house. Passers-by often slow down to admire it while walking their dogs, sometimes making the verbal calculation that a vegetable garden would, in fact, be smarter than a lawn. As a result, we have a bumper crop of greens, tomatoes and other summer produce to make use of during harvest season, and it's good to have an all-purpose drizzle on hand to liven them up.'

Sean says: 'Egusi is one of the staple dishes of Nigerian cooking, and there are as many versions as there are cooks. Instead of a more traditional soup or stew, I make a sauce, using egusi (also known as melon) seeds as the base (you can substitute pumpkin seeds but I'd encourage you to seek out the real deal). The addition of sumac makes for an interesting flavour profile – tart citrus to the egusi's bitter earthiness. Drizzle on any produce, raw or cooked. It's especially good over charred sweet potatoes.'

1. To make the egusi, sauté the onion and garlic in enough palm oil to coat the bottom of a sauté pan. Cook for 8–10 minutes until just translucent, then remove from the heat and leave to cool to room temperature. Blend all the egusi ingredients in a food processor, then salt to taste.

2. To make the sumac oil, in a small saucepan, gently steep the sumac in the oil over a low heat for about 30 minutes until the oil picks up some colour. Leave to cool at room temperature and then combine with the egusi purée. Keep refrigerated.

3. For the charred sweet potatoes, preheat the oven to 200°C (400°F), Gas Mark 6.

4. Pierce the sweet potatoes all over, place on a baking tray and bake for about 30 minutes until the potatoes are tender all the way through when pierced with a knife.

5. When they are cool enough to handle, cut the sweet potatoes in half lengthways and char over a grill or a gas flame on the hob until charred in places. Drizzle the egusi oil over the sweet potatoes to serve.

Natasha MacAller

Pineapple Mint Hawaiian Ceviche
with Blue Coconut Wafers

pineapple | mint | chillies

SERVES 2 AS A STARTER

120g (4 ¼oz) fresh firm white fish (I use opakapaka – Hawaiian pink snapper), skinned and boned
20g (¾oz) red onion, minced
60g (2¼oz) pineapple, peeled and cut into small cubes
50g (1¾oz) green papaya or mango, peeled and sliced into matchsticks
1–2 small red chillies, deseeded and chopped
20g (¾oz) small mint leaves, plus extra sprigs to garnish
60g (2¼oz) fresh or canned coconut cream
120g (4 ¼oz) passion fruit
4 dashes of Tabasco sauce (or to taste)
juice of 2 limes, plus zest of 1 lime and lime wedges, to garnish
small handful of coriander leaves and tender stems, to garnish
minced chives or spring onions, to garnish

For the Hawaiian blue coconut wafers
85g (3oz) unsweetened desiccated coconut
115g (4oz) granulated sugar or coconut sugar
35g (1¼oz) coconut flour
1 ½ teaspoons blue butterfly pea powder (blue matcha)
1 large egg, plus 2 egg whites
40g (1½oz) coconut butter, melted and cooled
zest of 1 lime
sea salt and freshly ground black pepper

There is no blue like Big Island Hawaii blue. From sea to sky, Hawaiian blue is a tropical holiday in my imagination and the blue coconut wafer is made with antioxidant-rich blue butterfly pea powder (also known as blue matcha powder), for some island inspo. Celebrate this island dish with the freshest white fish you can catch or find and enjoy alongside a refreshing tropical beverage.

---

1. To make the ceviche, cut the fish into 6cm/ ½ inch pieces and place in a non-reactive metal or glass bowl. Add the red onion, pineapple, papaya, chillies, mint leaves, coconut cream, passion fruit pulp, Tabasco, and lime juice and zest. Gently fold together, season with salt and pepper and more Tabasco if needed, then cover and chill for at least 1 hour.

2. While ceviche chills, make the wafers. Combine the dry ingredients in a medium bowl. Add the egg, egg whites and coconut butter, then the lime zest and season with salt and pepper. Cover and leave to stand for 30 minutes.

3. Preheat the oven to 130°C (300°F), Gas Mark 2. Lightly oil a silicone mat and place on a baking tray.

4. Using an offset or other small metal spatula, spread the batter thinly into 7.5cm (3 inch) rounds over the mat. Bake for 8–10 minutes until set and dried. Check often and turn the tray halfway through cooking to keep them from burning. (Reduce the oven temperature if needed). Carefully remove the wafers from the mat with an offset spatula, leave to air dry then, when fully cooled, store in an airtight container until ready to serve.

5. To serve, carefully spoon the ceviche into 4 decorative shells or martini glasses. Garnish with mint sprigs, chives, lime wedges and a scattering of coriander leaves and sprigs. Add a blue coconut wafer to each dish and serve immediately.

Natasha MacAller

Pan-grilled Stargazer
with Rainbow Relish

chilli | ginger | citrus

This fresh, bright and versatile one-dish meal is easy to make for lunch or dinner and can be cooked in a pan or on the barbecue.

SERVES 4

4 stargazer, grouper, halibut or salmon fillets, about 700g (1lb 9oz)
1 lemon grass stalk, harder outer layers removed and discarded, inside layers chopped
2 tablespoons light soy sauce
1 teaspoon toasted sesame oil
½ teaspoon fish sauce
2.5cm (1 inch) piece of fresh root ginger, minced
60ml (4 tablespoons) olive oil, plus extra for brushing
60ml (4 tablespoons) seasoned rice wine vinegar
1 makrut lime leaf, finely chopped, and juice of makrut lime, or zest and juice of 1 lime

For the relish
3 peppers – 1 red, 1 yellow and 1 green, cored, deseeded and sliced into thin strips
1 fresh red or green jalapeño, deseeded and thinly sliced into rings (or to taste)
3 medium tomatoes, peeled, deseeded and chopped
1 teaspoon grated fresh ginger
60ml (4 tablespoons) olive or grapeseed oil
1 garlic clove, minced or to taste
1 tablespoon light soy sauce, or to taste
2 tablespoons fresh lime or yuzu juice
60ml (4 tablespoons) seasoned rice wine vinegar
1 tablespoon finely chopped coriander leaves
sea salt and freshly ground black pepper

To serve
1–2 × 180–360g (6–12½oz) packets of soba, udon, hokkien or rice stick noodles, cooked
ketjap manis or sweet chilli sauce
coriander sprigs with tender stems
1 makrut or fresh lime, quartered
makrut lime leaves

1. To make the relish, mix all ingredients well and chill for 1 hour, or overnight.

2. Place the fish in a non-reactive container in a single layer. Mix all the remaining ingredients in a bowl and pour over the fish. Cover, transfer to the refrigerator and leave to marinate for 30 minutes, or up to 1 hour, turning the fish over once halfway through.

3. Remove the fish from the marinade and pat dry. Discard the marinade. Brush the fish with oil and place in a pan over a medium-high heat or on the barbecue. Cook without moving for 3–4 minutes, depending on thickness of the fish, then turn gently and cook for another 3–4 on the other side. Serve piping hot on a bed of noodles coated in a few spoonfuls of ketjap manis or sweet chilli sauce. Spoon the relish on top of the fish just before serving. Garnish with coriander, lime quarters and makrut lime leaves.

Chicken Chakalaka

lovage | alliums | coriander | chillies

SERVES 4–6

Simple herb-roasted chicken teams up beautifully with spicy moreish chakalaka, a hearty and spicy-as-you-like pairing inspired by Bibi's Kitchen, which hails from the South African diaspora. Experiment with your own herb and spice blends in any season, this satisfying, healthy and flavour-packed meal will have you coming back for seconds.

1 large chicken, about 1.8kg (4lb), patted dry
sea salt and freshly ground black pepper

For the marinade
2 tablespoons mustard powder
2 tablespoons sweet pimentón
½ teaspoon ground turmeric
½ teaspoon ground coriander
4 teaspoons minced garlic
2 tablespoons fresh lime juice
25g (1oz) herbs such as flat leaf parsley, basil, holy basil and lovage (or celery) leaves, chopped
20 grinds black pepper, or more to taste
1½ teaspoons sea salt
2 tablespoons local runny honey
235ml (8fl oz) rapeseed or vegetable oil
1 lemon, sliced into rings
1 medium onion, sliced into thick rings
a few sprigs of thyme

For the chakalaka
2 tablespoons sunflower oil
1 large brown onion, diced
2 garlic cloves, minced
2 jalapeños, deseeded and chopped
small handful of coriander leaves and stems, chopped
20g (¾oz) grated fresh ginger or ginger paste
4 dates, pitted and chopped
2 teaspoons pimentón
2 teaspoons ground turmeric
1½ teaspoons ground cumin
2 teaspoons flaky sea salt, plus extra to taste
1 small red pepper, cored, deseeded and cut into strips
1 yellow pepper, pepper, cored, deseeded and cut into strips
1 green bell pepper, cored, deseeded and cut into strips
3 carrots, about 250g (9oz), trimmed, peeled, then coarsely grated
½ small Chinese or green cabbage, about 300g (10½oz), grated
400g (14oz) very ripe tomatoes, peeled, cored and chopped, or 1 × 400g (14oz) can crushed tomatoes
300g (10½oz) canned black beans or cannellini beans, rinsed well
150g (5½oz) fresh or frozen sweetcorn kernels
2 tablespoons apple cider vinegar
juice of 3 limes, plus zest of 1 lime

1. Season the chicken all over and inside the cavity. Mix all the marinade ingredients, except the lemon, onion and thyme, together in a small bowl or jug. Place the chicken in a ziplock bag, pour over the herb mixture and leave to marinate in the refrigerator for 2–3 hours or overnight.

2. Preheat the oven to 180°C (350°F), Gas Mark 4.

3. Layer a bed of the onion and lemon rings in the bottom of a large casserole and top with the marinated chicken, breast side up. Drizzle over the marinade and scatter over the thyme. Roast for 1¾–2 hours until the juices run clear at the thickest part.

4. Meanwhile, make the chakalaka. In a large heavy-based pan set over a medium heat, heat the oil until it shimmers. Using a spoon you don't mind being stained with turmeric, stir in the onion, garlic, jalapeños, ginger and dates. Cook for about 7 minutes, stirring occasionally, until the onion begins to soften. Add the pimentón, turmeric, cumin and salt. Cook for about 30 seconds, stirring, just until fragrant. Add the peppers, carrots, cabbage and tomatoes, reduce the heat to medium-low and cook for about 10 minutes. Fold in the beans and sweetcorn and cook for another 20 minutes until the vegetables are just tender and most of the liquid has reduced. Turn off the heat, stir in the apple cider vinegar, lime zest and juice, then season the chakalaka to taste with flaky sea salt.

5. Remove the chicken from the oven, tent with foil and let it rest for 15–20 minutes. Carve the chicken and serve with a generous side of warm chakalaka. Store any leftover chakalaka in an airtight container in the refrigerator for up to a week.

Kathy Kordalis

Fattoush
with Charred Lamb, Pickled Beetroot & Whipped Sumac Feta

sumac

SERVES 4

For the quick pickled beetroot
50g (1¾oz) beetroot, peeled and julienned
50ml (2fl oz) apple cider vinegar
1 teaspoon salt
1 teaspoon runny honey

For the lamb
2 garlic cloves, crushed
1 red chilli, finely chopped (optional)
2 tablespoons pomegranate molasses
1 tablespoon smoked paprika
3 tablespoons extra virgin olive oil
450g (1lb) lamb rump steaks

For the whipped sumac feta
200g (7oz) feta cheese, crumbled small
200g (7oz) Greek yoghurt
2 tablespoons olive oil
zest of 1 lemon (reserve the juice for the salad)
1 teaspoon sumac (or more to taste)

For the fattoush
100ml (3½fl oz) olive oil
2 pieces of Middle Eastern bread or flatbread (thinner is better), torn into bite-sized pieces
1 red onion, thinly sliced
1 tablespoon sumac, plus extra to serve
300g (10½oz) mixed tomatoes, chopped into bite-sized pieces
2 Lebanese or baby cucumbers or 1 large cucumber, roughly chopped
30g (1oz) flat leaf parsley, coarsely chopped
30g (1oz) mint, leaves picked and coarsely chopped
1 red or yellow pepper, deseeded and finely chopped
5–6 radishes, thinly sliced
80ml (2½fl oz) extra virgin olive oil
½ pomegranate, seeds only
1 tablespoon pomegranate molasses
sea salt and freshly ground black pepper

'This is packed with the flavour of charred and succulent lamb alongside the tart, sour and tangy sumac with notes of citrus, earth and floral. Teamed with a crunchy and fresh Middle Eastern-inspired Fattoush, it melds beautifully with the creaminess of whipped feta.'

1. To make the quick pickled beetroot, add the beetroot to a jar or small bowl. Whisk together the vinegar, salt and honey, then add to beetroot. Set aside in the refrigerator until ready to top the whipped feta. This can be made a day ahead.

2. To marinate the lamb, mix and mash all the lamb ingredients, except for the lamb itself, in a medium bowl. Add the lamb and coat well with the marinade. Cover and leave to stand, turning occasionally, for at least 1 hour. For better flavour and tenderness, put the lamb into a Ziploc bag, seal and let marinate overnight in the refrigerator.

3. To make the whipped sumac feta, whisk all the ingredients together in a stand mixer to aerate, then chill in the refrigerator. Don't top with the beetroot until ready to serve (the beetroot juices will bleed into the feta but that's the beauty of it).

4. Gently heat the oil in a heavy-based frying pan over a medium heat and fry the flatbread for 3–4 minutes until golden and crispy. Drain on kitchen paper (this is the traditional way that the Lebanese do it). Set aside until ready to top the final dish.

5. Arrange the red onion on a serving platter and top with the reserved lemon juice and the sumac. Allow to sit and soften the onions a little.

6. Meanwhile, heat a frying pan over a high heat and sear the lamb for 4–6 minutes on each side, depending on thickness. The pomegranate molasses will char but that's the beauty of this dish. In the last few minutes of cooking, add the marinade and cook for 3 minutes until it's syrupy. You want to cook the lamb until pink on the inside. Allow to rest for 12–15 minutes, then slice.

7. Add the tomatoes, cucumber, parsley, mint, pepper, radishes, olive oil, pomegranate seeds, molasses and flatbread to the serving platter. Mix well and season with salt and pepper.

8. Top with the lamb and serve alongside the whipped feta topped with the pickled beetroot. Enjoy!

Natasha MacAller

Honey Mango Coconut Paletas
with Chilli Chamoy

citrus | chillies | ginger

So Cal summer memories: the tinkling bells of the ice cream truck offering chocolate dipped vanilla ice cream on a stick and colourful frozen fruit Mexican popsicles called Paletas, lemon and strawberry of course but also coconut-lime, tamarindo and, my absolute favourite, mango. On the counter was a bottle filled with a brightly coloured spicy fruit sauce. You had to ask for a squeeze on top. When I finally had the courage to try the Chamoy, it was spicy but super good!

MAKES 10

2 ripe juicy mangoes, peeled, pitted and cut into chunks, or 750g (1lb 10oz) frozen pieces, thawed
75g (2½oz) honey
75ml (2½fl oz) mango juice or water
75ml (2½fl oz) lime juice
100g (3½oz) coconut cream
pinch of salt
1 teaspoon cornflour, mixed with 25ml (1fl oz) coconut cream and 25ml (1fl oz) mango juice or water
1 teaspoon vanilla extract
½ teaspoon vegetable oil, for brushing

For the chilli chamoy
80g (2¾oz) dried apricots
25g (1oz) prunes
25g (1oz) crystallized ginger
50g (1¾oz) dried sour cherries
20g dried hibiscus flowers
7.5cm (3 inch) piece of lemon peel
7.5cm (3 inch) piece of orange peel
750ml (1⅓ pints) water
4 tablespoons fresh orange juice
4 tablespoons fresh lime juice
6g (⅛oz) chilli powder
1 tablespoon chilli flakes
½ teaspoon chipotle chilli powder

1. Put the mango and honey into a medium bowl and leave to macerate for 1 hour. Add 50ml (2fl oz) of the mango juice, all the lime juice, 75g (2½oz) of the coconut cream and the pinch of salt. Using a stick blender, blitz the mixture until smooth.

2. Add the remaining coconut cream and mango juice to a medium pan with the cornflour mixture and whisk until smooth. Gently heat until just warm. Add in the mango mixture and warm through, stirring until the mixture thickens. Do not simmer. Remove from the heat and continue stirring slowly until the mixture is thick and cooled. Mix in the vanilla. Cover and put in to the refrigerator while you prepare the chamoy.

3. Add the apricots, prunes, ginger, sour cherries, hibiscus, citrus peels and measured water to a medium pan over a low heat. Bring to a low simmer and cook for about 30 minutes until the liquid reduces by about half and the fruit is softened. While the fruit cooks, squeeze the juice from the orange and set aside. Spoon the softened fruit into the blender with the remaining ingredients and blitz to a smooth paste. Return the chamoy to the pan, add the orange juice and additional water if needed to give the chamoy a thick sauce consistency. Gently warm, stirring to meld the flavours together. Transfer to a glass jar and cool, then store in the refrigerator until ready to use. This makes 500ml (18fl oz) and will keep refrigerated for up to 2 months.

4. To make the paletas, dip a small, long-handled brush into the oil and paint the inside of 10 ice lolly (paleta) moulds with a very small amount of oil to ease the release of the paletas when ready to serve. Place the moulds on a flat tray that will fit inside the freezer. Using another brush, paint the insides of each mould with a little chamoy paste, being careful to not put too much at what will become the top of the paleta, so it will unmould cleanly. Using a small funnel, gently pour or spoon the mango purée into each mould, leaving a 5mm (¼ inch) space at the top. Snap the lids on top, then slide in a wooden lolly stick, being careful to not go too deep into the moulds. Transfer to the freezer and freeze for 2 hours or until set.

5. When ready to enjoy, remove the paletas from the freezer and leave to stand for 5 minutes. Spoon the chamoy into a little serving bowl. Then using the wiggle release method, slowly pull out the paletas one by one. If they become too soft return to the freezer to harden. Serve with a napkin and spoon some extra chamoy on top of your paleta if you wish. Indulge in this sweet and spicy hot yet frozen treat.

Sarah Johnson

Chocolate Cake
with Liquorice Espresso Buttercream

liquorice root

SERVES 6

95g (3¼oz) plain flour
45g (1½oz) unsweetened natural cocoa powder, plus extra for dusting
185g (6½oz) granulated sugar
1 teaspoon bicarbonate of soda
½ teaspoon baking powder
½ teaspoon salt
60ml (4 tablespoons) vegetable oil
1 large egg
1 teaspoon ground liquorice root, plus extra for dusting
100ml (3½fl oz) buttermilk, at room temperature
100ml (3½fl oz) strong coffee, cooled

For the buttercream
90g (3¼oz) granulated sugar
1 large egg, plus 1 large egg yolk
30ml (1fl oz) water
200g (7oz) unsalted butter, at room temperature, cubed
10g (¼oz) good-quality instant espresso powder
1 tablespoon ground liquorice root
½ teaspoon salt

'Chocolate, espresso and liquorice – what a revelation! I love how the liquorice elongates the flavour of the chocolate. Add in the deep, bitter notes of espresso, and you've got a trio of flavours that are truly meant to be together.'

1. Preheat the oven to 160°C (325°F), Gas Mark 3. Grease a 450g (1lb) loaf tin and line it with nonstick baking paper. Set aside.

2. In a medium bowl, sift together the flour and cocoa powder. Add the sugar, bicarbonate of soda, baking powder and salt. Whisk together and set aside.

3. In a separate bowl, whisk together the vegetable oil, egg, ground liquorice root and buttermilk. Then whisk in the coffee.

4. Create a well in the centre of the dry ingredients. Gradually pour the wet ingredients into the dry, whisking continuously until everything is well combined.

5. Pour the batter into the prepared loaf tin and bake for 25 minutes. Rotate the tin and continue baking for another 20–25 minutes, or until a skewer inserted into the middle of the cake comes out clean. Allow the cake to cool in the tin on a wire rack.

6. To make the buttercream, in the bowl of a stand mixer fitted with the whisk attachment, whisk together the sugar, egg and egg yolk. Add the measured water to the mixture. Then place the bowl over a pan of simmering water, ensuring the bottom of the bowl does not touch the water. Continuously whisk the egg mixture until it reaches 125°C (257°F), then immediately remove from the heat.

7. Attach the bowl to the stand mixer. Whisk on medium-high speed for about 5 minutes until the mixture is thick, satiny and cooled to room temperature.

8. While mixing on medium speed, gradually add the cubes of butter. Once all the butter is incorporated, increase the speed to high and beat until the buttercream thickens and becomes glossy. Beat in the instant espresso powder, liquorice and salt. Adjust the flavouring of liquorice and salt to taste.

9. Once the cake has cooled, remove it from the tin. Spread the buttercream evenly over the top of the cake. Store any leftover buttercream in the refrigerator for up to a week or in the freezer for up to 3 months. To use it again, bring it to room temperature and re-whip in the stand mixer before using.

10. Lightly dust the cake with cocoa powder, then follow with a light dusting of ground liquorice root. Slice and serve. This will keep in the refrigerator in an airtight container for up to 2 weeks.

Alan Bartos

Peppermint Panna Cotta
with Chocolate Tuile Shards

peppermint

MAKES 4–6

150ml (5fl oz) whole milk
15g (½oz) chocolate peppermint, chopped
2 gelatine leaves
450g (1lb) double cream
60g (2¼oz) caster sugar
extra melted dark chocolate (optional), to serve

For the chocolate tuile shards
50g dark chocolate (70–85% cocoa solids)

'This Chocolate Mint Panna Cotta was born when Natasha brought me an incredible batch of freshly picked chocolate peppermint from her garden. The unique, refreshing flavour of the mint immediately inspired me to incorporate it into a French, softer-style panna cotta, creating a delicate and aromatic dessert that is simple and easy to make at home.'

1. First, prepare the mint milk. Heat the milk in a saucepan until it begins to boil, then remove from the heat. Add the chopped mint to the hot milk and leave it to infuse overnight in the refrigerator or, for a quicker option, let it sit for at least 30 minutes. Strain the milk to remove the mint pieces.
Place the gelatine leaves in a bowl of cold water and let them soften (bloom) for about 5 minutes.

2. In a saucepan, combine the cream, mint-infused milk and sugar. Bring the mixture to the boil over a medium heat, stirring occasionally. Remove the saucepan from the heat. Squeeze the excess water from the gelatine leaves and add them to the hot cream mixture. Stir until the gelatine is completely dissolved.

3. Prepare a cold bain-marie (an ice water bath). Place the saucepan in the bain-marie and stir the mixture regularly as it cools. This prevents a skin from forming on the surface. When the mixture reaches room temperature, pour it into 4–6 serving bowls or glasses. Refrigerate for at least 3–4 hours, or overnight, until set.

4. To make the chocolate tuile shards, melt the chocolate over a bain marie or in the microwave in short bursts, stirring frequently. Spread the melted chocolate thinly (2mm/¹⁄₁₆ inch) between two sheets of baking paper and chill in the refrigerator for 30 minutes until firm. When chilled, peel off the top layer of paper and break the chocolate into shard sail pieces.

5. Serve the panna cotta, dot with some additional melted dark chocolate, if using, then insert the chocolate tuile shards as 'sails'. Enjoy your delicate and refreshing chocolate mint panna cotta!

Natasha MacAller

Balancing Balls

A balancing combination of beneficial ingredients formed into little balls of delight. Fresh, easy and handmade, these are great to enjoy on the go.

Chocolate Valencia Balance Balls

Intense chocolate orange ashwagandha bites can help to ease mental and physical stress.

ashwagandha

MAKES ABOUT 16

6 tablespoons chia seeds
50g (1¾oz) raw cacao or unsweetened black (Dutch) cocoa powder
40g (1½oz) date syrup or agave nectar
35g (1¼oz) coconut butter, plus extra if needed
2 pinches of sea salt
1 teaspoon vanilla bean paste
1 teaspoon ashwagandha powder
zest of 1 tangerine, plus 2 tablespoons juice

1. Pour the chia seeds into a shallow dish and set aside.

2. Combine the remaining ingredients in a small bowl. Use your hands to work it into a smooth mixture, adding a bit more coconut oil if needed. Divide and form the mixture into about 16 balls. If they are too soft to coat at this stage, chill on a small plate in the refrigerator. When cooled, roll in the chia seeds, then keep the balls in the refrigerator for up to 2 weeks.

Carrot & Coconut Sublime Spice Balls

Superhero maca root is an energy booster, supporting mood and hormonal health.

chilli | ginger

MAKES ABOUT 16

40g (1½oz) finely grated carrot
2 teaspoons maca root powder
60g (2¼oz) desiccated coconut, lightly toasted, plus extra for rolling
1 tablespoon coconut butter
2 tablespoons coconut sugar
50g (1¾oz) ground almonds
zest of ½ lime
¼ teaspoon chilli powder
pinch of sea salt
1 teaspoon chai spice blend

For the chai spice blend
2½ teaspoons each ground cloves, ground ginger and grated nutmeg
3 tablespoons ground cinnamon
2 tablespoons ground cardamom
1 tablespoon ground black pepper

1. Mix all the chai spice blend ingredients together well. Any extra will keep in a tightly sealed jar in a cool, dark place for up to 6 months.

2. In a small bowl, combine all the spice ball ingredients, then roll into 16 balls, rolling each in the extra coconut. These keep in the refrigerator for up to 2 weeks.

PB & J Balls

If you want a squidgy, colourful, veg-packed balance ball, this is the variation for you.

beetroot

MAKES ABOUT 16

4 teaspoons beetroot powder
60g (2¼oz) ground almonds
½ teaspoon freshly grated ginger
½ teaspoon maple syrup
1 teaspoon apple cider vinegar
pinch of salt
60g (2¼oz) cashew butter
3 small dates, pitted and cut into ¼ teaspoon pieces
puffed millet or puffed quinoa, for rolling

1. In a small bowl, mix all the ingredients, except the dates and millet, together. Shape into about 16 balls but leave a small opening for a piece of date in the centre of each. Push a piece of date into each ball and roll in puffed millet or quinoa to coat evenly. These keep in the refrigerator for up to 2 weeks.

Chapter 3

A SENSE OF CALM

Ben Shewry

Shiitake Broth
with Aromatic Herbs

kombu | shiso | fennel | tarragon

'This broth is all about reducing ingredients into their essential parts in a careful, considered effort to nurture a purity from them.'

SERVES 4

350g (12oz) fresh shiitake mushrooms, thinly sliced
1.6 litres (2¾ pints) cold water
2g (¹⁄₁₆oz) kombu
light soy sauce, salt, white sugar and white pepper, to taste
a large selection of soft herbs, such as tiny basil leaves, tarragon, chervil, sorrel, chives, fennel etc
a few drops of extra virgin olive oil, to serve

1. Combine the shiitake and measured water in a saucepan and heat to 70°C (158°F). Gently continue to heat at 70°C (158°F) for 2 hours. Remove from heat and allow to cool. Strain through a fine sieve, setting the cooked shiitake aside for another use.

2. Pour the stock back into a clean pan and heat to 70°C (158°F), until hot but not quite simmering. Add kombu and continue to heat at 70°C (158°F) for 15 minutes. Remove from the heat and strain out the kombu.

3. Season the broth to taste with a decent amount of light soy sauce, a little salt, a small pinch of sugar and a tiny grind of freshly ground white pepper.

4. In warm bowls, place the soft herbs and a few drops of olive oil. Reheat the broth and pour over the bowls tableside. Eat immediately.

Allen Arnette

Rosemary & Olive Oil Dressing

rosemary | honey | pine nuts

SERVES 6

2 teaspoons extra virgin olive oil
40g (1½oz) raw honey
115g (4oz) raw pine nuts, macadamia or pecan nuts
1/16–⅛ teaspoon Himalayan salt (or any high-quality naturally occurring sea salt)
120ml (4fl oz) rosemary tea, cooled (see below)

For the rosemary tea
235ml (8fl oz) pure clean water
1 large or 2 small rosemary sprigs, rinsed, plus extra to serve

To serve (suggestion)
mixed berries (blackberries, raspberries and strawberry halves)
picked mint leaves

'One of my favourite ways to enjoy fresh herbs is as a tea. The warmth of the water and the aromatic qualities of rosemary is a spa moment – taking me away with the lift of the rosemary and the grounding of the warmth, inspiring this tisane. The longer the steep and storage time, the more rosemary there will be in the final product. Basil or holy basil is also excellent added in rosemary tea.

'Or you can use the rosemary tea to make this dressing for freshly picked berries, blackberries and strawberries, if you can get them. For a more medicinal dressing, use manuka honey instead of ordinary honey, but always raw, or substitute maple syrup for honey for a vegan version. The combo of the olive oil, the fresh aromatic rosemary, the salt/sweet of the dressing all create an antioxidant "bomb" of amazing-ness and yumminess for all ages.'

1. To make the rosemary tea, bring the measured water to the boil, then turn off the heat, add the rosemary, cover and steep for 10 minutes. Set the rosemary aside on kitchen paper. Your tea is ready! You can consume as is – it can feel healing and rejuvenating – or use it to make the dressing below. Fresh tea will last about an hour.

2. For the dressing, in a 450g (1lb) jar (that a stick blender will fit into), combine all the ingredients, except the rosemary tea. Blend into a medium-thickness dressing. It'll take about 1–1½ minutes of blending. Then, when the tea is almost cool, start adding 2 tablespoons at a time into the dressing. Keep adding the tea until you've reached the desired consistency – probably 60–120ml (2–4 fl oz) of tea will be needed – adjust for your taste preference of sweet or salty.

3. Store in a jar with a small sprig of rosemary, in the refrigerator. The dressing is ready to eat immediately. However, the longer this can sit in the refrigerator – up to 3 days – the more it will infuse with the rosemary essence – both the flavour and smell.

4. Serve with a 2.5cm (1 inch) sprig of rosemary to top for the garnish but remove prior to eating. We've used it here over a simple berry salad garnished with mint leaves. This dressing will keep refrigerated for up to a week.

David Lebovitz

Tarragon Vinaigrette

tarragon

SERVES 4

120ml (4fl oz) extra virgin olive oil
18g (¾oz) tarragon leaves
3 tablespoons red wine vinegar or sherry vinegar
1 teaspoon water
1 small shallot, sliced
1 teaspoon Dijon mustard
½ teaspoon sea salt
¼ teaspoon runny honey

For a tomato and mozzarella salad, to serve (optional)
80g (2¾oz) lettuce leaves
300g (10½oz) ripe mixed coloured tomatoes such as heirloom cherokee, campari or yellow golden sunburst, sliced or cut in wedges
280g (10oz) fresh burrata or mozzarella cheese, sliced into rounds
1 large, sweet Walla Walla onion, or other sweet onion, about 100g (3½oz), thinly sliced into rings
40g (1½oz) pea tendrils
sea salt flakes and fresh ground pepper

'After we moved into our new apartment in Paris, I was thrilled to find a huge tarragon plant in the garden, which was not only growing, but thriving. While normally a little tarragon is chopped and added to salads, this lively herbal vinaigrette, which gets its punchy flavour from a generous handful of fresh tarragon, is delicious poured over sliced tomatoes, mozzarella or grilled vegetables, or served alongside roasted meat, chicken, or fish.

'It can be made in a mini-chopper, which I prefer, or a blender, which will make it smoother. If using a blender, feel free to take it as far as you'd like in terms of smoothness.'

---

1. Put all the vinaigrette ingredients in a mini-chopper (or blender). Pulse until all the ingredients are well-mixed. This will keep in a sealed jar in the refrigerator for up to a week.

2. This is great enjoyed with a tomato and mozzarella salad. On a large platter, or four separate plates, arrange the lettuce, tomatoes, cheese, onion rounds and a scattering of pea tendrils. Drizzle with the vinaigrette and season to taste. Bliss.

Nicola Shubrook

Flaxseed, Thyme & Sunflower Bread
with Smoked Mackerel

thyme | sunflower

MAKES ABOUT 10–12 SLICES

150g (5½oz) whole golden flaxseeds, plus extra for sprinkling
115g (4oz) whole brown flaxseeds, plus extra for sprinkling
35g (1¼oz) sunflower seeds, plus extra for sprinkling
4 tablespoons psyllium husks
1 tablespoon baking powder
2 tablespoons chopped thyme (or 2 teaspoons dried thyme)
½ teaspoon sea salt
½ teaspoon freshly ground black pepper
2 tablespoons apple cider vinegar
1 teaspoon extra virgin olive oil
354ml (12fl oz) warm water

For the mackerel spread (optional)
200g (7oz) smoked mackerel
4 tablespoons crème fraîche or Greek yogurt
30g (1oz) red onion, minced
juice of ½ lime, remaining half cut into wedges
15g (½oz) minced chives
freshly ground black pepper
torn flat leaf parsley leaves, to garnish

'This delicious, vegan, gluten-free, high-fibre nutty bread has the addition of fresh thyme to give it a sweet yet slightly peppery taste. You can add more or less of the herbs subject to taste, or try swapping the thyme for other herbs, like rosemary or oregano.

'This bread can be eaten cold, or it can be toasted. It's lovely spread with smoked mackerel for a light lunch or cut bread into squares, topped with mackerel spread and served as canapés.'

---

1. Preheat the oven to 170°C (340°F), Gas Mark 4. Line a 20 × 10cm (8 × 4 inch) loaf tin with greaseproof paper or brush the tin well with some olive oil.

2. Add the whole flaxseeds to a blender, or spice grinder, and blend until finely milled. Put the ground flaxseeds into a mixing bowl and add the sunflower seeds, psyllium husk powder, baking powder, thyme, salt and pepper. Stir to combine.

3. Pour in the apple cider vinegar, olive oil and warm water. Mix with a wooden spoon or spatula until fully combined and doughy. Don't overmix as this will make the dough heavier.

4. Allow to stand for a couple of minutes. Then transfer the dough into the prepared loaf tin and gently flatten it with a spatula. Top with some extra sunflower and flaxseeds and press gently into the top of the bread mixture.

5. Place the bread on the middle shelf of the oven and bake for 1 hour or until golden. Test with a skewer that the middle is baked – the skewer should be clean when you remove it.

6. Turn off the oven and leave the bread inside for a further 10 minutes. Do not open the door until the additional 10 minutes are up. This will prevent the bread from deflating.

7. Then, remove from the oven and allow to cool in the tin for another 10 minutes before turning out on to a wire rack to cool completely.

8. Store the loaf wrapped in greaseproof paper in the refrigerator for up to 7 days.

9. If you want to serve with the mackerel spread, peel the skin off the mackerel and discard any bones. Flake the meat into a small bowl, then add the remaining ingredients gently combining with a tablespoon. Season to taste and garnish with pepper and parsley leaves. Spread on to slices of bread or cut bread into squares and then spoon the mackerel spread on top and garnish with cracked black pepper and parsley leaves.

Allan Altschul

Crispy Asparagus
with Tarragon Mayonnaise & Crispy Nettles

nettles | tarragon

SERVES 2

mild olive oil, for frying
5–6 nettle leaves (from the top 4 leaves of the plant)
5–6 asparagus spears, woody ends removed and trimmed
flaky sea salt

For the batter
250g (9oz) plain flour
5g (⅛oz) baking powder
5g (⅛oz) salt
1 egg
350ml (12fl oz) sparkling water

For the tarragon oil
150g (5½oz) vegetable oil
100g (3½oz) tarragon
2g (a pinch) salt

For the mayonnaise
25g (1oz) egg yolks
15g (½oz) lemon juice
10g (¼oz) water
100g (3½oz) tarragon oil (see above)
100g (3½oz) vegetable or rapeseed oil
sea salt to taste

'Asparagus and nettles are very important ingredients for me, they are delicious signs of spring here in the UK, reminders that the cold, dark winter days are behind us, bringing renewed hope for a warm, sunny and fruitful spring and summer. I mark their arrival on the calendar each year, which never fails to fill me with joy and great expectation for the year ahead.'

1. To make the tarragon oil, blend all the ingredients until smooth and very green. Reserve in the refrigerator overnight. When you are ready to use it, strain through a muslin cloth.

2. To make the batter, mix all the dry ingredients together in a bowl. Add the eggs and sparkling water and whisk or blend it until smooth, adjusting the texture by adding extra water if needed. The batter should have a smooth texture and consistency slightly looser than custard. Set aside for about 30 minutes before using it.

3. To make the mayonnaise, add the yolks, lemon juice and water to a blender and blend until pale. Then start slowly adding the oil. Pour in all the tarragon oil and then the vegetable or rapeseed oil until you have your desired texture. Season with salt to taste.

4. Once you have made the mayonnaise and the batter, fill a pan large enough to fit your asparagus spears three-quarters full of oil. Heat to 180°C (350°F) or when a cube of bread added to the oil browns in 30 seconds. First add the nettles and deep-fry until they are dark green and crispy, about a minute. Remove from the pan and leave to rest on kitchen paper.

5. Submerge the asparagus spears in the batter and, using a pair of tongs, remove them allowing excess batter to drip off. Drop gently into the oil and fry until golden brown. Remove carefully to kitchen paper and sprinkle with flaky salt.

6. To serve, plate the asparagus randomly on a suitable plate, add a generous dollop of mayo on the side and garnish with the fried nettles. Any remaining Tarragon Mayonnaise can be kept, sealed, in the refrigerator for up to 3 days.

Natasha MacAller

Pan-seared Snapper,
with Nasturtium & Poor Man's 'Capers'

nasturtium

SERVES 4

4 sustainably caught pink snapper, cod, plaice, rockfish or other firm white fish fillets, skinned and boned, about 115–175g (4–6oz) each
60g (2¼oz) plain flour
big pinch of pimentón
1 tablespoon avocado oil
3 tablespoons unsalted butter
flaky sea salt and freshly ground black pepper
4 stems of nasturtium flowers and leaves, to serve

For the poor man's 'capers'
60g (2¼oz) bright green and firm nasturtium seed pods, separated into single-bud pods and rinsed well (make sure they are free of dark or soft spots)
40g (1½oz) sea salt
435ml (15½fl oz) lukewarm water
120ml (4fl oz) white wine vinegar
1 teaspoon honey
1½ teaspoons sea salt
6 coriander seeds
6 pink peppercorns
1 bay leaf
2.5cm (1 inch) piece of orange peel, pith removed

For the brown butter caper sauce
55g (2oz) cold unsalted butter, cut into 8 pieces
2 tablespoons poor man's 'capers' (see above)
zest and juice of ½ lemon
3–4 nasturtium flowers, broken into petals
8–10 small nasturtium leaves

Poor Man's 'Capers' are fun to forage, tasty and, similar to pricey authentic Italian capers, a perfect pairing with fish. Forage or harvest the large pea-sized triple seed clusters of the nasturtium buds that seem to grow like weeds, just as their sunshine-orange flowers start to droop. If you are lucky enough to gather a cupful, simply double the recipe. They become deliciously like classic capers if brined first.

---

1. Start by making the poor man's 'capers', at least 4 days before using. In a 1 litre (1¾ pint) jar, dissolve the salt in the lukewarm water. Add the pods and swirl the jar to settle them. Fill a small ziplock bag with water, seal and place on top to keep the pods submerged. Leave them to sit, out of sunlight, for 2 days. Lift out the ziplock bag then, using a strainer, drain the nasturtium pods, rinsing well to remove any excess salt. You will see the pods have become more of an army green colour at this stage and have a less pungent flavour.

2. Add the vinegar, honey, salt, coriander seeds and peppercorns to a small saucepan. Bring to a simmer for 2 minutes to dissolve the honey, then remove from the heat. Fill a 225g (8oz) sterilized lidded jar with the pods, then pour over the pickling liquid, submerging the pods completely. Tuck the bay leaf and orange peel down the sides, then dry and tightly seal the jar. Allow to stand until cool. Store in a dark, dry pantry until ready to use. Once opened, store in the refrigerator for up to a year.

3. When you're ready to cook the fish, pat it dry with kitchen paper. Mix the flour with ¼ teaspoon of freshly ground black pepper, ¼ teaspoon of crushed flaky sea salt and the pimentón. Dredge the fish in the seasoned flour, shake off any excess and set on a tray.

4. In a medium to large pan that will fit the fish fillets, add the oil and butter over a medium heat, swirling the mixture to coat the pan. Bring to a good sizzle, then arrange the fillets in the pan. Cook for about 2 minutes on each side, depending on the thickness of the fish, until golden and crisp. Carefully lift the fillets from the pan and place on a warmed plate. Remove any excess oil from then pan, then return it to a low heat.

5. To make the sauce, melt the butter over a medium heat and cook for 3–5 minutes until browned. Add the poor man's 'capers' and 1 teaspoon of the lemon juice, then remove from the heat and gently fold in the nasturtium flowers and leaves. Season with salt, pepper and additional lemon juice and zest if needed. To serve, arrange the fish on plates and spoon over the sauce. Garnish each plate with a stem of nasturtium flowers and leaves. Serve immediately. This dish goes beautifully with a glass of crisp dry white wine.

Natasha MacAller

The Oak Smoked Artichoke
with Zesty Mayonnaise

artichoke

SERVES 2

2 tablespoons lemon juice
4 large globe artichokes
80ml (2¾fl oz) olive oil
1 garlic clove, minced

For the zesty mayonnaise
120g (4¼oz) mayonnaise
3 tablespoons Worcestershire sauce
2 tablespoons lemon-infused olive oil
1 tablespoon chilli oil
1 tablespoon toasted sesame oil
35g (1½ tablespoons) richly flavoured honey, such as Manuka or buckwheat
1 tablespoon fresh yuzu or lemon juice
1 tablespoon minced fresh basil leaves, plus extra picked leaves to serve
¾ teaspoon garlic salt
¼ teaspoon fresh cracked black pepper

One childhood evening, my mom decided to create something 'different', inspired by that day's episode of Julia Child's 'The French Chef' cooking show… The Artichoke. My dad arrived home, sat down, saw what he thought looked like a cross between a tumbleweed and a flower, stared at it for a moment, then took his knife and started buttering it like a piece of bread – Scots-Irish all the way! As a devout globe artichoke lover and native Californian (99% of US artichokes are grown in Castroville, CA) I'm happy to share an addictively delicious artichoke preparation finished on the grill and inspired by the late Walt's Wharf restaurant on Seal Beach California, in which I joyfully worked a summer in their pastry kitchen. Artichokes are at their peak in the mid to late spring. Choose ones that are firm, heavy for their size and with closed leaves and little give.

---

1. To make the zesty mayonnaise, whisk all the ingredients together in small bowl to blend well. Cover and refrigerate until cold.

2. To prepare the globe artichokes, fill a large bowl with enough cold water to cover the artichokes and add the lemon juice. Cut off the stem and top quarter of 1 artichoke. Bend back the dark green outer leaves and snap them off at the artichoke base until only pale green and yellow leaves remain. Cut any dark green areas off the base. Trim the tip of each leaf and discard any prickles. Cut the artichoke into single-serve wedges, then immediately submerge the trimmed artichoke in the lemon water to keep it from browning. Repeat with the remaining artichokes.

3. Place a metal steamer over a pan of just boiling water. Remove the artichokes from the lemon water and place them in the steamer. Steam the artichokes until the stems are just fork tender, about 30 minutes.

4. When steamed, remove from the steamer and place on a cooking rack to drain and dry. Using a teaspoon, scoop out the thistley choke and any purple-tipped leaves from centre of the artichoke wedges.

5. Prepare a barbecue or kitchen grill to a medium-high heat. Whisk the olive oil and minced garlic in a small bowl then brush it over the steamed artichokes. Season with salt and pepper and grill the artichokes until slightly charred, turning occasionally, for 4–8 minutes depending on size.

6. Transfer the artichokes to platter, garnish with the extra basil leaves and serve with the sauce on the side. This pairs wonderfully well with an oaky Californian Chardonnay.

Natasha MacAller

Sticky Chicken Meatballs & Ketjap Manis
on Steamed Greens

lemongrass | pineapple | ginger

Easy to make, flavourful and memorable, freshly made ketjap manis, aka Indonesian ketchup, tastes far better than store-bought. Feel free to add more or less of these ingredients to your preference – it's delicious on noodles, vegetables and even scrambled eggs! Once made, keep covered in the refrigerator where it will last for 6 months.

SERVES 4

For the ketjap manis (Makes 350ml/ 12fl oz)
200ml (7fl oz) light soy sauce
275g (9¾oz) palm or coconut sugar
50g (1¾oz) molasses
3 garlic cloves, peeled and smashed
5cm (2 inch) piece of fresh root ginger, sliced into coins
20g (¾oz) lemon grass stalks (tough, outer leaves removed), smashed
1 star anise
3 allspice berries
1 bay leaf
¼ teaspoon black peppercorns
½ teaspoon cracked cardamom pods
½ teaspoon coriander seeds
1 dried jalapeño or serrano chilli, crushed
60g (2¼oz) pineapple pieces, crushed
zest and juice of 1 makrut lime
1 tablespoon yuzu juice or lime juice

For the meatballs
700g (1lb 9oz) minced chicken
260g (9½oz) chicken sausage meat
2 eggs, beaten
2 shallots, minced
15g (½oz) fresh chives and flat leaf parsley, minced
zest of 1 lime
1 tablespoon flaky sea salt
2 teaspoons cracked black pepper
70g (2½oz) panko breadcrumbs
sunflower or canola oil, for greasing

To serve
steamed greens, such as baby bok choi, Chinese cabbage and gai lan
1 tablespoon sesame seeds (optional)
120g (4¼oz) diced pineapple pieces

1. To make the ketjap manis, add all ingredients, except the makrut lime zest and juice and the yuzu juice (if using), to a small pan. Bring to the boil, then reduce to a simmer and cook for 12–18 minutes, stirring slowly but constantly, until sauce begins to thicken. Add the makrut lime zest and juice and continue cooking for another 3–5 minutes. Test for doneness by putting a small plate in the freezer, then pour a little spoonful of the sauce on the frozen plate. Run a finger through – it should keep separate. If the sauce is still runny, cook for a few minutes more and test again. Cool, then store sealed in a sterilized jar in the refrigerator.

2. In a medium bowl, gently mix the chicken, chicken sausage meat, eggs, shallots, chives, parsley, lime zest and salt and pepper until well combined. Gently fold in the panko until evenly distributed. Using a large ice-cream scoop or 2 serving spoons, portion into twelve 80g (2¾oz) balls and set on a lightly oiled tray. Spritz or brush each one lightly with oil, then cover and refrigerate until ready to cook.

3. Preheat the oven to 200°C (400°F), Gas Mark 6. Line a roasting tray with foil and grease with oil.

4. Place the meatballs in the tray, spacing each about 1cm (½ inch) apart. Brush each meatball all over with ketjap manis, letting it run down the sides. Bake in the oven for about 20 minutes, turning halfway through cooking, until the sauce caramelizes and balls are firm and cooked through.

5. To serve, arrange the warm steamed greens on serving plates, then top each with 3 meatballs, drizzle with some additional ketjap manis, then add a spoonful of pineapple pieces and a sprinkle of sesame seeds, if liked. Serve immediately.

Natasha MacAller

Pear, Rosemary & Walnut Bundt Cake

rosemary | pear | citrus

SERVES 8–10

For the cardamom candied walnuts
125g (4½oz) fresh walnut halves
½ teaspoon ground cardamom
zest of 1 tangerine
1 teaspoon vanilla extract (I use Heilala)
105g (3½oz) granulated sugar
60ml (4 tablespoons) water
½ teaspoon flaky sea salt

For the salted caramel sauce
225g (8oz) butter
450g (1lb) caster sugar
2 teaspoons lemon juice
450ml (16fl oz) double cream, slightly warmed
½–¾ teaspoon flaky sea salt

For the cake
sunflower oil or cake release spray
300g (10½oz) plain flour, plus extra for dusting
1 teaspoon ground ginger
1 teaspoon bicarbonate of soda, sifted
1 teaspoon sea salt
2 teaspoons dried rosemary, or 1 tablespoon finely chopped fresh rosemary
2 teaspoons ground cinnamon
3 large eggs
zest of 1 lemon
270ml (9½fl oz) olive oil
200g (7oz) granulated sugar
150g (5½oz) light brown sugar
25g (1oz) molasses
3 pears, about 500g (1lb 2oz), peeled with stems removed
80g (2¾oz) walnut pieces, toasted and finely chopped

An old-fashioned treat made with tummy-calming pears and molasses, plus good-for-the-heart black walnuts and good-for-the-memory rosemary, as well as iron-rich sticky dark molasses. We had a bumper crop of pears this season and we were poring through recipes thick and fast to take advantage of our unexpectedly massive harvest before the birds managed to find the tiniest opening in the netting and peck away at those gently-scented fruits of the gods. The pear shapes were, how do I put it, only a Mom could love, some tiny, some huge, even a palm sized pear with belly button that made me giggle, but all delicious. I made cinnamon-steamed pears with maple and whipped ricotta, my fenugreek poached pear with dessert dukkha, orange and vinegar pickled pears and a twice-weekly salad of baby spinach, red onion, crumbled blue cheese and thinly sliced ripe and crunchy sliced pears, drizzled with David's tarragon vinaigrette on page 76. I saved some of my just-right, tall-enough-to-fit-standing-in-a-Bundt-pan pears for this moreish recipe.

This Bundt cake is best served with a cuppa at teatime or after dinner and offered naked or decadently drizzled with caramel and cardamom candied walnuts.

---

1. First, make the candied walnuts. Lightly toast the walnuts in a dry pan over a medium heat until fragrant, about 5–6 minutes. Then set aside to cool.

2. Mix the cardamom, tangerine zest and vanilla together and set aside.

3. Add the sugar, measured water and salt to a small, very clean pan and cook to a soft ball stage, where it measures 112–115°C (234–240°F) on a sugar thermometer (or until a small spoonful of the syrup dropped into a glass of cold water forms a soft, pliable ball). Remove from the heat and, working quickly, stir in the cardamom-vanilla mixture, then fold in the walnuts to coat. Transfer the nuts on to a silicone mat or baking paper and separate the hot walnuts quickly with gloved hands or a butter knife before they set. Leave to cool completely, then store the candied nuts in an airtight container for up to 2 weeks until ready to use.

4. To make the salted caramel sauce, begin to melt the butter in a large saucepan. Slowly stream in the sugar and stir with a wooden spoon until combined. Continue stirring and when the sugar begins to caramelize, drizzle in the lemon juice carefully as it may splatter. (Lemon juice keeps the sugar from caramelizing too quickly.) Continue cooking until the sugar syrup is a deep golden brown.

continued overleaf

Carefully remove from the heat and stream in the cream in two stages, stirring carefully to prevent splattering. Once combined, pour the hot caramel into a metal bowl placed inside a larger bowl of ice and water. Keep stirring the caramel occasionally as it cools and thickens. Once cooled, transfer the caramel to a sturdy container, such as a preserving jar with a lid. Seal and store in the refrigerator until ready to use. It will keep refrigerated, tightly sealed, for up to 6 weeks.

5. Preheat the oven to 160°C (325°F), Gas Mark 3. Grease a 2.8-litre (5-pint) Bundt tin or 2 1.4-litre (2½-pint) Bundt tins with oil or cake release spray, then dust evenly with flour, knocking out any excess flour.

6. Prepare the pears by cutting in them in half vertically, then thinly (about 6mm/¼ inch thick) slicing so the pieces will fit snugly inside the Bundt tin. Line the sides of the Bundt tin with the pear slices and set aside. Core and cube any remaining pear to add to the batter.

7. Add the flour, ground ginger, bicarbonate of soda, salt, rosemary and cinnamon to a medium bowl and whisk together then set aside. Put the eggs into the bowl of a stand mixer or a large mixing bowl. Add the lemon zest, oil, both sugars and the molasses. Attach the flat beater to the mixer, or use an electric hand whisk in the mixing bowl, and beat on medium speed for 1 minute until blended.

8. Add the flour spice mixture to the egg mixture in 2 stages and beat on a low speed for 20 seconds, just until incorporated. Scrape down the sides of the bowl. Detach the bowl from the stand and, with a large spoon, fold in the pear cubes and chopped walnuts.

9. Scoop the batter into the prepared Bundt tin, being careful that the pear slices sides remain standing, and level the top. Bake for 50 minutes–1 hour, turning the cake halfway through cooking. At 50 minutes, test if the cake is ready by seeing if a skewer, or wire cake tester, inserted into the centre comes out clean and the cake springs back when pressed lightly in the centre. Leave the cake to cool in the tin on a wire rack for 30 minutes. (If using a straight-sided tin, run a metal spatula between the sides of the tin and the cake.) Invert the cake on to a wire rack that has been lightly coated with nonstick cooking spray and leave to cool completely for about 1½ hours.

10. Carefully lift and transfer the cake to a serving plate. Using a serving spoon or jug, pour the caramel sauce on the top of cake and let it run down the sides, as pictured. Decorate the top with candied walnuts and scatter with rosemary flowers, if you like.

Natasha MacAller

Herbal Apothecary Sweets Jar

citrus | ginger | liquorice | peppermint

MAKES 60 OF EACH FLAVOUR

non-stick coin-sized silicone moulds (optional)
anti-moisture silica packets, to store

For White Sage Orange and Pepperleaf
350ml (12fl oz) freshly-boiled water
15g (½oz) dried white sage
10g (¼oz) dried hoja santa leaves (or any other sturdy, fragrant leaves, such as New Zealand horopito)
zest of 2 oranges
200g (7oz) granulated sugar
a pinch of sea salt
70g (2½oz) mild manuka or mild local honey
3–4 drops orange or fiori de sicillia extract
cooking oil spray, for oiling (optional)
icing sugar, for dusting

For Angelica, Lemon Balm, Fennel and Ginger
350ml (12fl oz) freshly-boiled water
15g (½oz) fennel seeds
10g (¼oz) angelica powder
10g (¼oz) dried lemon balm
10g (¼oz) fresh root ginger, grated
zest of 1 lemon
200g (7oz) granulated sugar
a pinch of sea salt
70g (2½oz) mild manuka honey or mild local honey
⅛ teaspoon ground turmeric
3–4 drops lemon extract
cooking oil spray, for oiling (optional)
icing sugar, for dusting

Old-fashioned boiled sweets using herbs and honey to support and soothe. You'll need a good kitchen or jam thermometer to make this recipe as it is important to record the temperature accurately. Do not attempt this on a humid day either, as the moist air will make the sweets sticky rather than hard and dry.

For Liquorice, Peppermint, Thyme and Marshmallow Root
350ml (12fl oz) freshly-boiled water
20g (¾oz) dried chopped liquorice root
15g (½oz) dried peppermint leaves
10g (¼oz) dried thyme leaves, or 15g (½oz) fresh leaves and flowers
2 teaspoons marshmallow root powder (optional)*
200g (7oz) granulated sugar
a pinch of sea salt
70g (2½oz) mild manuka honey or mild local honey
1 teaspoon black liquorice powder (optional)
½ teaspoon peppermint extract
cooking oil spray, for oiling (optional)
icing sugar or fruit powder (available from whole foods stores), for dusting

1. Place the herbs and zest for your chosen version into a 500ml (18fl oz) glass jar. Pour the measured water over all the contents and swirl around. Screw the lid on and set aside to infuse for 1–2 hours, swirling occasionally to thoroughly combine.

2. While the herbs are infusing, prepare a flat baking tray covered in lightly oiled (use a spray) baking paper, or simply use non-stick coin-sized silicone moulds.

3. When the measured water is infused, strain the mixture through a fine mesh strainer or several layers of muslin, squeezing the solids to get every drop of liquid. Reserve 240ml (8½fl oz) of the strained infusion.

4. Set everything up before you start cooking as once the mixture reaches the right temperature you will need to act quickly. Attach a confectionary thermometer to the inside of a large pot (this needs to be larger than you think, at least 3 litres/5¼ pints). Place a small bowl of iced cold water and a few teaspoons next to a large glass measuring jug on the countertop.

5. When ready to cook, add the reserved strained infusion, sugar, salt, honey and extract, if using, to the pot over a medium heat. Gently stir the mixture using a long-handled silicone spatula until the sugar is dissolved. Let the syrup come to a gentle rolling boil, occasionally stirring and scraping the bottom of the pot to prevent the sugar from burning. Continue stirring occasionally until the syrup reaches 121°C (250°F), then begin stirring continuously and scraping the bottom of the pot (be careful not to scrape too hard as this could cause the sugar to crystalize) until the temperature reaches 150°C (302°F). This will take approximately 15–20 minutes. The liquid sugar will expand, puff up and darken in colour. Keep a close eye on the thermometer, it must reach exactly 150°C (302°F) for hard crack stage, 149°C (301°F) will leave you with tooth-sticking sweets.

6. As soon as the correct temperature is reached, working quickly, turn off the heat and use a teaspoon to drop a tiny bit of the hot sugar into the cup of cold water. It will chill quickly. Using your fingers, pull the cooled sugar out, snap it and taste it to make sure it is not sticking to your teeth. If it is sticky, wait 30 seconds–1 minute longer and try again. If still sticky, return to a low heat, then repeat the process.

7. Pour the syrup into the reserved glass measuring jug, then slowly and carefully pour it into your prepared moulds, is using. If not using moulds, slowly pour little coin shaped sweets, or a large circle, onto your oiled baking paper. If the sugar becomes too cool to pour, pop the jug in a microwave oven for 10–15 seconds, then swirl until it looks pourable again. Let stand to cool.

8. If you have made a large circle, as soon as it is partially set, use a long sharp knife to score the sugar into diamonds or squares that can be broken off once completely cooled. If using moulds, or you have created coin-shaped sheets, allow the sweets to cool completely, about 3 minutes.

9. When cooled, pop the sweets out of the moulds or remove them from the baking paper (snapping along the score lines if you made one big circle). Dust the individual sweets with icing sugar or fruit powder and either wrap in cellophane or transfer the unwrapped, powdered sweets into an airtight decorative glass jar with a few anti-moisture silica packets. These will keep for up to 4 weeks. If they do become sticky in this time then dry them in an oven set to its lowest heat, cool, then tightly seal.

*If using marshmallow root powder for the liquorice, peppermint, thyme and marshmallow root variation, the marshmallow root powder should be added to the cooled herb infusion, swirled to hydrate and left to infuse with the lid back on for an additional hour before straining and cooking.

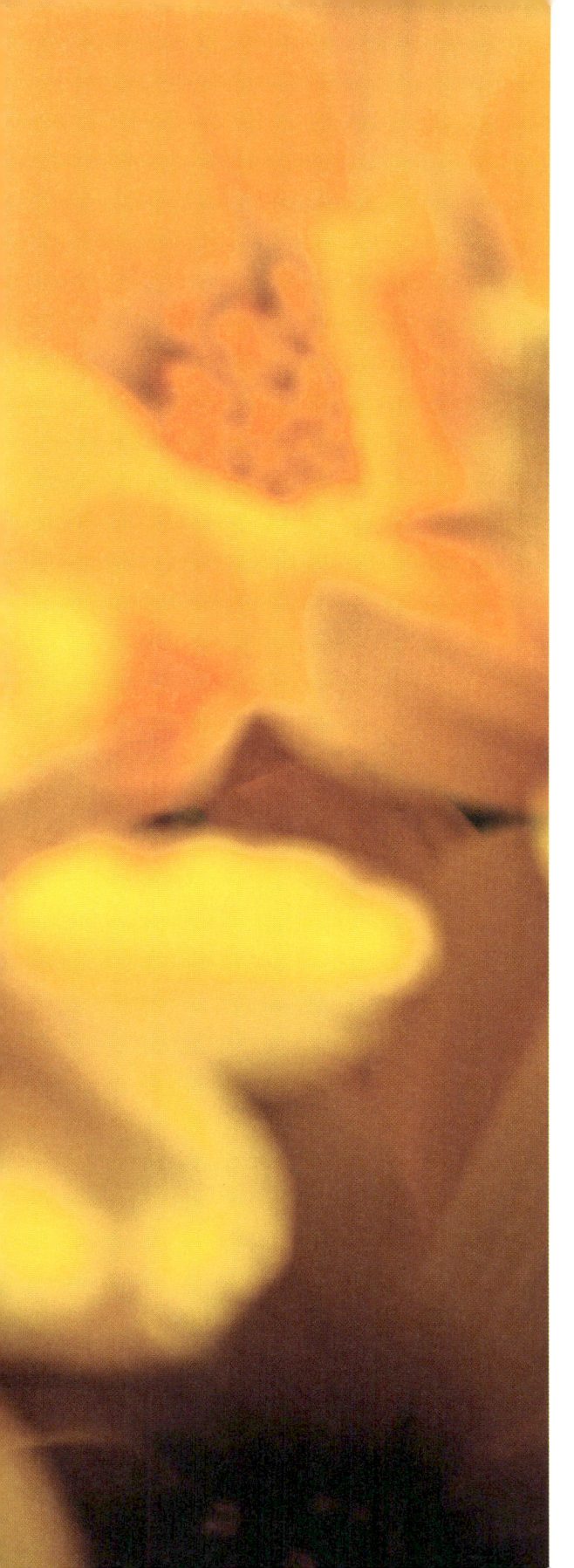

Chapter 4

IMMUNITY BOOSTERS

Natasha MacAller

Root, Rice, Leek & Nettle Soup

nettles | garlic | horseradish

SERVES 6–8

90g (3¼oz) mixed wild, red, brown and black rice
475ml (16fl oz) water
3 tablespoons extra virgin olive oil, plus extra for drizzling
½ large onion, sliced into half-moons
4 garlic cloves, chopped
1 tablespoon peeled and grated ginger
2–3 jalapeños, trimmed and chopped (deseeded if you like), or chilli paste to taste
1 teaspoon mustard powder
1 teaspoon medium chilli powder
150g (5½oz) carrots, peeled and cut into 1.5cm (⅝ inch) coins
150g (5½oz) parsnips, peeled and cut into 1.5cm (⅝ inch) coins
170g (6oz) trimmed leeks, rinsed, cut in half lengthways, then into 1.5cm (⅝ inch) semicircles
1.75 litres (3 pints) vegetable or scrap stock (see introduction) or water, plus extra if needed
45g (1½oz) brown lentils, rinsed
2 tablespoons grated horseradish, fresh or jarred
1–2 tablespoons molasses
2–3 tablespoons apple cider vinegar, to taste
80g (2¾oz) nettles, rinsed well, plus extra to serve (or baby spinach if nettles are not in season)
20g (¾oz) flat leaf parsley, chopped
light soy sauce, to taste
sea salt and freshly ground black pepper

This hearty vegan dish is a flexible and bountiful soup allowing you to use up an overabundance of vegetables hiding in your fridge or root cellar. Save your vegetable and herb odds and ends – from stringy celery to carrot tops, ginger root ends, tomato bits and woody basil stems. Simply discard the bad bits to the mulch pile, rinse the good stuff well and store in a freezer bag until you have enough to make a batch of scrap stock. To make the scrap stock, add the scraps to a pot, cover with water or stock, bring to a simmer and cook down until you have a rich broth. Strain and cool then pack and freeze until needed.

1. To cook the rice, follow the packet instructions or rinse the rice well in a colander, then add it to a saucepan with a tight-fitting lid along with the measured water. Bring to the boil, cover with the lid, reduce the heat and cook on a low simmer for 40–45 minutes. Check to see if the rice is cooked but a little al dente. If it's still too hard, cook for a further 5–7 minutes, adding additional water if needed. With the lid on, turn off the heat and let it sit for 10–15 minutes to steam. Remove the lid, season with salt and pepper, mix through, then scoop and spread the rice evenly onto a baking tray. Set aside to cool completely.

2. Set a 4 litre (7 pint) pan or casserole over a medium-low heat, swirl the oil into the pan, then add the onion and cook for 7–8 minutes until translucent. Add the garlic, ginger, jalapeños, mustard and chilli powders, stir and cook for 2 more minutes.

3. Add the carrots, parsnips and leeks, stir, then cover with the lid and sweat the veggies for 5–7 minutes. Add the stock and lentils and bring to a low simmer, adding additional stock or water as needed. Let the lentils cook for about 15–20 minutes until tripled in size and al dente.

4. Stir in the horseradish, molasses and apple cider vinegar. Add the nettles to the soup with the parsley, reserving some parsley and a few nettle leaves to garnish. Gently stir in the rice and taste and season with salt and pepper, apple cider vinegar and soy sauce.

5. To serve, ladle the soup hot into warmed soup bowls and garnish with the reserved nettle leaves and chopped parsley, and a drizzle of extra virgin olive oil. Enjoy immediately. This soup can be stored in the refrigerator for up to a week.

Natasha MacAller

Sorrel & Watercress Bisque

sorrel | watercress

SERVES 4 AS A STARTER

300g (10½oz) small ice cubes
30g (1oz) unsalted butter or olive oil
150g (5½oz) sweet onion, such as Vidalia, Maui, Cipollini Grande or Sweet Domenica), chopped
2–3 garlic cloves, roughly chopped
250g (9oz) common sorrel, small to medium leaves (stems removed), washed well
150g (5½oz) watercress or land cress with tender stems attached, washed well
85g (3oz) baby spinach leaves, washed well
100g (3½oz) peeled cooked starchy potato, such as Russet or Maris Piper
300ml (10fl oz) freshly-boiled water
sea salt and freshly ground black pepper
80ml (2¾fl oz) crème fraîche or Greek or unsweetened coconut yogurt, to serve

This simple soup is lemony-tart with a rich vegetal flavour from the watercress. If you don't have a fresh-flowing stream nearby you can easily grow land cress (Barbarea verna) in a garden bed as well as sorrel. Sorrel comes in many varieties; my favourite is pucker-up common sorrel. Cress and sorrel are both favourites for foraging, and it's so satisfying to gather and make this flavourful immune-boosting dish. Serve this glorious garden bisque hot or cold with a dollop of Greek yogurt, crème fraîche or vegan coconut yogurt. A bisque traditionally includes shellfish, but this spring to summer soup has the same creamy texture. Trade butter for olive oil and top with coconut yogurt for a vegan alternative.

---

1. Fill a bowl with the ice cubes.

2. Set a 2 litre (3½ pint) saucepan over a medium-low heat, then add the butter and heat until it sizzles. Add the onion and cook for about 5 minutes, stirring occasionally, until it becomes translucent. Add the garlic, stir and cook for a few minutes longer. Increase the heat to medium, add the sorrel, cress and spinach and cook for 3 minutes until the leaves have wilted and softened.

3. Add the potato, a big pinch of salt and pepper, then pour in the freshly-boiled water. Cook for 1½ minutes, then add the ice to shock the leaves, stirring to melt the ice and keep the vibrant green colour and beneficial nutrients of the leaves. Using a stick blender or high-spend blender, blitz the soup in a few batches until smooth and creamy.

4. Ladle the soup into small bowls, garnish with a dollop of crème fraîche or yogurt and sprinkles of salt and pepper, and indulge in this healthy and satisfying spring-summer moment.

Natasha MacAller

Quick-Pickled Coriander

coriander

MAKES 1 × 350ML (12FL OZ) JAR

60g (2¼oz) granulated sugar
60ml (4 tablespoons) water
1 teaspoon coarse sea salt
235ml (8fl oz) rice wine or apple cider vinegar
1 small shallot, minced
½–1 jalapeño, minced
½–1 teaspoon dried fenugreek leaves
¼ teaspoon celery seeds
4cm (1½ inch) piece lime peel, white pith removed
1 bay leaf
1 teaspoon coriander seeds
15g (½oz) coriander or 2 lovage or celery sticks, trimmed and cut on an angle into 2cm (¾ inch) pieces

A quick tasty brine for soft herbs is especially useful when you suddenly have a bumper crop and can't bear to relegate them to the garden compost bin. You not only preserve their flavour, but also their vivid green colour. Pickle the entire bunch with stems on and you can use both stems and leaves when garnishing your dish. Trade the coriander for other soft herbs, such as parsley, tarragon, lovage chervil or even sage leaves and use complementary pickling spices, such as toasted peppercorns and thinly sliced garlic when pickling parsley or tarragon.

This recipe also makes a quick brine for vegetables, such as lovage or celery stalks, baby carrots, fennel, bell peppers, chillies and baby onions. The brine can be refrigerated for up to 1 week before adding the herbs. Very delicate herbs such as coriander or chervil may become a deeper shade of green as they pickle, but that won't affect the flavour.

Garnish or stir the pickled coriander into the Chakalaka (see page 58), or use it to top the tomato gratin (see page 104) or hard-boiled eggs, or to garnish a refreshing michelada.

1. Combine the sugar, measured water, sea salt and vinegar in a small pan over a medium heat, stirring until the sugar and salt are dissolved. Add the shallot, jalapeño, fenugreek leaves, celery seeds, lime peel, bay leaf and coriander seeds to the saucepan. Cover and bring to a full simmer over a medium heat, then immediately remove from the heat, swirling the pan to make sure the sugar is completely dissolved. Steep uncovered until cool.

2. Pour the brine, seeds and all, into a sterilized 500ml (18fl oz) jar with a lid, loosely close the lid and refrigerate until cold, then tighten the lid.

3. Unscrew the jar of brine and set aside. Rinse the coriander in a large bowl of cold water then, holding them by the stems like a bunch of flowers, shake the herbs dry. Press the herbs down into the jar of cold brine, making sure all bits are completely submerged. Using a clean cloth or paper towel, dry the screw top of the jar then seal tightly and store in the refrigerator at least 2 hours before uisng. This will keep in the refrigerator for about 4 weeks.

Natasha MacAller

Farro Power Bowl
with Dua Gia, Charred Wild Garlic & Tahini Fig Vincotto Dressing

garlic | wild garlic | sorrel | onion

This all began with a bottle of tahini dressing and some Emmer Farro, which I then paired with sweet, aromatic cumin carrots. The carrots are nutrient-packed and also make a lovely side accompaniment to pork and chicken dishes. The recipe makes more than needed but will keep for a week chilled and can be used as a great soup and sauce base.

SERVES 4

160g (5¾oz) farro
4 fresh garlic scapes or spring onions (roots and all), well-washed, dried, then lightly charred on a barbecue or in a griddle pan
small handful of lemon sorrel, shredded
small handful of baby spinach, shredded
small handful of fresh soft garden herbs (such as dill, basil, parsley, lovage, cress and pea sprouts)
180g (6oz) ricotta salata (or vegan alternative), sliced into chunks
2 teaspoons black sesame seeds

For the dua
120ml (4fl oz) white wine vinegar
120ml (4fl oz) warm water
170g (6oz) palm sugar, chopped
1 tablespoon sea salt
200g (7oz) mung bean sprouts
½ medium red onion, thinly sliced
115g (4oz) spring onions, sliced diagonally
1 small cucumber, about 100g (3½oz), peeled, deseeded and cut into cubes
60g (2¼oz) mangetout, thinly sliced on the diagonal
1 large red pepper, cored, deseeded and thinly sliced

For the cumin carrots
500ml (18fl oz) fresh carrot juice
80g (3oz) dried apricots, chopped
1 teaspoon toasted cumin powder
20g (¾oz) fresh root ginger, grated
8 small whole carrots, about 140g (5oz), peeled and halved lengthways

For the sesame sprinkle
1 tablespoon sesame seeds
1 teaspoon salt flakes
¼ teaspoon each cumin seeds
¼ teaspoon dried sumac

For the tahini fig dressing
40g (1½oz) tahini
1 tablespoon white miso paste
1 tablespoon soy sauce
1 tablespoon fig vincotto or balsamic syrup
1 teaspoon chilli paste
1 tablespoon apple cider vinegar
juice of 1 large lemon, or to taste
2 teaspoons maple syrup
50g (1¾oz) fresh, or rehydrated then drained dried, garden figs (about 3), stems removed, figs chopped
2–3 garlic cloves, peeled and smashed
big pinch of sea salt

1. First make the dua gia. Whisk together the vinegar, water, palm sugar and salt in a medium non-reactive bowl until dissolved. Add the beansprouts, onions, cucumber, mangetout and red pepper to a large bowl. Pour the liquid into the bean sprout mixture and combine. Transfer to a large container and refrigerate for at least 6 hours.

2. To make the cumin carrots, add all the ingredients except the carrots to a small pan. Bring to a simmer over a low heat for about 5 minutes, add a pinch of salt, then use a stick blender to puree. Add the carrots and gently simmer until fork tender and the juice is reduced and thick, about 10–12 minutes. Refrigerate in the sauce until ready to serve.

3. Rinse and drain the farro into a medium pan with a lid. Add 750ml (1⅓ pints) of water and bring to the boil. Reduce to a low simmer, cover and cook for 20–25 minutes until toothsome and tender. Cool, then set aside until ready to assemble.

4. To make the sesame sprinkle, add all the ingredients to a small sauté pan and gently toast until fragrant.

5. Using a bullet or stick blender, blitz all the tahini fig dressing ingredients with 150ml (5fl oz) water until smooth and creamy. Check the seasoning and thin with a little more water if needed.

6. To assemble, remove the carrots from the sauce and generously top them with the sesame sprinkle. Toss the farro with a little dressing, then add to a serving bowl. Arrange the greens, dua gia, cumin carrots and ricotta salata on top. Top with the charred wild garlic. Drizzle over the remaining dressing, sprinkle with black sesame seeds and serve.

Natasha MacAller

Allotment Tomato, Anchovy & Parmesan Gratin

parsley | chives | alliums

One of the many joys of late summer is picking heavy fragrant multi-coloured heirloom tomatoes at their peak of flavour and making this quick gratin, to serve as an al fresco lunch or an evening side dish.

SERVES 4

4 large heirloom tomatoes (your favourite varieties)
2 teaspoons flaky sea salt crumbled with 1 teaspoon granulated sugar
3 tablespoons extra virgin olive oil, plus extra for drizzling
130g (4½oz) fresh sourdough bread, torn into chunks
1 onion, chopped
1–2 garlic cloves, chopped (optional)
3–4 anchovy fillets in oil, drained and chopped
small handful of flat leaf parsley leaves, chopped
1 tablespoon capers, drained
60g (2¼oz) freshly grated hard cheese, such as pecorino or Parmesan

To serve
chopped chives
freshly ground black pepper

1. Core, then horizontally slice the tomatoes into 1cm (½ inch) thick circles. Arrange the tomatoes in a single layer on a grated cooling rack on top of a baking tray, sprinkle with the salt and sugar mix and leave to drain for 1–1½ hours.

2. Preheat the oven to 160°C (325°F) Gas Mark 3. Brush a gratin dish with olive oil and set aside.

3. Heat 1 tablespoon of the olive oil in a medium saucepan. Add the sourdough chunks and cook, stirring frequently, for 6–8 minutes until toasted golden brown. Transfer the croutons to kitchen paper to drain.

4. Put the remaining olive oil into a small pan. Add the onion and cook over a low heat for 5–7 minutes, stirring occasionally, until translucent. Add the garlic (if using), anchovies, parsley and capers, combine well, then remove from the heat.

5. Fan the drained tomatoes in the bottom of the gratin dish in 2–3 layers, then spoon the onion mixture in an even layer on top. Sprinkle over the croutons, then sprinkle cheese over everything. Drizzle with olive oil and bake for 40 minutes, or until golden brown. Sprinkle the chives over top, garnish with black pepper and serve warm.

Note: A tasty technique to make croutons is to cut or tear open a fresh loaf of sourdough and pull random-sized pieces of bread with your fingers from the centre to the crust. Toast in a low oven until dry, cool completely then freeze tightly wrapped until needed.

Pierre Koffmann

Tourte de Pommes de Terre à l'Ail
Potato & Garlic Pie

garlic | parsley

'A take on a classic dish from the Limoges region of France.'

SERVES 4

400g (14oz) all-butter puff pastry
plain flour, for dusting
500g (1lb 2oz) potatoes, such as Désirée, unpeeled and very thinly sliced
2 garlic cloves, finely chopped (you can add a few chopped wild garlic leaves if in season)
2 tablespoons chopped flat leaf parsley
1 egg yolk lightly beaten with 1 tablespoon milk
100ml (3½fl oz) double cream
1 egg yolk
salt and freshly ground black pepper

1. Preheat the oven to 200°C (400°F), Gas Mark 6.

2. On a lightly floured surface, roll out three-quarters of the pastry and use it to line a medium gratin dish (about 16 × 20cm/6¼ × 8 inches).

3. Put the potatoes, garlic, parsley and seasoning in a bowl, mix well, then place in the pastry-lined gratin dish. Roll out the rest of the pastry and place it on top of the potatoes to make lid. Carefully seal the edges and brush the top with the beaten egg yolk mixture. Cut a hole in the lid to let the steam escape and bake the pie for 55 minutes.

4. Mix together the cream and egg yolk. Remove the pie from the oven and, using a funnel, pour the cream mixture into the pie through the hole in the pastry. Return the pie to the oven for 5 minutes, then remove and serve warm from the oven.

John La Puma

Nasturtium & Miner's Lettuce Pesto Pasta
with Butter Beans

miner's lettuce | nasturtiums | alexanders

SERVES 10

130g (4½oz) raw cashew nuts
3 garlic cloves, roughly chopped
75g (2½oz) packed miner's lettuce or Alexanders (small stems are fine)
30 nasturtium leaves, measuring about 7.5–10cm (3–4 inches) each
1 whole large (or 2 small) lemons (ideally Meyer), peeled
⅔ teaspoon salt
¼ teaspoon ground black pepper
250ml (9fl oz) extra virgin olive oil (preferably organic), plus extra for drizzling
400g (14oz) dried pasta bowties or your favourite shape
1 × 400g (14oz) can of butter beans, drained and rinsed
grated Parmesan cheese, to serve (optional)

'Every spring, these two greens pop up on our Santa Barbara farm, often at the edge of the oak woodlands meditation trail. Gathering them in the morning, still dew dropped, for this thrillingly iridescent spread couldn't be easier. Garnish with nasturtium petals and blooming miner's lettuce seeds, if you can find them.

'These greens are easily found and grown, nearly anywhere it is cool and moist. And they're not only delicious but powerfully part of your garden medicine cabinet. The Miner's Lettuce variety "Naturita" is especially high in lutein, the eye-protecting antioxidant that fights against macular degeneration, the leading cause of blindness in people over 65. Miner's lettuce is tops in vitamin C – in fact, Gold Rush miners ate it to stave off scurvy.

'Alexanders found in the UK and Europe can be substituted for miner's lettuce. Macadamia nuts can be used instead of cashews. Finely grated Parmigiano Reggiano can be added if you wish: reduce the salt to ¼ teaspoon if so.'

1. Place the cashew nuts and garlic in the bowl of a food processor fitted with a steel blade. Process for about 10 seconds until coarsely chopped. Add the lettuce and the nasturtium leaves, lemon, salt and pepper and process for about 1 minute until it resembles a stiff paste. Drizzle the olive oil through the processor tube while processing and continue until the pesto is blended completely. If not dolloping on to pasta, gigante beans or an omelette right away, keep in the refrigerator and cover the container with a thin layer of olive oil to prevent oxidation and preserve the brilliant green colour.

2. Cook the pasta according to the packet instructions until al dente. Drain well, add the butter beans to warm them and drizzle with a little olive oil. Arrange in bowls and spoon a generous amount of the pesto on top. Sprinkle with grated Parmesan, a drizzle of oil and serve immediately.

Natasha MacAller

Four Fish & Herb Stew

lovage | dill | fennel | chillies | lemon sorrel

SERVES 4

300g (10½oz) monkfish, skinned, boned and cut into bite-sized pieces (skin and bones reserved)
300g (10½oz) sustainable fresh, white fish (snapper, cod or grouper), skinned, boned and cut into bite-sized pieces (skin and bones reserved)
300g (10½oz) salmon, skinned, boned and cut into bite-sized pieces (skin and bones reserved)
400g (14oz) shell-on large prawns, peeled, deveined and sliced lengthways (shells reserved)

For the fish stock
1 litre (1¾ pints) fish stock
235ml (8fl oz) water
½ onion, unpeeled, roughly chopped
1 carrot, about 70g (2½oz), halved
6–8 black peppercorns, toasted
1 garlic clove, unpeeled and crushed
2 bay leaves
5g (⅛oz) lovage sprigs
5g (⅛oz) dill fronds and stems

For the lemon sorrel aioli
3 large egg yolks
1 tablespoon Dijon mustard
2 garlic cloves
175ml (6fl oz) extra virgin olive oil
2 tablespoons fresh lemon juice, or to taste
½ teaspoons sea salt
60g (2¼oz) lemon sorrel leaves, finely chopped

For the stew
1 garlic clove, minced
5g (⅛oz) dill fronds, roughly chopped

This light flavoursome stew is packed with beneficial omegas and nutrients from the fish, herbs and a veritable cornucopia of vegetables. Feel free to mix and match the fresh fish and seafood to your taste. Dressed up with the lemon sorrel aioli it becomes an elegant go-to dinner party dish. Serve with toasty garlic bread and boiled baby potatoes.

20g (¾oz) lovage or celery leaves, chopped
5g (⅛oz) flat leaf parsley, chopped
1 tablespoon chopped tarragon, or ½ teaspoon dried tarragon
2 shallots, about 50g (1¾oz), minced
½ fennel bulb, about 80g (2¾oz), thinly sliced
160g (5¾oz) courgette, cubed
½ red pepper, deseeded and chopped
1 small pak choi, about 170g (6oz), halved and cut into bite-sized pieces
35g (1¼oz) carrot, peeled into ribbons
120ml (4fl oz) dry white wine or zero-alcohol white wine
1 tablespoon cornflour, whisked with 3 tablespoons cold stock or water
lemon juice, to taste
1½ teaspoon sriracha, or to taste
sea salt and freshly ground black pepper

1. Pat dry the fish and prawns, then store chilled on a kitchen paper-lined tray until ready to serve.

2. To make the fish stock, add all the ingredients to a 3–4 litre (5¼–7 pint) pan with the reserved fish skin and bones, and the prawn shells. Bring to a low simmer for about 45 minutes, the remove from the heat and leave to cool. Strain. (The stock can be made ahead of time and kept frozen for 1 month.)

3. To make the lemon sorrel aioli, put the egg yolks, mustard and garlic in blender and process on low for 2 minutes. With the motor running, slowly drizzle in the olive oil. Add the lemon juice, salt and sorrel and blend until smooth. Check and adjust the seasoning. Alternatively, the aioli can be made by hand in a big bowl with a whisk. Cover and chill until ready to serve. This makes 225g (8oz) and will keep in the refrigerator for up to 3 days.

4. To make the stew, return the strained stock to the pan and add the garlic, dill, lovage, parsley, tarragon, shallots, fennel, courgette and red pepper and return to a low simmer. Once the fennel is just fork tender, add the pak choi, carrot and wine and cook until the pak choi is just fork tender. Gently stir in the cornflour mixture to thicken. Add the fish and prawns, put the lid on and gently simmer for 2–3 minutes until the fish and prawns are just cooked. Season with lemon, salt, pepper and sriracha to taste.

5. To serve, ladle the fish stew into individual bowls, then swirl a large spoonful of lemon sorrel aioli over the top. Pour or spoon the remaining aioli into a little jug to pass around at the table.

Cyrus Todiwala

Patrani Macchi

coriander | lime | chillies

SERVES 4–6

3 pomfret, cut into 2.5cm (1 inch) thick pieces
¾ teaspoon ground turmeric
1–2 banana leaves (available in Thai, Philippine or Indian food stores)
malt vinegar, for sprinkling
salt

For the coconut chutney
1 coconut, grated or 200g (7oz) finely ground desiccated coconut
200g (7oz) coriander, plus extra to serve
4–5 green chillies
6–8 garlic cloves
1 heaped teaspoon cumin seeds
1 tablespoon sugar
juice of 2 limes or lemons, plus extra to taste
200g (7oz) mint

'Patrani macchi is a classical Parsee fish preparation and is very popular at weddings and other festive occasions. If banana leaf is not available, substitute it with foil. You can also top a fish fillet, or a whole fish, with the chutney and cook directly under a grill. Pomfret is a flat roundish fish quite like a pompano. You can use filleted plaice, or any other white fish if you like but there is no doubt pomfret is the best. Alternatively, use 150–200g (5½–7oz) bass fillets per portion. This recipe will produce enough chutney for 5–6 fillets.'

1. Preheat the oven to 190°C (375°F), Gas Mark 5.

2. Rub each slice of fish with salt and turmeric and set aside while you make the coconut chutney.

3. Grind all the chutney ingredients into a paste in a food processor or high-powered blender, using only as much water as you think the machine needs to grind. Refrigerate for at least an hour to allow the flavours to infuse.

4. Coat each slice of the fish with the coconut chutney on both sides.

5. Remove the stems from the banana leaves and cut them into squares big enough to cover each fish piece. The leaf squares have to be warmed over an open flame to make them soft and supple. To do this, just run them over a gas burner or hot plate and you will see them change colour and become soft and a bit shiny. Do not overdo it, just one pass on either side is often sufficient.

6. Place each piece of coated fish on a banana leaf and gently fold the sides of the leaf over into a parcel. Tie each parcel with string to prevent the chutney from coming out. Alternatively, you can wrap the fish in foil or greaseproof paper and follow the same method. However, I cannot guarantee the same flavour.

7. Put the wrapped fish on a flat tray, sprinkle some vinegar over the parcels, then a little water and put them in the oven. Steam for about 20 minutes.

8. Just before serving, remove the strings. Serve the fish on the banana leaf with a scattering of coriander.

Peter Gordon

Curry Leaf-crusted Fish in a Lemon Myrtle Coconut Sauce
with Finger Lime & Sweet Potato Salad

lemon myrtle | finger lime | sweet potato

'Most fish will work well for this recipe, although you want the flesh to be between 2–3cm (¾–1¼ inches) thick for the best result. John Dory, snapper, sea bass, salmon, halibut and trevally all work well.'

SERVES 4

4 skinless, boneless fish fillets (see intro)
3 curry leaf stalks, leaves picked and coarsely shredded
1–2 shallots, finely diced (about 2 tablespoons)
1 tablespoon vegetable, grapeseed, olive, extra virgin rapeseed or sunflower oil, plus extra for cooking
1 teaspoon finely diced fresh ginger
1 garlic clove, finely diced or crushed
2–3 fresh lemon myrtle leaves, rolled in the palm of your hand to help release their essential oils (or ½ teaspoon ground lemon myrtle)
¼ teaspoon finely grated fresh turmeric (or ⅛ teaspoon ground turmeric)
¼ teaspoon coriander seeds, slightly crushed
300ml (½ pint) fish stock
400ml (14fl oz) coconut milk
flaky sea salt

For the salad
500g (1lb 2oz) sweet potatoes, scrubbed and cut into 1cm (½ inch) dice
1 finger lime, flesh squeezed out
10 Vietnamese mint leaves, shredded lengthways about 3mm (⅛ inch) across
1½ tablespoon thinly sliced chives
⅛ teaspoon coarsely ground black pepper
1 tablespoon extra virgin olive oil
flaky sea salt, to taste

1. Lightly salt the fish fillets on both sides and chill in the refrigerator for 20 minutes. Pat dry with kitchen paper and place on a clean tray or plate. Sprinkle half the curry leaves on top and press them in, then flip the fish over and sprinkle the remainder of the leaves on, pressing them in firmly. Seal tightly with clingfilm and leave in the refrigerator while you make the rest of the components.

2. In a medium pan, sauté the diced shallot in the extra vegetable oil over a medium heat for 4 minutes until it has become slightly translucent. Add the ginger and garlic and fry for 3 minutes until aromatic. Add the lemon myrtle, turmeric and coriander seeds and sauté for another 30 seconds, stirring gently. Add the fish stock and bring to the boil, then reduce the heat to a simmer until the liquid has reduced by a third. Add the coconut milk and bring to the boil, then reduce the heat and simmer until reduced by a third. Taste for seasoning.

3. Steam or boil the sweet potatoes in lightly salted water until just done – a little al dente is better than overcooked. Drain and leave to cool on a tray to come to room temperature. Once cooled, transfer them to a large bowl and squeeze in half the finger lime pulp. Add the Vietnamese mint, chives, black pepper, extra virgin olive oil and 1 teaspoon of flaky sea salt and gently mix it all together. Taste for seasoning.

4. Drizzle ½ teaspoon of oil over each fish fillet (2 teaspoons in total). Heat a pan and, when medium-hot, carefully place the fish fillets in. If your pan can only hold 2 or 3 fillets, then cook 2 at a time. You want the curry leaves to crispen up before you carefully flip them over and cook the same way on the other side. The fish should be slightly undercooked in the centre before you remove the fillets. The easiest way to check is to use a sharp knife to cut into the thickest part of the fillet – it shouldn't be fully cooked all the way through. Once cooked, remove the fish fillets to a warm plate.

5. Divide the sweet potato salad between 4 plates and lay a fillet of fish on top of each one. Give the coconut sauce a good stir, then spoon it on top of the fish. Squeeze over the remaining finger lime pulp.

Elizabeth Falkner

Out-of-this-World Vegan Tacos
with Sweet Potato, Salsa Macha & Coconut Yogurt

sweet potato | avocado | chilli | coriander

SERVES 6

2 purple or orange sweet potatoes

For the salsa macha
2 ancho chillies, deseeded
2 guajillo chillies, deseeded
4–6 Chile de arbol chillies, deseeded
350ml (12fl oz) olive or rapeseed oil
20g (¾oz) pumpkin seeds
3–4 garlic cloves, chopped
35g (1½oz) roasted peanuts
½ teaspoon cumin seeds
1 tablespoon sesame seeds
3 tablespoons apple cider vinegar
1 teaspoon Mexican oregano
good pinch of salt, to taste

For the corn tortillas (optional)
325g (11½oz) masa harina
pinch of coarse sea salt
415ml (15fl oz) room temperature water

For the flour tortillas (optional)
275g (9¾oz) plain flour
½ teaspoon coarse sea salt
1 teaspoon baking powder
1 tablespoon rapeseed oil
175ml (6fl oz) room temperature water

For the guacamole
2 ripe avocados, pitted and roughly chopped
½ white or red onion, chopped
juice of 1–2 limes
½ jalapeño, minced
a handful of coriander leaves and a few stems, chopped
1 makrut lime leaf, minced
coarse sea salt and black pepper

'I love to use the vibrant colours of different ingredients and I just adore the flavour and nutrition in roasted sweet potatoes. This recipe adds to that the earthy and spicy salsa macha and… wow. I made up this guacamole with lime leaf a few years ago and it's a real people pleaser with amplified lime flavour.

'Recipes such as this are the Cliff Notes of my personal journey through tasting, cooking and learning more about food. It's a shorthand study of ingredients combined with art, history, science, culture and, ultimately, the love of balancing poetry and architecture with the pleasure of eating.

'Very early on I learned to respect the culinary traditions of preparing everything from scratch and without shortcuts. The gratification from making pasta, noodles, sourdough bread, filo and homemade tortillas, in this case, is worth it! Making homemade tortillas such as the ones in this is not that difficult and it's so satisfying. I promise you are going to love these.

'In the last decade, I have been obsessed with all the varietals of different fruits and vegetables grown in different parts of the world. And I always look for vibrant natural colours and textures in foods for the nutrition they provide and for the artistry of how they appear at the table. In the interests of seasonal and regional eating, please feel free to experiment and utilize other ingredients from wherever you are in the world and don't feel like you have to use everything listed here. Mixing it up is part of the fun!'

To serve
salt
120ml (4fl oz) coconut yogurt or other yogurt
60ml (4 tablespoons) salsa macha
handful of coriander sprigs
1–2 limes

continued overleaf

1. Make the salsa macha ahead of time to allow the flavours to meld together. In a dry cast-iron pan over a medium heat, roast the chillies until they begin to blister, then remove from the pan and set aside.

2. Add a tablespoon of the oil to the pan, turn the heat to low and add the pumpkin seeds and garlic. Cook for a few minutes until toasty. Turn off the heat, then add the peanuts, roasted chillies, cumin and sesame seeds and stir to toast the seeds for 1 minute. Then add the apple cider vinegar, stir and set aside to cool.

3. When cooled, add the oregano and a good pinch of salt, then half of the remaining oil. Pour into food processor or blender and pulse a few times until combined. Add the rest of the oil and season with salt as needed. Store in a tightly sealed sterilized jar for up to 4 weeks.

4. To make the corn tortillas, if using, combine the ingredients with most of the water then, using your hands, knead until for a few minutes into a smooth mass, adding more water if needed. Divide into 6 and shape into balls, then roll flat into tortillas. If you don't have a tortilla press, place a sheet of baking paper on top of 1 ball and roll with a rolling pin until thin and even. Repeat the process with the remaining 5 balls.

5. To make the flour tortillas, if using, combine the ingredients with most of the water to form a cohesive dough. Knead for a few minutes into a smooth dough, adding more water if necessary. Cover the dough and leave to rest for 15–20 minutes. Divide into 6 and shape into balls then roll into tortillas as in step 4 above.

6. Preheat the oven to 200°C (400°F) Gas Mark 6. Put the sweet potatoes into the oven and roast for about 30 minutes until tender. Remove from the oven, split the potatoes apart and salt to taste.

7. Meanwhile, make the guacamole. Add the avocado, white or red onion and juice of 1 lime to a bowl and sprinkle with salt, then mix together with a fork. Add the jalapeño, coriander and lime leaf and mix. Taste and add more salt, lime juice or black pepper, as needed. Set aside until ready to serve.

8. Whether you are using corn or flour tortillas, cook each tortilla in a griddle or a cast-iron pan over a high heat for about a minute on each side until it starts to brown a little and puff up. Cover the cooked tortillas with a clean tea towel so they will steam and finish cooking as you cook the remaining tortillas.

9. To serve, reheat the tortillas in microwave or steamer, or directly over a fire. Scoop the sweet potato into tortillas and spoon some of the yogurt and guacamole next to it. Finish with the salsa macha, a sprig of coriander and a squeeze of lime.

Natasha MacAller

Bittersweet Chocolate Chicory Fandango

chicory | pine tips

SERVES 6

A fandango of tastes and textures that will have you dancing on the tabletop. This sultry smooth chicory chocolate delice is cut into triangles and suspended on shiny vanilla gelée for a dramatic effect. A showstopper dessert which can be made and plated ahead of time, reserving the crunchy chocolate pine-scented brownie bark and blue chicory flowers to arrange just before serving.

For the pine-scented brownie bark
80g (2¾oz) 70% dark chocolate, broken into medium pieces
60g (2¼oz) unsalted butter, softened
2 large pinches of sea salt flakes, crumbled
1 large egg and 2 large egg whites, beaten
1½ teaspoons vanilla extract
180g (6oz) granulated sugar
50g (1¾oz) plain flour
35g (1¼oz) rye flour
25g (1oz) black (Dutch) cocoa powder
2 teaspoons ground chicory
¼ teaspoon baking powder, sifted
70g (2½oz) cacao nibs
1½–2 teaspoons spruce pine salt flakes* or plain flaky sea salt

For the chocolate chicory delice
400ml (14fl oz) double cream
140ml (5fl oz) whole milk
2 tablespoons ground chicory root or ground chicory
6 large egg yolks
360g (12½oz) 72% dark chocolate, chopped
¼ teaspoon sea salt
1 tablespoon vanilla bean paste (I use Heilala)

For homemade sweetened condensed milk
80ml (3fl oz) double cream
80g (3oz) caster sugar
a pinch of salt

For the vanilla cream gelée
homemade sweetened condensed milk (see above) or 4 tablespoons sweetened condensed milk from a can
75ml soured cream
pinch of sea salt
2 teaspoons vanilla bean paste (I use Heilala)
75ml (2½fl oz) whole milk
2¾ silver gelatine leaves or 5g (⅛oz) powdered gelatine and 30ml (1fl oz) water
90ml (3fl oz) cream
80g (3oz) sugar

1. Preheat the oven to 180°C (350°F), Gas Mark 4. Line 2 baking trays each measuring 33 × 25cm (13 × 10 inch) with baking paper or silicone mats.

2. To make the pine-scented brownie bark, melt the chocolate and butter with the salt in a heatproof bowl over a saucepan of simmering water, making sure the bottom of the bowl does not touch the water. Gently stir until nearly melted. Remove from the heat and leave to cool on a work surface, stirring until smooth and cooled. Whisk in the egg mixture and vanilla until well combined.

3. In a separate bowl, sift together the sugar, flours, cocoa, ground chicory and baking powder, then stir into the chocolate and egg mixture. It will be grainy and tight. Using the back of an offset, or a regular, spatula, spread the dough from edge to edge of both prepared baking trays, levelling and then smoothing the top. Sprinkle with the cacao nibs and lightly dust with the spruce salt flakes.

4. Bake for 25–27 minutes. Remove from oven and leave to cool completely before breaking into crisp shards. Store any leftovers in an airtight container for up to 2–3 weeks.

5. To make the delice, warm the cream and milk with the chicory in large pan until steamy. Turn off the heat and leave to infuse for 20–30 minutes. (If using ground chicory root, strain it out before continuing with the recipe.)

continued overleaf

6. In a separate bowl, whisk the egg yolks, then add a little of the warmed milk to the yolks and stir. Whisk this egg mixture back into the pan with the cream and milk and gently stir, scraping down the sides of the pan occasionally until the custard mixture coats the back of a spoon and a finger drawn through leaves a set line.

7. Lightly spray a 33 × 25cm (13 × 10 inch) baking tin with water then line it with clingfilm with the edges hanging over sides. Smooth the clingfilm down and set aside. Transfer the chopped chocolate into a bowl and pour the custard over, give it a wiggle to settle the chocolate, sprinkle in the salt, then let it stand for 1 minute. Stir gently in a slow motion (no bubbles) until combined and the chocolate is melted and smooth. Cover with clingfilm and chill until ready to use.

8. If you are making your own condensed milk, set a small saucepan over a low heat. Add all the ingredients and whisk until the sugar is dissolved. Turn the heat up to medium and simmer, using a spatula to keep the mixture from sticking to bottom and sides of the pan. Cook until the mixture has thickened and reduced down, about 12–15 minutes. Transfer to a small bowl and set aside to cool.

9. To start making the gelée, whisk the room-temperature condensed milk with the soured cream, salt and vanilla bean paste until smooth and set aside.

10. When ready to finish the gelée, warm the whole milk in the microwave or a pan until steamy. Squeeze out the water from the gelatine leaves, then add the softened gelatine to the whole milk and stir to dissolve. Whisk in the soured cream/condensed milk mixture and strain the combined liquid into a jug. Carefully divide the liquid evenly between 6 rimmed dessert plates. Place in the refrigerator and chill until set.

11. When ready to serve, place the vanilla gelée plates on a work surface. Lift the chocolate delice from the tin pan using the clingfilm edges and place on a chopping board. With a hot sharp knife, cut the delice into clean-edged triangles. Then peel off the clingfilm and arrange a triangle on each plate as shown in the photo opposite. Garnish with shards of pine-scented brownie bark and chicory or edible flowers. Serve immediately.

* To make your own spruce pine salt, blitz 25g (1oz) fresh pine tips, 40g (1½oz) coarse sea salt and 1 tablespoon of water in a spice grinder until it forms a smooth paste. Spoon the paste onto a smooth, solid dehydrator tray and spread it into an even layer. Dry at 40°C (104°F) until completely dried, about 1 hour. If you don't have a dehydrator, spread the mixture thinly (about 3mm/⅛in thick) over a large dry baking tray or silicone baking sheet and dry out in an oven on its lowest setting, checking every 10 minutes or so, until dried. When dried, allow to cool completely, then break into flakes and store in the freezer in an airtight container for up to 6 months.

Note: You can use this recipe for rosemary salt too using the same quantities, but make sure you use small rosemary tips from the top of branches as rosemary needles can be bitter and overpowering.

Henrietta Inman

Mantulky
Honey Cookies from Ukraine

dill | sunflower | honey

MAKES 24

100g (3½oz) unsalted butter
100g (3½oz) golden caster sugar
30g (1oz) runny honey
1 egg
290g (10¼oz) wholemeal flour
2g (¼ teaspoon) coarse sea salt
30g (1oz) linseeds
20g (¾oz) sunflower seeds
20g (¾oz) hulled hemp seeds
30g (1oz) raisins
20g (¾oz) candied squash or candied orange peel
3g (1 tablespoon) dill seeds

'These fragrant honeyed biscuits were inspired by my dear friend Olia Hercules' recipe in her book, 'Summer Kitchens'. When she was young, Olia's friend Katrya, a wonderful baker (see her Instagram @seldonenko), read about a character in Ukrainian literature munching these, only to discover the recipe for them years later in a classic Ukrainian cookbook from 1913! "Manty" means dumpling. These are sweet little, crunchy-soft dumplings, bejewelled with fruit and seeds; the dill seeds add a little bit of extra Ukrainian magic. Spelt works in place of wheat flour, or try a delicious wholemeal blend, such as wheat, spelt, buckwheat and rye. You can vary the seeds and dried and candied fruit. Thank you Olia and Katrya.'

1. Cream the butter and sugar together until really light and fluffy, this is so important for the texture of the biscuits, making them lighter. Add the honey and egg and incorporate thoroughly, then add the remaining ingredients.

2. Roll the dough into a log on a sheet of nonstick baking paper, using a dough scraper or knife. Chill for about 45 minutes in the refrigerator, you can also freeze some of the dough for later.

3. Preheat the oven to 180°C (350°F), Gas Mark 4.

4. Cut the dough into 26–28g (1oz) rounds, then roll each round between your palms into a ball. Place each one on a baking tray with 2cm (¾ inch) between each biscuit and press down with a floured fork to make a crisscross pattern. If the biscuits have become very soft while shaping, place the tray into the refrigerator to chill for 10–20 minutes before baking. This helps them to retain their shape when they are baked.

5. Bake from cold for 10 minutes, then turn the tray and bake for another 6–8 minutes, or until a good golden brown.

6. The biscuits keep well in a sealed container for at least 2 weeks.

Allen Arnette

Echinacea Tisane

echinacea

SERVES 2

350ml (12fl oz) pure, filtered water
2 tablespoons echinacea leaves, stems and flowers, dried and cut or chopped into 1.25cm (½ inch) pieces

'This immune-stimulating tisane is so helpful when the weather changes. Wind alone can create the need for immune balancing. According to the ancient medical traditions, bitter taste in herbs creates a cooling effect, calming the immune system. Like many teas from flowers, this won't keep – it will need to be made fresh each time. Whether using fresh-from-your-garden echinacea or purchased from a trusted source, the plant material will need to be dried ahead of time. Use a dehydrator, low oven or the sun to fully dry the echinacea. All parts of the plant can be used for making this tisane.'

1. Pour the water into a saucepan, bring to the boil, then turn off the heat. Add the echinacea to a reusable teabag or a tea ball, cover with the water and steep for 5–15 minutes depending on the desired strength (the stronger, the more bitter the flavour). Or, place the chopped echinacea into a teapot, pour in the freshly-boiled water and cover with the lid.

2. Once ready, strain and pour the tisane into cups. Serve and enjoy with any of the options below:

3. Add 30–50ml (1–2fl oz) cashew milk per cup for a creamy treat. We suggest cashew, but all plant-based milks (coconut, hemp, oat, almond) are great and beneficial.

4. You can also replace the water with a plant-based milk to steep the echinacea in for a creamier final product.

5. For a sweeter taste, maple syrup is a great match for the bitter taste from the herb. Add 1–2 teaspoons per cup.

6. Lemon juice is a common addition (1–2 teaspoons per cup). Fresh lime juice is amazing if you also use coconut milk.

7. Add 1–2 drops of orange essential oil and mix well into the tisane to bring a tension-relieving quality to the experience.

Chapter 5

LONGEVITY & RESILIENCE

Natasha MacAller

Corn, Leek, Cauli & Chilli Crisp Chowder
with Preserved Lemon Gremolata

alliums | parsley | chilli

This moreish, rich chowder is not only vegan but gluten-free and lighter than a traditional chowder, substituting the usual potatoes for cauliflower cubes. So, celebrate corn season, dig in with that spoon and feast on these flavours!

SERVES 4

For the chowder
100ml (3½fl oz) rapeseed, vegetable or sunflower oil
4 large leeks, about 800g (1lb 12oz), trimmed, cleaned, halved lengthways and sliced into 1cm (½ inch) semicircles, outer peel reserved
4 large corn on the cobs
½ cauliflower, florets and stems cut into bite-sized cubes
1 head garlic, roasted, cooled and squeezed into a paste
235ml (8fl oz) coconut, soya or nut milk mixed with 1 tablespoon cornflour
2 tablespoons coconut oil
2–3 tablespoons freshly squeezed lime or lemon juice
120ml (4fl oz) crispy chilli oil
sea salt and freshly ground black pepper

For the gremolata
60g (2¼oz) flat leaf parsley
2–3 teaspoons Greek oregano leaves
4–5 garlic cloves, smashed
2–3 strips preserved lemon peel, cut into 1cm (½ inch) thick strips
3 tablespoons lemon juice, to taste
175ml (6fl oz) extra virgin olive oil

1. To make the chowder, put the rapeseed, vegetable or sunflower oil into a large frying pan with a lid over a medium heat to warm. Then add the leeks and a good pinch of salt, stirring to coat the leeks in the oil. Once the leeks begin to sizzle, turn the heat down to low, cover with the lid and sweat gently, stirring and adding a little water to the oil to help soften the leeks but not brown them. Continue to cook for about 30 minutes, stirring occasionally, until the leeks soften and 'melt'.

2. Meanwhile, to make the gremolata, place the herbs, garlic, lemon peel and a big pinch of salt on a chopping board. Using a sharp chef's knife, chop all the ingredients together until minced and fragrant. Scrape into a bowl, mix in the olive oil, then add salt to taste. Cover and refrigerate until ready to serve.

3. For the chowder, bring 750ml (1 ⅓ pints) of cold salted water to the boil in a 4.5–6 litre (8–10½ pint) pan with a lid. While the water heats, place a corn cob in the centre of a low rimmed bowl or a plate with a rim. Using a sharp paring or chef's knife, hold the cob tip on its end with your fingers and gently cut downwards in a sawing motion from top to bottom to release the kernels from the cob into the bowl (and not all over the floor). Rotate the cob and repeat. Continue with remaining cobs and leave the kernels in the bowl. Add the stripped corn cobs to the water with the leek scraps, put the lid on and bring to a simmer for 8–10 minutes. Skim and discard or compost the cobs and leek scraps from the corn water.

4. Add the cauliflower and simmer for 4–5 minutes, then add the garlic purée and corn kernels. Stir in the cornflour mixture, coconut oil and melted leeks and cook for about 5 minutes until the chowder thickens, is warmed through and steamy. Add salt, pepper and the lime juice to taste, adjusting seasoning to your liking.

5. Ladle into 4 large, warmed bowls, top with a spoonful of crispy chilli oil and a generous spoonful of the gremolata. Serve immediately.

Palmiro Ocampo Grey

Green Pea & Calendula Soup
with Golden Peruvian Potato Shells

calendula

SERVES 4

3 tablespoons olive oil
6 green pea pods, the cellulose from the inside of the green pea shells carefully removed
½ red onion, diced
2 medium boiled potatoes (we use Peruvian), peeled and skin reserved, cut into 4 pieces each
1 teaspoon diced calendula leaves
dried oregano, to taste
calendula pollen (or edible organic golden flower powder – available online and made from pulverized calendula petals), to taste
200ml (7fl oz) water
sea salt and freshly black ground pepper

'Ccori cocina óptima is a non-profit organization that I founded to promote optimal cooking and avoid food waste. We develop social programmes to teach everyone who cooks, from an award-winning fine dining restaurant to a prison inmate, to a woman in a community kitchen. We believe food is for everyone. For this reason, we promote the use of the entire ingredient. The name CCORI comes from the ancient Quechua language of the Incas and means gold.'

This dish celebrates the edible pollen and petals of the golden Calendula plant. In-keeping with CCORI's zero-waste ethos, the inedible stems and roots can be composted to enrich your soils.

1. Add 2 tablespoons of the olive oil to a pan and sauté the clean pea peels with the onion over a low heat for 3–4 minutes until soft. Then add the boiled potatoes, stir and cook for 3 more minutes. Add the calendula, oregano and calendula pollen and season with salt and pepper. Stir for another minute so that the seasonings are incorporated and finally add the measured water. Cook, covered, for 1 minute.

2. To make crispy potato skin, simply brown the reserved potato peel in a pan using the remaining olive oil for 3–4 minutes until crisp. Sprinkle with a little salt and calendula pollen to create the effect of actual mineral gold bits.

3. Once cooked, transfer the soup to a blender and blitz to a smooth purée. Serve hot with the crispy potato skin on top.

Julia Komp & Anne Kratz

Summer's Day

sunflower

SERVES 10

This 'Summer's Day' was co-created by Julia Komp and her lauded pastry chef, Anne Kern. Julia says: 'Using sunflower seeds and petals, plus rowanberries and wheatgrass, this dish recreates a perfect summer's day. Imagine cycling to the sea with the smell of freshly cut grass in the air, floral notes from sunflowers, wild berries and pure nature.'

Rowanberries

100g (3½oz) rowanberries, washed
5g (⅛oz) rowanberry alcohol (or other clear, fruity alcohol such as crème de cassis)
25g (1oz) sugar
125g (4½oz) apple juice
1 vanilla pod

1. Put the rowanberries in the freezer for 1 day to reduce their bitterness. The following day, put all the ingredients into a saucepan over a medium-high heat and boil for 20 minutes. Pour it into a glass preserving jar or vacuum pack and let it rest for at least 1 week.

Sunflower blossom tea

1g aniseed, roasted and ground
½ cinnamon stick
1 vanilla pod
300g (10½oz) apple juice
3g dried sunflower petals, or 20g (¾oz) fresh petals
1 tablespoon rowanberry purée (see above)
petals from 1 nelke carnation

1. Carefully toast the spices and vanilla in a dry pan over a low heat until fragrant, then add the apple juice and bring to the boil. Add the sunflower petals. Remove from the heat and leave to cool. Put into a vacuum pack and chill in the refrigerator for 2 days.

Apple blossom

2 green apples, thinly sliced
250g (9oz) sunflower blossom tea (see above)
50g (1¾oz) passion fruit purée
50g (1¾oz) mango purée
¼ of a vanilla pod
1 tablespoon lime juice

1. Use a blossom cookie cutter to cut out the apple slices into blossom shapes. Put them together with the other ingredients into a vacuum pack and chill for 1 day. Make green apple juice out of the rest from the apples and keep it tightly sealed to avoid browning by oxidation (this will be used for the sunflower blossom sauce)

Sunflower milk

100g (3½oz) roasted sunflower seeds
550g (1lb 4oz) freshly-boiled water
25g (1oz) light brown sugar
12g (⅜oz) sunflower oil
½ a vanilla pod

1. Mix all the ingredients together in a large bowl, then pass through a mesh strainer, discarding the solids. Set the milk aside until needed.

Sunflower seed paste

250g (9oz) roasted sunflower seeds
50g (1¾oz) light brown sugar
40g (1½oz) sunflower oil, plus extra to store
25g (1oz) pumpkin seed oil
25g (1oz) grapeseed oil

1. Place all the ingredients into a food processor or blender and mix into a smooth paste. Set aside, with a little extra oil on top, until needed).

Sunflower seed nougat

200g (7oz) sunflower seed paste (see above)
100g (3½oz) roasted sunflower seeds
30g (1oz) light brown sugar
30g (1oz) milk chocolate, about 35% cocoa (I use Valrhona Azélia)
large pinch of Maldon sea salt

1. Place all the ingredients into a food processor or blender and mix into a smooth paste. Set aside until needed.

continued overleaf

Sunflower seed mousse

300g (10½oz) sunflower milk (see above)
50g (1¾oz) light brown sugar
½ vanilla pod
35g (1¼oz) egg yolk (about 1½ eggs)
16g (½oz) cornflour
2 leaves of gelatine, soaked for 5 minutes in cold water and squeezed dry
85g (3oz) sunflower seed nougat (see above)
150g (5½oz) cream, whipped

1. Put 250g (9oz) of the sunflower seed milk, the sugar and vanilla pod into a medium pan and bring to a simmer. Whisk in the yolks, cornflour and remaining sunflower milk, then stir using a silicone spatula until thickened, scraping down the sides occasionally. When thickened and smooth, remove from the heat and stir in the gelatine until dissolved. Add the sunflower seed nougat and, when it's cooled to 35°C (95°F), carefully fold in the whipped cream. Pipe or spoon the mixture into 10 spherical moulds, about 60g (2½oz) in size. Allow to set in the refrigerator for 30 minutes, then transfer to the freezer until ready to serve.

Sunflower seed cream

200ml (7fl oz) sunflower seed milk (see above)
200g (7oz) sunflower seed paste (see above)
5g (⅛oz) gellan gum or agar-agar
15g (½oz) caster sugar
seeds scraped from ¼ of a vanilla pod
20g (¾oz) egg yolk (about 1 egg)
20g (¾oz) white chocolate, chopped
10g (¼oz) butter
50g (1¾oz) apple juice from Apple Blossom (see above)

1. Whisk together the sunflower seed milk and paste with the gellan gum, sugar and vanilla. Let it rest for 10 Minutes. Bring to the boil over a high heat and carefull mix in the egg yolk and chocolate until combined. Remove from the heat and allow to cool until it is more solid. Then cut into small pieces and mix with the apple juice into a nice smooth cream.

Sunflower blossom sauce

100g (3½oz) sunflower blossom tea (see above)
80g (2¾oz) apple juice
40g (1½oz) passion fruit purée
10g (¼oz) mango purée
10g (¼oz) rowanberry purée
30g (1oz) rowanberry juice
1 tablespoon lemon juice
1g guar gum, or carob or locust bean gum

1. Mix all the ingredients, except the gum, together. Stir through the gum to thicken a little into a creamy consistency. Set aside until needed.

Sunflower blossom ganache

100g (3½oz) sunflower blossom tea (see above)
25g (¾oz) rowanberry purée
25g (¾oz) passion fruit purée
25g (¾oz) mango purée
50g (1¾oz) double cream
2g fresh sunflower petals
1½ leaves of gelatine, soaked for 5 minutes in cold water and squeezed dry
1 vanilla pod
200g (7oz) white chocolate, chopped
50g (1¾oz) cold butter

1. Add the sunflower blossom tea, purées and cream to a pan and heat to a low simmer, then remove from the heat. Add the sunflower petals, gelatine, vanilla and chocolate and stir to combine. Remove from the heat and when the mixture has cooled to 35°C (95°F), add the butter and slowly stir until melted and combined. Allow to cool until needed.

Sunflower seed cookies

100g (3½oz) light brown sugar
100g (3½oz) hazelnut flour
200g (7oz) sunflower seed flour
1 egg
10g (¼oz) butter, softened
10g (¼oz) plain flour, plus extra for dusting

1. Preheat the oven to 180°C (350°F), Gas Mark 4. Put all the ingredients into a mixing bowl, or into a stand mixer on low speed, and combine until smooth. Transfer the dough to a lightly floured surface and roll out thinly. Use a 5cm (2 inch) cookie cutter to cut out 10 circles. (You can chill the dough for a short time in the refrigerator to make it easier to cut through.) Transfer the cookies to a baking tray and bake for 6 minutes. Remove from the oven and allow to cool until needed.

Gooseberry & wheatgrass sorbet

200g (7oz) gooseberries, topped and tailed
50g (1¾oz) gooseberry juice
50g (1¾oz) fresh apple juice
75g (2¾oz) sugar syrup/gomme
20g (¾oz) fresh wheatgrass, cut into small pieces
1 tablespoon lime juice

1. Mix the ingredients together until smooth then check the taste. Add the mixture to an ice cream maker (we use a Ninja Cremi), following the instructions until an even sorbet is formed.

Gooseberry gel

250g (9oz) gooseberry juice
100g (3½oz) apple juice
100g (3½oz) water
50g (1¾oz) caster sugar
5g (⅛oz) gellan gum or agar-agar
1 vanilla pod

1. Put all the ingredients into a medium pan and give them a good stir. Set aside to rest for 10 minutes. Set the pan over a medium-high heat and bring to the boil, stirring constantly. Now transfer the mixture to a metal container or bowl and leave to cool and harden. Once cold, cut the gel into small pieces and mix it until it's a nice, smooth and tasty gel.

Sunflower seed crumb

100g (3½oz) butter, cut into cubes
100g (3½oz) light brown sugar
125g (4½oz) plain flour
50g (1¾oz) sunflower seed flour

1. Preheat the oven to 180°C (350°F), Gas Mark 4. In a large bowl, rub all the ingredients together with your fingers. Transfer to a baking tray and bake for 10 minutes. Set aside.

To assemble

1. Set a big dot of Sunflower Seed Cream off centre on each plate. Carefully spread a thin layer of Sunflower Ganache and Sunflower Sauce over each Sunflower Seed Cookie and add it to each plate on top of the Sunflower Seed Cream. Set the Apple Blossom around the cookie to resemble the petals of a flower, then add a globe of Sunflower Mousse on top of the centre of the cookie to create a 'sunflower'.

2. Add a small oval of Sunflower Seed Crumb to each plate and top with a scoop of Gooseberry and Wheatgrass Sorbet.

3. Decorate the plates with several small dots of gooseberry gel and top a few with rowanberries. Finally, garnish the sunflower with curls of orange and lime zest and serve.

Natasha MacAller

Sunshine Citrus Salad
with Lemon Balm Vinaigrette

citrus | lemon balm | fennel

This sparkly fresh citrus salad, full of digestive support ingredients, makes a light midday dish or a spectacular side for the brunch table.

SERVES 4

120g (4¼oz) small fennel bulbs, thinly sliced and fronds reserved to garnish
2 tablespoons apple cider vinegar
¼ teaspoon sea salt
big pinch of sugar
2 grapefruit, about 500g (1lb 2oz)
2 oranges, about 300g (10½oz)
2 tangerines, about 240g (8½oz)
2 gem or small romaine lettuce
2 large handfuls of baby kale leaves
2 firm ripe avocadoes, about 300g (10½oz), peeled, pitted and thinly sliced
1 red onion, thinly sliced
1 large handful of pea shoots or microgreens
fennel fronds, poppy seeds and petite violas (edible flowers from the garden), to garnish

For the lemon balm vinaigrette
1 shallot, minced
7g (¼oz) lemon balm leaves, chopped
zest and juice of 1 lemon
20ml (4 teaspoons) tangerine or orange juice
45ml (3 tablespoons) rice wine vinegar
2 teaspoons runny honey
1 teaspoon Dijon mustard
¼ teaspoon toasted and finely ground fennel seeds
60ml (4 tablespoons) sunflower oil

1. Put the fennel into a small bowl, then stir in the vinegar, sea salt and sugar and set aside to pickle for 20–30 minutes.

2. Remove the peel and pith from the citrus fruit. Cut one of each fruit into wheels, then cut the remaining citrus into 'supreme' segments. Reserve 20ml (4 teaspoons) of the orange or tangerine juice for the vinaigrette and set aside.

3. To make the vinaigrette, put all of the ingredients, except the oil, into a small blender or food processor and whizz until smooth. With the motor running, drizzle in the oil until emulsified. Decant into a small jug until ready to use.

4. To assemble and serve, arrange the lettuce and kale leaves on a serving platter and scatter over the pickled fennel. Tuck in the thinly sliced avocado and citrus, adding flecks of red onion, pea shoots and fennel fronds. Drizzle with the lemon balm vinaigrette and sprinkle with poppy seeds and fresh edible flowers. Serve immediately.

April Bloomfield

Polenta with Bitter Greens
& Pan-fried Sweet Potato Cubes

cavolo nero | sweet potato | garlic

'Simple, delicious vegetarian comfort.'

SERVES 4 AS A MAIN

875ml (1⅓ pints) water
2 teaspoons sea salt
160g (5¾oz) coarse stone-ground polenta (I like Anson Mills or Bob's Red Mill)
2 tablespoons extra virgin olive oil
1 large sweet potato, about 450g (1lb), peeled and cut into 2cm (¾ inch) cubes
3 tablespoons mascarpone
55–85g (2–3oz) Pecorino Romano cheese, grated
freshly ground black pepper

For the bitter greens purée

5 garlic cloves, peeled
2 shallots, peeled and halved lengthways
500g (1lb 2oz) mixed fresh bitter green leaves, such as cavolo nero, spinach and Swiss chard, thick stems removed, about 170–250g (6–9oz) after trimming
1 chilli, stem removed and deseeded
1 teaspoon flaky sea salt
120ml (4fl oz) extra virgin olive oil

1. Combine the measured water and salt in a medium pot, cover and bring the water to the boil. Stream in the polenta, stirring constantly with a wooden spoon. Reduce the heat to medium and continue stirring for about 2–3 minutes until it looks like it's one with the water. Reduce the heat to low, cover and stir briefly every 10 minutes until tender, creamy but still slightly al dente: about 40 minutes in total. Cover and keep warm.

2. While the polenta is cooking, make the bitter greens purée. Put 4 of the garlic cloves and the shallots into a medium pot, fill it with water, cover and bring to the boil over a high heat. Add enough salt so that the water tastes slightly salty, then add the bitter greens, prodding the veggies down to submerge in the water. Simmer, uncovered, for 2–3 minutes until the greens are tender and tear easily. Drain the greens in a colander, fish out the garlic cloves and shallots, then set them aside.

3. Squeeze as much water out of the greens as you can, then roughly chop the greens, chilli, shallots and boiled and raw garlic.

4. Add the greens mixture and salt to a food processor and blitz for about 45 seconds, stopping occasionally to scrape down the sides. Alternatively, you can do this in a bowl with a stick blender. Add the olive oil and whizz into a fairly smooth purée. Cover and keep warm while you make the pan-fried sweet potatoes. Leftover purée will keep tightly covered and chilled for 5 days.

5. Add the diced sweet potato to a small pot of boiling salted water and simmer for 2–3 minutes until just al dente. Drain, then spread on kitchen paper to dry. Over a medium heat, warm the oil in a medium sauté pan until it shimmers.

6. Add the pieces of sweet potato without overcrowding the pan and fry and turn until they are crisped and browned. Transfer the first batch to dry kitchen paper and keep warm. Repeat with the remaining sweet potato.

7. To serve, swirl the mascarpone and grated cheese and a few grinds of black pepper into the polenta. Spoon the polenta into 4 warm bowls. Ladle the bitter greens purée on top, give the purée a swirl with a large serving spoon, then top with crispy sweet potato cubes. Sprinkle with salt and a few grinds of pepper. Serve immediately.

Natasha MacAller

Pan-seared Scallops
on Silky Avocado Crema

avocado | coriander | yuzu

Dreamy creamy and silky. The yuzu juice adds a whisper of floral citrus fragrance to this South American-inspired crema.

SERVES 2 AS A MAIN OR 4 AS A STARTER

16 large scallops, about 600g (1lb 5oz) in total, at room temperature
1 avocado, peeled, stoned and halved
120ml (4fl oz) buttermilk
120ml (4fl oz) Greek yogurt
1 tablespoon yuzu juice
1 jalapeño, trimmed, deseeded and roughly chopped
1 small shallot, roughly chopped
20g (¾oz) fresh coriander leaves and tender stems
2 teaspoons Mexican tajín salt blend* or 1½ teaspoons flaky sea salt, plus extra to serve
1 teaspoon dried oregano, crumbled
1 teaspoon manuka honey
juice of 3 small limes, plus zest of 2 limes
avocado oil or butter, for searing

To serve

90g (3¼oz) cucumber ribbons
4 teaspoons rice wine vinegar
big pinch each of flaky sea salt and sugar
100g (3½oz) thinly sliced cherry tomatoes
60g (2¼oz) mango, peeled and cut into small pieces
2 finger limes, cut into wedges
freshly ground black pepper (optional)

1. Pat dry the scallops and set aside on a kitchen paper-lined plate, covered, until ready to use.

2. Using a small blender or bullet blender, blitz the avocado, buttermilk and yogurt into a thick creamy mixture. Add the yuzu juice, jalapeño, shallot, most of the coriander (reserving a small handful of leaves to serve), salt, oregano, honey, lime juice and zest, then blitz again until well combined and smooth. Taste and adjust with additional yuzu juice and seasonings, if you like.

3. Put the cucumber ribbons and vinegar in a small bowl and season with the salt and sugar.

4. Divide the avocado crema between serving plates. Arrange the tomatoes, mango, reserved coriander leaves and a little swirl of cucumber, as pictured. Finish with the lime wedges and set aside until ready to serve.

5. Set a medium pan over a medium-high heat until sizzling hot. While the pan is heating, remove and discard the kitchen paper from the scallops. Brush the scallops with oil and place them back on the plate. Add 1 tablespoon of oil to the pan and swirl to coat the pan evenly. Place the pan back on the heat. Working quickly, add the scallops, flat-side down, one at a time. They will only need 1–1½ minutes per side, depending on their thickness. When the edges are golden brown, using tongs or a small spatula, turn the scallops over and cook for another minute. Remove to the serving plates and divide evenly. Sprinkle with flaky sea salt, black pepper or tajín and serve immediately.

* Tajin is a delicious Mexican seasoning of equal parts sea salt, dried lime juice powder and chilli powder.

Natasha MacAller

Omakase Nigiri
with Yuzu Wasabi Snow

ginger | yuzu | wakame seaweed

SERVES 4

For the granita
250ml (9fl oz) water
40g (1½oz) caster sugar
10g (¼oz) fresh root ginger, peeled and grated using a Microplane
20g (¾oz) wasabi root, peeled and grated using a Microplane
60ml (4 tablespoons) rice wine vinegar
120ml (4 fl oz) yuzu juice

For the rice crackers
55g (2oz) sweet rice flour or glutinous rice flour
pinch of sugar
1 teaspoon coconut oil
85ml (6 tablespoons) room temperature water
onion seeds, sesame seeds and sea salt flakes, for sprinkling

To serve
350g (12oz) fresh sushi-grade ahi (yellowfin) tuna or Hamachi (yellowtail), sliced
60g (2¼oz) wakame seaweed
1 ripe avocado, peeled, pitted and thinly sliced (optional)
light soy sauce or tamari, to taste
sesame seeds, to garnish

My California take on a dainty omakase sashimi starter delights the taste buds with flavour, temperature and texture. Get fresh wasabi if you can, it is a hot but sublimely fragrant taste you'll not forget. My favourite method to enjoy this is to stack the wakame on the cracker, top with tuna, then spoon the yuzu snow on top and down the elegant snack all in one bite!

1. To make the granita, place a shallow glass 500ml–1 litre (1–1¾ pint) baking dish flat in the freezer. Also put a 750ml–1 litre (1 ⅓–1¾ pint) airtight container with a tight-fitting lid in the freezer to chill.

2. In a saucepan, stir together the measured water and sugar. Set the pan over a medium-low heat and simmer for 2 minutes, or until the sugar has dissolved. Remove from the heat, add the ginger and wasabi and allow to infuse for 10 minutes. Stir in the rice wine vinegar and yuzu juice. Let the mixture come to room temperature, then strain into pre-frozen shallow dish, pressing firmly on the ginger and wasabi as you strain to release more flavour.

3. Transfer to the freezer. Every 30 minutes, use a fork to stir and scrape the ice crystals around the edges, corners and top, moving them to the centre of the dish. Continue until the mixture is completely frozen and has a fine snowy texture; about 2–3 hours. Quickly spoon into the pre-chilled container with a tight-fitting lid, return to the freezer and keep frozen until ready to serve.

4. To make the rice crackers, preheat the oven to 190°C (375°F), Gas Mark 5. Grease two flat baking trays with oil or cover with silicone baking mats (do not use baking paper).

5. In a small bowl, stir the flour, sugar and coconut oil together, then whisk in the measured water until smooth. Let stand for 10 minutes or cover and chill until ready to use – it will be very runny but it works! Using a teaspoon, drip spoonfuls of batter into rounds, or creative shapes, on to the prepared baking trays, spacing the batter 2.5cm (1 inch) apart. Let stand for 5 minutes, then top with a sprinkle of furikake or onion seeds, sesame seeds and salt.

6. Carefully place in oven to bake for 12 minutes until thin, crispy and light brown around the edges. Gently remove from the tray to a cooling rack and leave to cool to room temperature. Transfer and store in an airtight container until ready to use. These crackers can be made up to 2 days in advance.

7. To serve, plate the fish first, then rice crackers, wakame and soy sauce/tamari as pictured, adding the granita last. Serve immediately.

Rudolph van Veen

Vegetable Garden Tea Cakes

apple | ginger | maple syrup

'This divine treat is specially created for bakers with green fingers. Vegetables and fruits give flavour and structure to these gluten- and sugar-free tea cakes. The topping is made of fresh cream cheese mixed with carrot purée, turmeric and maple syrup. Decorated with edible flowers, baby carrots and delicate cress, these cakes are just perfect for a summer afternoon tea in your garden.'

MAKES 8-10

4 teaspoons olive oil
200g (7oz) almond flour
½ teaspoon baking powder
pinch each of finely ground cinnamon and white pepper
80g (2¾oz) grated carrots
50g (1¾oz) grated courgette
1cm (½ inch) piece of fresh ginger, finely grated
1 small, apple, grated (skin on)
50ml (2fl oz) extra virgin olive oil
60ml (4 tablespoons) maple syrup
1 teaspoon vanilla extract
2 large eggs
30g (1oz) pecans, rougly chopped

For the topping
30g (1oz) baby carrots, roughly chopped
pinch of ground turmeric
80g (2¾oz) cream cheese, softened
1 tablespoon maple syrup
1 teaspoon vanilla extract

To decorate
10 baby carrots
edible flowers
micro watercress
1 tablespoon apricot jam (optional)

1. Preheat the oven to 180°C (350°F), Gas Mark 4. Use the olive oil to grease 8–10 cake moulds. I use 5 × 6cm (2 × 2½ inch) cake moulds but you can also use muffin moulds, mini loaf moulds or even heatproof teacups.

2. Mix the almond flour with the baking powder, cinnamon and white pepper. Combine this with all the remaining cake ingredients, except the pecans. Fill the greased cake moulds about halfway up the sides and sprinkle with the pecans. Bake for 30 minutes.

3. Unmould the cakes and leave them to cool on a wire rack.

4. Cook the baby carrots for decoration in boiling water for 30 seconds, then shock in ice-cold water. Drain on kitchen paper.

5. To make the topping, cook the chopped baby carrots until soft, then shock in ice-cold water and drain well. Blend in a food processor with the turmeric, cream cheese, maple syrup and vanilla.

6. Top the cakes with the cream cheese spread.

7. For a beautiful finish, you can brush the baby carrots with the apricot jam to give them some shine before placing on top of the cream cheese spread. Then add the edible flowers and cress. Arrange on serving plates or a cake stand and serve with your favourite pot of tea.

Nyesha Arrington

Persimmon Pudding

persimmon

SERVES 8–10

3 ripe Hachiya or Fuyu persimmons (freeze to ripen instantly)
3 large eggs
200g (7oz) granulated sugar
4oz (115g) unsalted butter, melted and cooled to room temperature, plus extra for greasing
180g (6oz) plain flour
1 teaspoon bicarbonate of soda
1 teaspoon baking powder
1 teaspoon grated fresh ginger
½ teaspoon ground cinnamon
½ teaspoon ground allspice
½ teaspoon sea salt
¼ teaspoon ground cardamom
235ml (8fl oz) milk
235ml (8fl oz) double cream

For the maple whip
500ml (18fl oz) whipping cream
1 teaspoon vanilla extract
pinch of salt
90g (3¼oz) maple syrup

'This persimmon pudding cake is a true celebration of autumn's bounty, combining the sweet, honeyed flavour of ripe persimmons with warm spices to create a tender dessert. Whether you're using Hachiya or Fuyu persimmons, their rich, luscious texture brings a unique depth. Perfect for gatherings, this cake can be made ahead and pairs beautifully with a dollop of whipped maple cream or a scoop of vanilla ice cream. Enjoy a slice with a cup of tea or coffee for a cosy, seasonal treat. Cheers!'

1. Preheat the oven to 180°C (350°F), Gas Mark 4. Butter a 23cm (9 inch) springform cake tin.

2. Remove the stems from the persimmons and quarter them. Place the quarters in the bowl of a food processor and blend until smooth. Strain the purée through a medium-mesh strainer, leaving behind and discarding any bits of seed or skin. You should have about 500g (1lb 2oz) of purée. Set aside.

3. In a large mixing bowl, whisk together the eggs and sugar until fully combined. Whisk in the melted butter. In a medium mixing bowl, sift in the flour, then add the bicarbonate of soda, baking powder, ginger, cinnamon, allspice, salt and cardamom. Stir it all together until well combined and then stir it into the egg mixture. Slowly pour in the milk and cream, stirring until combined. Finally, stir in the persimmon purée. The batter should be quite thick.

4. Pour the batter into the prepared tin and bake for 40–45 minutes until a skewer inserted into the centre comes out clean. Allow it to cool for 10 minutes before serving and note that the pudding will sink as it cools.

5. To make the maple whip, in a large mixing bowl with a whisk, or a stand mixer with a whisk attachment, add the cream, vanilla and salt and whisk until you have stiff peaks. Fold in the maple syrup.

6. Carefully remove the springform ring and slide the pudding on to cake platter. Use a large spoon to dollop creamy clouds of maple whip on top. Serve warm.

7. If you are making the pudding in advance, reheat it in a 160°C (325°F), Gas Mark 3 oven for 15 minutes to warm through before serving.

Fennel Seed & Ginger Gems

ginger | lemon | fennel

Ginger gem tins and recipes are New Zealand classics. You can still find these tins – cast-iron baking tins for small cake/muffin bites called gems – in great grandmothers' kitchens or online, but any cast-iron tin with smallish wells, such as rounded gem tins or Danish aebleskiver (pancake ball) tins will also work beautifully.

MAKES 12

1 tablespoon fennel seeds, freshly ground
115g (4oz) granulated sugar
60g (2¼oz) salted butter, softened, plus 85g (3oz) for greasing
1 egg
2 tablespoons mild Manuka honey
zest of 1 lemon
15g (½oz) fresh root ginger, peeled and grated
120g (4¼oz) plain flour
1 teaspoon ground ginger
½ teaspoon ground cardamom
¼ teaspoon baking powder
pinch of salt
80ml (2½fl oz) whole milk
1 teaspoon bicarbonate of soda, sifted
fennel pollen or flowers, to garnish

To serve
cream
marmalade

1. In a small sauté pan over a medium-low heat, toast the ground fennel seeds until fragrant. Transfer to a bowl then remove 1 teaspoon of the fennel seeds into a separate bowl and mix it with 1 tablespoon of the sugar. Reserve the toasted seeds and the fennel sugar for later.

2. Preheat the oven to 180°C (350°F), Gas Mark 4.

3. In a medium bowl with a spoon, or using an electric hand whisk, or a stand mixer fitted with the paddle attachment, beat together the butter and remaining sugar until light and fluffy. Add the egg, beat well, then add the honey, lemon zest and grated fresh ginger. Sift the flour, ground ginger, cardamom, baking powder and salt into the bowl with fennel, then fold into the butter and sugar mix.

4. Add the milk and bicarbonate of soda to a separate small bowl, making sure the soda is dissolved with no lumps. Add to the batter, combining well and leave for at least 30 minutes while you heat the gem iron in the oven.

5. When you are ready to bake the gems, melt the reserved butter and brush into each gem opening, making sure each little bit is well greased. Using a tablespoon, scoop a large spoonful of batter into each gem hole. Bake for 15 minutes or until evenly golden. Remove from the oven and leave to cool for 5 minutes before removing from the gem tin. Turn the gems upside down and sprinkle with the reserved fennel sugar and fennel pollen. Serve with lashings of cream and marmalade, plus a hot cuppa, of course.

Lemon Buttermilk Muhallebi Puddings

ginger | sumac | lemon

SERVES 4

200g (7oz) caster sugar
½ teaspoon sea salt
zest of 1 lemon
½ teaspoon sumac
50g (1¾oz) cornflour
235ml (8fl oz) whole or semi-skimmed milk
475ml (17fl oz) double cream
475ml (17fl oz) buttermilk
60ml (4 tablespoons) lemon juice (I use Meyer)
100g (3½oz) blueberries, to serve
2 tablespoons stem ginger syrup (see below), to serve

For the stem ginger syrup (makes 150g/5½oz)
180g (6oz) peeled fresh ginger root, cut into 5g (⅛oz) pieces and rinsed
475ml (17fl oz) cold water
150g (5½oz) granulated sugar
pinch of sea salt

These soothing elegant puddings are egg- and gluten-free. Instead of traditional Middle Eastern rose water, this version is flavoured with fresh lemons and sour sumac. A generous spoonful of ginger syrup tops off this custard-like dish, which is also finished with fresh blueberries. Buttermilk has a sour rich flavour similar to natural yogurt. The ginger brings a bit of heat and additional digestive support. It's also a great method of preservation so that you can have a taste of sweet spicy stem ginger all year long.

1. To make the stem ginger syrup, add the fresh ginger to a small saucepan, cover with the measured water, top with a lid and bring to a boil over a high heat. Once boiled, reduce the heat to a gentle simmer and cook, uncovered, until reduced by half, about 25–30 minutes. Strain the ginger water into a measuring jug, reserving the ginger pieces – you should have about 240ml (8¾fl oz), so add more water if needed.

2. Rinse the pan, then return the ginger water to it and place over a medium-low heat. Stream in the sugar and salt, stirring to dissolve. Add the ginger pieces, bring up to a boil, then turn down to a simmer and cook uncovered for 40 minutes, skimming away any foam, as needed. Remove from the heat and let stand for 2 minutes. Using a funnel, pour into a sterilized 250ml (9fl oz) preserving jar and seal. Let cool at room temperature then transfer to the refrigerator where it will keep for a year.

3. To make the muhallebi pudding, put the sugar, salt, lemon zest and sumac into a small bowl and rub together to release the citrus oils. Add the cornflour and combine well. Whisk in the milk to make a slurry and set aside.

4. Add the cream and buttermilk to a medium pan over a medium-low heat and gently stir with a spatula, scraping the sides and bottom of the pan until warm and steamy.

5. Slowly stream the slurry into the hot cream and buttermilk mixture, whisking continuously until the mixture thickens. Reduce the heat to low and, using a spatula, slowly stir for another 5 minutes to cook out the cornflour: low and slow!

6. Turn off the heat and whisk in the lemon juice. Strain and pour into 4 tall glasses, leaving a bit of room at the top for garnishes. Top with clingfilm and chill until set.

7. To serve, swirl 2 tablespoons of ginger syrup evenly over each pudding and top with a generous handful of blueberries.

Roger Pizey

Meadowsweet Mousse Globes

meadowsweet

'Meadowsweet's softly scented flowers disguise this plant's heroic ability to relieve pain and swelling of arthritic, muscular and head aches.'

MAKES 15

100g (3½oz) milk chocolate, to decorate

For the meadowsweet custard
290ml (9¾fl oz) organic whole milk
8g (¼oz) dried meadowsweet
60g (2¼oz) egg yolks
60g (2¼oz) liquid glucose
290g (10¼oz) 75% Venezuelan dark chocolate, melted
425g (15oz) semi-whipped double cream

For the raspberry coulis
85g (3oz) frozen raspberries, thawed
½ teaspoon lime juice
10g (¼oz) caster sugar
a tiny pinch of sea salt

For the chocolate glaze
250ml (9fl oz) double cream
175g (6oz) 75% Venezuelan dark chocolate, broken into pieces
50ml (2fl oz) liquid glucose

For the chocolate sponge
60g (2¼oz) plain flour
13g (½oz) cornflour
10g (¼oz) cocoa powder
85g (3oz) caster sugar
3 large eggs
6g (⅛oz) unsalted butter, melted

1. To make the meadowsweet custard, add the milk and meadowsweet to a medium pan over a medium heat and bring to the boil. In another pan, whisk the egg yolks and glucose together. When boiled, strain the milk through a mesh strainer into the egg yolk mixture and whisk again to combine. Continue whisking over a medium heat until it reaches 85°C (185°F). Pour the mixture into the melted chocolate and emulsify with a hand blender for at least 2 minutes. Allow to cool to 45°C (113°F) then fold in the whipped cream. Chill in the refrigerator.

2. To make the coulis, mix all the ingredients together in a bowl. Strain through a mesh strainer and discard the seeds. If the liquid seems too thin, gently simmer in a small pan for 10 minutes until thickened. Cover and chill in the refrigerator.

3. To make the chocolate glaze, add the cream to a pan over a medium-high heat and bring to the boil. Pour over the chocolate and mix with a spoon until emulsified. Allow to cool slightly, then stir in the glucose and set aside at room temperature.

4. To make the sponge, preheat the oven to 180°C (350°F), Gas Mark 4, and grease and line a 25cm (10 inch) cake tin with baking paper. Sift the dry ingredients together and set aside. Place a heatproof bowl over a pan of boiling water and whisk the eggs and sugar together in the bowl until doubled in volume and hot to the touch. Transfer the mixture to a stand mixer and mix on a high speed until lukewarm and fluffy. Fold the butter, then the dry ingredients, into the mixture. Bake for 25 minutes, or until a cocktail stick inserted into the centre comes out clean. Remove from the oven, cool for 10 minutes in the tin, then turn out onto a wire rack. When cool, strip off the baking paper and cool completely.

5. To assemble, cut the cooled sponge into 15 small circles, approximately 4cm (1½ inch) in diameter, then carefully slice each horizontally to 5cm (2 inch) thick. Line a tray with baking paper. Dip an ice-cream scoop into some hot water, shake it, then scoop a globe of custard on to the baking paper. Repeat until you have 15 scoops. Spoon 1 teaspoon of coulis on to each globe, then place the tray in the freezer to chill until the globes are firm.

6. Place a wire rack over a baking tray and arrange the cake discs on the rack. Remove the globes from the freezer and, quickly but carefully peel 1 from the baking paper and place onto a cake disc. Repeat with the remaining globes. Gently pour the chocolate glaze, with a small ladle, in circles over the globes, fully coating them. Let stand for a few minutes, then transfer to the refrigerator to chill.

7. Melt the milk chocolate until just runny. Remove the globes from the refrigerator and use the melted chocolate to drizzle decorations over them. Allow to set, then transfer to small plates to serve.

Natasha MacAller

Santa Barbara Date Shake

citrus | honey

Salad days, smoothies and visits to the local health food market and juice bar Kayser's – these are my happy memories whilst a student at UC Santa Barbara. Kayser's date shake was a generous and filling little bit of heaven. I have updated my collegiate taste memory with homemade tahini gelato and my Santa Barbara Citrus triple orange infusion. Sub coconut milk and cream to make it dairy free.

SERVES 2–4

180g (6oz) organic unhulled tahini, well stirred
80g (2¾oz) local honey, preferably raw
¼ teaspoon ground cardamom, plus extra to serve
pinch of sea salt
330ml (12fl oz) cream
330ml (12fl oz) milk
2 teaspoons vanilla bean paste
100g (3½oz) pitted dates
120ml (4fl oz) hot water
4 tablespoons citrus triple orange infusion (see below)
130g (4½oz) crushed or chipped ice

For citrus triple orange infusion (makes about 120ml/4fl oz)
zest and juice of 1kg (2lb) oranges (this should yield about 350ml/12fl oz juice and 10g/¼oz zest)
zest and juice of 1 lemon
2 green cardamom pods, crushed
1 tablespoon orange blossom water

To serve
softly whipped cream
orange leaves and blossoms

1. Warm the tahini, honey, cardamom and sea salt in a medium pan over a low heat and stir until melted together.

2. Whisk the cream and milk into the tahini mixture until warmed and well mixed, then mix in the vanilla bean paste. Cover and refrigerate until cold.

3. Pour the tahini mixture into an ice-cream machine and spin according to the manufacturer's instructions until set. Transfer to a covered storage container and freeze until ready to serve, at least 1½ hours.

4. Alternatively, if you don't have an ice cream machine, place a deep baking dish into the freezer. Create an ice bath in a large bowl or sink and nestle a metal bowl in the ice bath. Once you have made the gelato base, add to the metal bowl to chill. When chilled, pour the gelato paste into the frozen baking dish and return to the freezer. After 40 minutes, remove from the freezer and use a rubber spatula to scape down the sides and stir together thoroughly. Return to the freezer. Remove after 30 minutes and blitz with a stick blender to break up any clumps, until smooth and creamy. Return to the freezer and continue to check every 30 minutes, stirring or blending as it hardens, about 2 hours.

5. To make the citrus triple orange infusion, add all the ingredients except the orange blossom water to a non-reactive pan over a low heat. Bring to a gentle simmer and reduce by half. Remove from the heat and chill completely. When chilled, add the orange blossom water. Store, covered, in the refrigerator for up to 1 week.

6. To make the shake, soak the pitted dates in the hot water until soft. Then, using a stick blender, blitz to a smooth purée. Chill until cold.

7. Spoon the date purée into the bottom of the blender, add the citrus triple orange infusion and blitz until smooth. Add the crushed ice and the tahini ice cream. Blitz until smooth and creamy, then pour into tall, chilled glasses. Top with unsweetened softly whipped cream, orange leaves and blossoms, a sprinkle of cardamom and indulge.

Chapter 6

BREATH & BALANCE

Natasha MacAller

Baby New Potato, Egg & Herb Salad
with Basil Buttermilk Horseradish Cream

lovage | basil | horseradish | dill | parsley | tarragon | mint

A go-to weekend dish, especially if you have successfully grown deep-in-the-soil baby new potatoes. There is such a huge difference in the taste and texture of a freshly dug potato and this recipe spotlights the humble spud in a celebration of freshly grown herbs, zingy pickled celery or lovage and a bit of pepper sauce heat. Mix up your garden herbs, blitz together in just moments for a moreish dressing.

SERVES 8–12

1 large fennel bulb with fronds, thinly sliced
2 tablespoons apple cider vinegar
¼ teaspoon sea salt
pinch of sugar
3kg (6lb 8oz) baby new potatoes, brushed and washed
4–5 large, hard-boiled eggs, peeled
180g (6oz) pickled lovage or sliced celery stalks in coriander pickle (see page 100)
2 large red onions, minced
450g (1lb) herb cream

For the herb cream
12g (¼oz) basil leaves, roughly chopped, plus extra for garnish
4.5g (1/8oz) fresh dill fronds, plus extra for garnish
6g (1/8oz) lovage or flat leaf parsley leaves, roughly chopped
2 tablespoons roughly chopped tarragon leaves, plus extra for garnish
2 tablespoons mint leaves, plus extra for garnish
¼ teaspoon sweet basil seeds (optional)
juice of 1 lemon
30ml (1fl oz) rice wine vinegar
2 tablespoons Dijon mustard
20g (¾oz) garlic paste
1 teaspoon celery salt
½ teaspoon dried sumac
2 teaspoons freshly ground black pepper, plus extra to serve
2 tablespoons freshly grated horseradish or hot horseradish sauce
2 teaspoons sriracha sauce, or to taste
235g (8½oz) mayonnaise
120ml (4fl oz) buttermilk
120ml (4fl oz) Greek yogurt

1. Add the first 14 herb cream ingredients to a food processor and blitz to a smooth paste. Transfer to a medium bowl, stir in the remaining herb cream ingredients and adjust the seasonings. Chill.

2. While the herb cream is chilling, pickle the sliced fennel. Put the fennel into a small bowl, then stir in the vinegar, sea salt and sugar and set aside to pickle for 20–30 minutes.

3. Submerge the baby potatoes in a pan of water and boil until just fork tender but firm, about 10–12 minutes, extending the cooking time if you are using larger potatoes. Drain and leave the potatoes to cool for 15 minutes, then, if needed, cut into bite-sized cubes and add to a large bowl.

4. Cut the eggs into cubes and add to the bowl. Then add the pickled fennel, pickled lovage, red onion and herb cream. Gently fold and mix the potato salad with a spatula to coat the potatoes all over. Taste and adjust the seasonings. If possible, cover and chill for an hour or more to let the flavours meld. Spoon into a large bowl and serve family-style, scattered with more fresh herbs and grinds of black pepper.

Natasha MacAller

Honey, Pine Nut & Sage Tart

sage | honey | pine tips

MAKES A 25CM (10 INCH) TART

For the rubbed sage pastry
140g (5oz) butter, softened
90g (3¼oz) granulated sugar
1 small egg, beaten
230g (8oz) plain flour
2 teaspoons dried rubbed sage or 1 tablespoon finely minced fresh common, golden or pineapple sage

For the pine nut filling
160g (5¾oz) sage honey
100g (3½oz) granulated sugar
1 teaspoon crumbled flaky sea salt
225g (8oz) butter
120ml (4fl oz) double cream
1 large egg and 1 egg yolk, whisked together
175g (6oz) pine nuts, lightly toasted
pine salt or rosemary salt (see page 120), for sprinkling

I've previously had the great pleasure of working with the late NYC pastry chef Gina De Palma. This adapted recipe of hers adds fresh or dried sage leaves and aromatic pine tips to give the tender buttery pine nuts an extra flavoursome layer. Serve with a large spoonful of whipped tangerine ricotta (see page 174) or shown here as Gina recommends: with divine vanilla gelato. This includes my simple recipe for a tart dough. Adapt for other tart recipes by switching out the sage leaves for other herbs, citrus zest or vanilla powder. If a recipe calls for a par-baked tart shell: remove from the oven, remove the baking beans and cool. If needed completely baked: remove the baking beans, return to the oven and bake until just lightly browned.

1. First make the dough. In a stand mixer fitted with the paddle attachment, beat the butter on medium speed until smooth. With the mixer on low, stream the sugar into the butter until well combined but not fluffy. Mix in the egg until well incorporated. Add the flour and sage a bit at a time just until combined. Don't overwork the dough. Turn the dough out onto a board and work with a plastic dough scraper, or your hands, until smooth. Shape into a pad, wrap tightly in clingfilm and chill until firm and ready to shape into the tart tin. (It can also be frozen for up to a month until needed.)

2. While the tart dough chills, make the filling. Scoop the honey, sugar and salt into a medium saucepan over a low heat and stir to combine. Add the butter and, over a medium-high heat, bring the mixture to the boil, stirring for about 3 minutes with a heat-resistant spatula. Turn off the heat, then pour the mixture into a large mixing bowl or jug and leave to cool for 20 minutes, stirring occasionally.

3. While the filling cools, remove the dough from the clingfilm and pat out into a 25cm (10 inch) fluted tart tin with a removable base (round or square). You can also roll the chilled dough into a 30cm (12 inch) round between layers of clingfilm, then peel off the bottom layer and unroll into the tart tin, shaping the sides to fit snugly. Lastly, trim the tart dough edges gently with a small knife. Lightly cover the tin and chill again until firm.

4. Preheat the oven to 160°C (325°F), Gas Mark 3 and position a rack in the centre.

5. Place the tart tin in the middle of a baking tray to catch any drips and, using a fork, lightly dock the dough. Whisk the cream into the cooled filling, followed by the beaten egg mixture.

6. Sprinkle the pine nuts evenly over the bottom of the tart case, then gently pour in the custard until it reaches the very top of the crust (you may not use all the custard depending on the size of your tin). Carefully place in the oven and bake for 30–55 minutes, depending on the depth of your tin, until both the crust and the filling have turned light golden brown and the custard is softly set but still jiggly. Allow the tart to cool completely on a rack before carefully removing the sides of the tin.

7. Sprinkle with pine salt or rosemary salt, cut into wedges and serve while still slightly warm. Cooled and wrapped in clingfilm, any leftovers will keep in the refrigerator for 2–4 days.

Pim Techamuanvivit

Seared Sea Scallops
with Buttered Naam-jim & Lemon Basil

chillies | basil | lime

SERVES 4

12 large sea scallops, about 450g (1lb) in total
3 tablespoons lime juice
1 small shallot, thinly sliced
3 tablespoons butter
1–2 tablespoons fish sauce
pinch of palm or white granulated sugar
2 bird's eye chillies, thinly sliced (optional)
1 tablespoon fried shallots
6g (⅛oz) lemon basil leaves

'Taking this bright, citrusy chilli-garlic sauce (that we Thais love to pair with seafood) and softening it just a bit with butter, is my favourite way to cook and eat scallops. Sometimes I even share with friends!'

1. Pat the scallops dry with kitchen paper.

2. Add the lime juice to the sliced shallot and set aside.

3. Place a large carbon-steel or nonstick pan over a medium heat and, when the pan is hot, add 2 tablespoons of the butter and let it melt. Swirl the pan to coat it with the butter. Sear the scallops in the pan for no more than a minute each side until caramelized and golden. Do not overcrowd the pan or your scallops won't have a lovely caramelized crust. Work in batches if necessary. Transfer the seared scallops to a large serving plate and set aside while you finish the sauce.

4. Add the remaining tablespoon of butter the pan, then turn the heat down to low. Add the fish sauce and sugar. (Because different brands of fish sauce can vary in salinity, add 1 tablespoon first, then add more if you need more salt.) Add the shallots and lime juice. Swirl the pan to combine everything. Add the chilli, if using, and turn off the heat. Pour the sauce over the scallops. Scatter the fried shallots and lemon basil over the top. Serve immediately.

Adam Brydon

New Zealand Rack of Lamb
Lamb with Goats' Cheese Parfait & Cavolo Nero Pesto

cavolo nero | beetroot | sea purslane

'New Zealand lamb is the best and is the preferred choice of chefs around the world. This dish celebrates it.'

SERVES 4

1 × 8-rib rack of lamb (preferably New Zealand), French trimmed
rosemary salt (see page 120)
sea purslane and baby beetroot leaves, to garnish

For the goats' cheese parfait
250g (9oz) goats' cheese, softened
50g (1¾oz) cream cheese, softened
1 tablespoon manuka honey
1 tablespoon lemon juice
pinch of salt

For the salt-baked beetroot
4 beetroots, scrubbed clean
2 yellow beetroots, scrubbed clean
700g (1lb 9oz) rock salt
1 egg white, well beaten
50g (1¾oz) butter
1–2 tablespoons sherry vinegar
1 tablespoon brown sugar

For the cavolo nero pesto
100g (3½oz) cavolo nero, blanched and refreshed in ice water
50g (1¾oz) pine nuts, toasted
50g (1¾oz) Parmesan cheese, grated
120ml (4fl oz) olive oil
1 garlic clove
juice of 1 lemon
sea salt and freshly ground black pepper

1. First, make the goats' cheese parfait. Blend the cheeses and honey in a food processor or blender until smooth. Season with the lemon juice and salt. Spoon into 4 of your desired moulds (even ice-cube trays will work). Freeze.

2. Place the beetroot in a steamer or boil it in a small pot of water until al dente. Leave to cool.

3. Meanwhile, preheat the oven to 180°C (350°F), Gas Mark 4 and make the salt crust. Mix the salt and beaten egg white together until the mixture is the consistency of wet sand. Place the beetroots on a baking tray and coat thoroughly with the salt mix, being careful not to let the yellow and purple beetroots touch. Bake for about 1 hour. Remove from the oven and leave to cool for 5 minutes, then peel and discard the salt crust and beetroot skin.

4. Using 5cm (2 inch) round cutters, make 4 large rings of purple beetroot. Also make four small thick rounds of yellow beetroot using 3cm (½ inch). Assemble as in the photo opposite. The remaining yellow beetroot will last for up to 2 weeks, covered in the refrigerator, and is great to have lying around to use in salads.

5. Thinly slice the remaining purple beetroot and sweat in the butter over a low heat for 15–20 minutes until super soft. Deglaze with the sherry vinegar and add the brown sugar. Blend and pass through a sieve. Check and adjust the seasoning with salt and pepper if needed. Set aside.

6. Season the lamb with a little rosemary salt. Sear evenly in an ovenproof sauté pan over a high heat, then roast in the oven for about 12 minutes to ensure a nice rose-pink centre. Remove from the oven and leave to rest for at least 12 minutes.

7. While the lamb is resting, make the pesto. Blend all the ingredients together and season to taste with salt and pepper.

8. To serve, slice the lamb rack to show the beautiful pink centre. Put 2 ribs on each plate, followed by one rocher (spoonful) of beetroot purée. Drizzle the pesto in a circular motion around the plates. Add the beetroot rounds and, finally, the goats' cheese parfait. Garnish with sea purslane and baby beetroot leaves. Enjoy.

Lee Westcott

Isle of Wight Tomatoes
with Chamomile, Ricotta, Cherries & Green Almonds

fennel | chamomile

SERVES 4

8 fresh green almonds in their husks
500g (1lb 2oz) variety of Isle of Wight or heritage tomatoes in different colours and sizes, at room temperature, cut into 1.5cm (⅝ inch) slices
4 English cherries, pitted and halved
24 fresh bronze fennel fronds

For the ricotta
380ml (13fl oz) full-fat milk
95ml (3fl oz) double cream
50ml (2fl oz) buttermilk
5g (1 teaspoon) lemon juice
a pinch of sea salt

For the chamomile oil
100g (3½oz) freshly picked/foraged chamomile buds
500ml (18fl oz) cold-pressed rapeseed oil

For the fennel pollen salt
40g (1½oz) sea salt
6g (⅛oz) fresh fennel pollen (easily grown in a pot, or you can buy dried if needed but halve the quantity)

For the baby tomatoes
fine salt
8 red cherry tomatoes
8 yellow cherry tomatoes

'Cooking with the British seasons means you can really utilize the wonderful produce grown here at the peak of their individual seasons. Isle of Wight tomatoes are a true example of this; in my opinion, they are one of the best seasonal products available to us.

'This dish is all about highlighting a beautiful ingredient alongside other seasonal ingredients, which truly complement each other.

'The tomatoes work incredibly well with the addition of chamomile and fennel pollen – two ingredients that we forage during the summer season in the UK. Hence, why I think they really pair well together, as they all grow in harmony together.'

---

1. First make the ricotta. Mix all the ricotta ingredients in a bowl. Split the mixture evenly into vacuum pack bags and vacuum tightly. Place each bag into another bag and vacuum tightly again. Cook in a water bath at 88°C (190°F) for 2 hours. Remove and chill in an ice bath until very cold. Strain through muslin, hang and leave for at least 1 day. Keep the whey. Once fully strained, transfer the hung ricotta to a bowl and whisk it well. Season with a little fine salt.

2. You may need to add a little bit of the whey if needed. You are looking to achieve a nice thick, but glossy and smooth texture. Keep the excess whey to use for future recipes.

3. For the chamomile oil, vacuum both the ingredients tightly in a vacuum bag and water bath at 65°C (149°F) for 6 hours, or use a large pot on the stove with a thermometer. Remove from the heat and leave to cool in the refrigerator for 24 hours. When needed, strain through a muslin, keeping the oil and discarding the buds.

4. To make the fennel pollen salt, place the ingredients in a bowl and scrunch together well using your fingers. Don't scrunch them together too much, as you still want it to be quite coarse salt, but you just want to marry the flavours together more. Transfer to a tray and leave somewhere warm to air dry for 3 hours, mixing occasionally. Place in an airtight container and store at room temperature in a cool, dry place until needed.

continued overleaf

5. For the baby tomatoes, bring a large pan of water to the boil. Season the water well with fine salt. Lightly score a criss-cross into the top of each tomato (where the tomato was attached to the vine). Get a bowl of iced water ready. Now, plunge the tomatoes into the boiling water for 5 seconds and quickly remove. Plunge the tomatoes into the ice water for 5 minutes. Remove the tomatoes from the ice water and into a colander to drain. Using your hands and a small paring knife, peel the tomatoes. Once peeled, gently rub a J cloth on to each tomato to remove any residue. Place the peeled tomatoes in a dehydrator at 55°C (131°F) for 1½ hours, or in an oven on the lowest heat. You just want to dry them out a bit, you do not want to over-dry them.

6. Take the almonds and carefully, using a hammer, gently hit the crease of the husk until the husk forms a crack. Do not hammer it any more once this happens. Now, using your hands, gently prise the husks open until you can see the almond kernel inside. Gently remove the kernels and reserve. Discard the husks and soak the nuts in cold water for 2 minutes. Drain well.

7. Using a small paring knife, carefully peel the skin off each almond kernel. Once all peeled, gently rinse them in ice cold water for a few seconds to remove any leftover skin. Now, split each kernel in half, down their natural seam, using a small paring knife. Dry well on kitchen paper and store in an airtight container in the refrigerator until needed.

8. Place the sliced tomatoes on a tray ready to be dressed and seasoned.

9. Wash the bronze fennel well in ice water and then drain in a colander. Spin the fronds in a small salad spinner to remove any excess water. Store in a container with kitchen paper on the bottom in the refrigerator until needed.

10. To plate, dress the sliced tomatoes, baby red cherry and baby yellow cherry tomatoes with the chamomile oil and fennel pollen salt. Arrange the sliced tomatoes on a plate as desired. Place one nice spoonful of the ricotta on to the tomatoes. Now arrange your baby cherry tomatoes and cherry halves on and around the above. Add the almonds and the sprigs of bronze fennel to garnish. Keep it organic and natural looking. Ensure the tomatoes are well seasoned and served at room temperature to really encourage their natural flavours. Enjoy.

Natasha MacAller

Swiss Meringue Pamplemousse Pavlova

grapefruit | basil

SERVES 8–10

For the meringue
200g (7oz) egg whites
350g (12oz) caster sugar
1¼ teaspoons vanilla extract
2 teaspoons grapefruit juice, strained
2 teaspoons cornflour

For the grapefruit curd (makes 750ml/1⅓ pints)
zest of 1 large grapefruit, about 400g (14oz), plus the segments to garnish
285g (10oz) granulated sugar
5 large eggs
185ml (6fl oz) grapefruit juice
170g (6oz) butter, cut into 1cm (½ inch) pieces

For the ricotta cream
180g (6oz) fresh ricotta cheese
160ml (5½fl oz) whipping cream
30g (1oz) runny honey
1 tablespoon vanilla bean paste
1 tablespoon lemon juice
pinch of salt

For the sweet basil drizzle
2 bunches of liquorice basil, lemon basil or classic basil, leaves picked
3–4 tablespoons agave syrup, runny honey or simple syrup
pinch of salt
¼ teaspoon sweet basil seeds (optional)
a few grinds of toasted pepper

To serve
2–3 tablespoons hibiscus flowers and syrup from a jar
4 tablespoons pistachios (optional)
edible flowers and citrus blossoms

The New Zealand grapefruit is like no other – it looks like a large orange and its flesh is a 60s neon orangey-pink. Less bitter and pithy than other varieties, its flavour is tart, sweet and extremely fragrant. Use your favourite variety of grapefruit in this recipe, ideally one that is homegrown or from the local farmers' market. 'Pamplemousse' means grapefruit in Flemish and when I danced in the Royal Ballet of Flanders in Belgium I grew to love pavlovas and say 'grapefruit' repeatedly in Flemish, much to the annoyance of my dance colleagues.

This dessert does justify the phrase so often heard on TV Baking Shows, 'This dish is a showstopper!' Filled with colour, flavour and fragrance, reminiscent of childhood nostalgia of the famous Brown Derby Restaurant next to Capitol Records at Hollywood and Vine, it is a sweet, tart, gluten-free showstopper. Make all the components a day ahead and assemble just before serving. Make sure the finished meringue is stored in a dry airtight container if making ahead of time.

1. First make the meringue. If you have a fan oven, ensure the fan is turned off, then preheat the oven to 170°C (340°F), Gas Mark 3½. Line a baking tray with the baking paper. Place a 20cm (8 inch) cake tin in the centre of a sheet of baking paper and trace around the tin with a pencil to make a circle. Turn the paper upside down and set aside.

2. In the clean, dry bowl of a stand mixer, or in a heatproof bowl, combine the egg whites, sugar and vanilla extract, whisking to combine. Set the bowl over a pan of gently simmering water to create a bain-marie – make sure that the water does not touch the bottom of the bowl. Attach an instant-read thermometer inside the bowl then whisk continuously, heating the egg and sugar mixture until it reads 76°C (169°F) and the sugar has completely dissolved. Using a dry tea towel, carefully transfer the hot bowl to the stand mixer fitted with the whisk attachment. Whisk on high speed until the mixture is glossy and holds stiff peaks, about 3–4 minutes. Turn the mixer to low and add the grapefruit juice and cornflour, then turn the mixer speed back to high and whisk for a further minute to ensure that the mixture is well combined.

3. Using a little of the meringue on an offset spatula or spoon, place a big dot in each corner of the baking tray, to stick the baking paper to the tray so that it does not move when you shape the pavlova. Using an offset spatula or large spoon and staying within the outlined ring on the paper, shape and spread the meringue into a sloping mound, then form and shape the sides so that it resembles a straight-sided cylinder. Smooth and level the top.

continued overleaf

4. Using the back of a small spoon with the handle facing upwards, go around the entire meringue from bottom to top, moving the spoon upwards to make decorative shell-like waves, leaving little points at the top. Carefully place the pavlova in the oven and immediately reduce the temperature to 110°C (225°F), Gas Mark ¼. Bake for 2 hours, then, *without opening the oven door,* turn the oven off. Leave the pavlova to cool in the oven for at least 2 hours. I leave myself a sign taped on the door in case I forget!

5. After the wait you may find cracks on the top and edges of the pavlova which is perfectly normal – the cream will cover the cracks! Remove the pavlova from the oven and either carefully transfer to a serving platter or store in an airtight container until ready to decorate and serve.

6. While the pavlova is baking and cooling, make the grapefruit curd. Prepare an ice bath to cool the curd. Add the grapefruit zest to the sugar and, using your fingertips, work them together until fragrant. Whisk the eggs in a heavy-based, non-aluminium 1 litre (1¾ pint) saucepan until well combined. Whisk in the grapefruit zest and sugar mix, then add the grapefruit juice. Set over a low heat. Using a wooden spoon or heat-resistant spatula, stir in the butter. Continue stirring slowly but constantly over a low heat for about 10 minutes until the curd thickens. Immediately strain into a large, sterilized glass jar or non-reactive metal container and cool in the ice bath, stirring occasionally until chilled. The curd will keep, tightly covered and stored in the refrigerator, for up to 2 weeks.

7. To make the ricotta cream, use a stand mixer on a medium speed to whisk all the ingredients together until thick and fluffy. Cover and chill for at least 1 hour or up to overnight.

8. For the sweet basil drizzle, quickly blanch the basil leaves in boiling water, then shock them in ice-cold water. Dry on kitchen paper, then add to a bullet blender with the agave, salt and basil seeds (if using). Blitz to a smooth purée. Check and adjust the seasonings, then store chilled in a small jar with a lid.

9. To assemble and serve, carefully peel away the baking paper and place the pavlova on a serving plate or cake stand, using a dab of ricotta cream to hold it steady. Dollop large spoonfuls of ricotta cream in the centre of the pavlova and swirl to the edges. Spread and swirl the grapefruit curd on top as pictured opposite, letting it run down the sides. Decorate with grapefruit segments, the sweet basil drizzle, fresh citrus or other edible blossoms, dot with the hibiscus flower syrup and arrange the hibiscus flowers and optional pistachios over the top. Serve within an hour of assembling.

Natasha MacAller

Pickled Magnolia Petal Compote with Mascarpone & Triple lime Sablés

citrus | magnolia | sea buckthorn

An aromatic afternoon indulgence. Make sure you pick the tender leaves close to the flower's centre for melt-in-the-mouth pickled leaves.

SERVES 4–6

For the homemade raspberry vinegar
200g (7oz) fresh or frozen raspberries
250ml (9fl oz) white wine vinegar
2.5cm (1 inch) piece of vanilla pod, chopped
4 teaspoons granulated sugar
pinch of salt

For the magnolia petal compote
100g (3½oz) fresh small and tender magnolia petals
4 tablespoons homemade raspberry vinegar*
200–300g (7–10½oz) caster sugar (depending on how bitter the magnolia is)
300ml (10fl oz) water
big pinch of salt flakes

For the sablés
120g (4¼oz) unsalted butter, softened
200g (7oz) plain flour
75g (2½oz) icing sugar, sifted, plus extra for dusting
1 egg, separated
4 teaspoons makrut lime juice
1 teaspoon lime zest
2 finger limes, tips cut off, then rolled on a work surface to release the caviar
big pinch of flaky sea salt
crystal sugar, for sprinkling

For the mascarpone
200g (7oz) mascarpone cheese
2 teaspoons sea buckthorn powder
2 teaspoons caster sugar

To serve
100g (3½oz) blackberries
caviar from 1–2 plump finger limes

1. Make the raspberry vinegar at least 1 day before serving. Add the ingredients to a high-speed blender and blitz until combined. Pour into a sterilized jar, cover with a small piece of dry muslin and let stand overnight, or up to 2 days. Remove the muslin, then pour the vinegar into a small non-reactive pan and warm to a simmer. Cook for about 5 minutes until the sugar dissolves. Strain the vinegar through muslin, decant into a sterilized bottle and seal. This will keep in the refrigerator for 3 months.

2. For the magnolia petal compote, add all the ingredients to a medium pan. Simmer over a low heat for 20 minutes, stirring occasionally, until the petals soften to almost opaque. Remove from the heat, cool, then pour into a sterilized jar, cover and refrigerate overnight to infuse. This will keep, tightly sealed, in the refrigerator for 1 month.

3. To make the sablés, beat the butter, flour and icing sugar in the bowl of a stand mixer with a paddle attachment, or using a hand mixer, until crumbly. Add the egg yolk, lime juice, zest, finger lime caviar and salt and mix to well combined. Gather together into a disc, then wrap tightly with clingfilm. Chill for about 30 minutes until firm.

4. Preheat oven to 160°C (325°F), Gas Mark 3. Line a baking tray with baking paper.

5. Lightly dust a work surface with icing sugar then roll out the dough to 5mm (¼ inch) thick and cut into shapes with a cookie cutter. Place the cookies on the lined baking tray and brush with beaten egg white, sprinkling the tops with crystal sugar. Bake for 5–7 minutes until the edges are lightly browned. Remove from the oven and leave to cool on a wire rack. When completely cool, store in an airtight container to maintain their crispiness until ready to serve.

6. For the mascarpone, add the cheese, sea buckthorn powder and sugar to a small bowl and whisk until smooth and creamy, adjusting the sweetness to taste. Cover and chill if not using immediately.

7. When ready to serve, scoop the mascarpone into flat bowls. Use the back of a serving spoon to create a swirly bowl inside the mascarpone, then divide the magnolia compote and juice between the bowls. Top with blackberries and spoon or sprinkle the finger lime caviar to serve over all. Serve with 1–2 crisp sablés.

Natasha MacAller

Dutch, Dutch Baby
with Tangerine Ricotta Whip

sunflower | garlic | citrus

SERVES 4

For the whipped tangerine ricotta
50ml (2fl oz) double
  or whipping cream
225g (8oz) ricotta
1 tablespoon tangerine juice
zest of 1 tangerine
10g (¼oz) small peppermint
  leaves, torn

For the filling
1 teaspoon sunflower oil
1 tablespoon salted butter
100g (3½oz) minced onions
½ jalapeño, minced
100g (3½oz) butternut squash or
  pumpkin, peeled, deseeded and cut
  into 1cm (½ inch) pieces
1 tablespoon roasted garlic
1 tablespoon local runny honey
15g (½oz) basil, chopped
sea salt and freshly ground black
  pepper

For the Dutch baby batter
70g (2½oz) plain flour
½ teaspoon grated nutmeg
30g (1oz) salted butter
5 large eggs, at room temperature
1 teaspoon caster sugar
90ml (6 tablespoons) milk,
  at room temperature
15g (½oz) basil, chopped

To serve
1 tablespoon toasted salted
  sunflower seeds
1 tablespoon pomegranate seeds
baby salad leaves
sunflower petals (optional)

Dutch, Dutch baby: the dancing sunshine yellow-orange glow greets the weekend morn as this oven-baked, brightly-coloured, puffed Dutch Baby is gently pulled from the oven, dressed in orange, green and red with orange whipped ricotta, then served to share!

1. Make the ricotta. In a medium bowl using a hand-held electric whisk, in a stand mixer or in a big bowl with a whisk, beat the cream and ricotta together until smooth and thickened. Whisk in the tangerine juice, zest and mint leaves. Cover and chill until ready to serve. The ricotta will thicken as it continues to chill.

2. Preheat the oven to 220°C (425°F), Gas Mark 7.

3. For the filling, heat the oil and butter in a small pan heat over a medium heat until it sizzles. Add the onion to the pan and cook for about 3 minutes until translucent. Add the jalapeño, squash and garlic with a good pinch of salt. Continue to cook for about 3 minutes until squash is al dente, then gently fold in the honey and basil. Season to taste. Transfer to a plate to cool, setting aside.

4. To make the Dutch baby batter, add the flour to a medium bowl, mix in the nutmeg and set aside.

5. Over a medium-high heat, warm the butter in a 20cm (8 inch) cast-iron pan, swirling the to coat the sides of the pan for about 5 minutes until the butter becomes a nutty brown colour.

6. While the butter heats, use a balloon whisk to beat the eggs with the sugar and a pinch of salt until smooth. Whisk the milk into the flour until well combined, then fold in the eggs, whisking until the mixture is smooth.

7. When the butter is browned, pour the egg mixture into the hot buttered pan and spoon half of the squash mixture around the pan. Bake for 12 minutes until puffed up and golden brown.

8. While the Dutch baby is baking, line up the sunflower and pomegranate seeds, baby leaves and tangerine ricotta. When the Dutch baby is ready, carefully remove it from the oven. Working quickly, add the ricotta to the centre, scatter with the pomegranate and sunflower seeds, garnish with the baby leaves, slice and serve immediately.

Natasha MacAller

Fig, Pear & Cranberry Mostarda
for Cheese

mustard | pears | honey

MAKES ABOUT 1 LITRE (1¾ PINTS)

160ml (5½fl oz) dry white wine
4 tablespoons mild honey
4 tablespoons agave syrup
1 firm ripe Bosc or homegrown pear, about 230g (8oz), peeled, cored and cut into bite-sized pieces
200g (7oz) fresh or frozen cranberries
1 small shallot, chopped
180g (6oz) fresh ripe firm figs, stems trimmed and sliced into bite-sized pieces
4 teaspoons yellow mustard seeds
2 bay leaves
big pinch of chilli flakes, or to taste
1 tablespoon Dijon mustard
1 tablespoon apple cider vinegar
½ teaspoon coriander seeds
1 teaspoon pimentón
1 teaspoon ground ginger

To serve
cheeses of your choice, energize flatbreads (see page 44), bread, crackers, nuts or fruit
1 tablespoon pomegranate seeds
baby salad leaves
sunflower petals

A New Zealand take on the traditional northern Italian accompaniment to boiled meats, this hearty mostarda uses mustard and coriander seeds, plus Dijon mustard and fresh fruit from the garden with cranberries for a tart and healthy zing. Served here with a modern moreish cheeseboard.

1. In a 2 litre (3½ pint) pan, whisk together the wine, honey and agave and bring to a simmer. Add the pear, 100g (3½oz) of the cranberries and the shallot, then cook gently, stirring occasionally, for about 7 minutes until the cranberries pop and the pear is just fork tender.

2. Add the remaining cranberries and simmer a few minutes longer, then gently fold in the figs. Stir in the remaining ingredients and gently simmer for another 3 minutes. Remove from the heat, leaving in the uncovered pan to let the flavours blend together and cool to just warm.

3. To serve, spoon into a serving bowl and serve with a platter of your favourite cheeses, bread, crackers, nuts and fruit. Transfer any remaining mostarda into a large jar to store in the refrigerator for up to 3 weeks. Allow the chilled mostarda to come to room temperature before serving.

Sequanna Manzenita

Soothing Summer Switchel

ginger | lemon | maple

SERVES 20

200g (7oz) fresh root ginger, washed or just peeled and chopped
15g (½oz) dried hibiscus flowers
2 vanilla pods, cut in half lengthways with the seeds scraped out
4 cinnamon sticks
2 litres (3½ pints) spring water
235ml (8fl oz) apple cider vinegar with mother
180ml (6fl oz) lemon juice
120ml (4fl oz) maple syrup
90ml (3fl oz) agave syrup
2 tablespoons molasses
1 teaspoon mineral salt (I use grey/Celtic sea salt)

This soothing summer switchel comes courtesy of Sequanna Manzenita and I have paired it here with my Rhubarb, Raspberry and Peppermint Shrub, the cold process of which keeps the flavours and colours bright and sassy! Sequanna says: 'Dating back to the 17th century, Switchel's appeal lies in its combination of tartness from the vinegar and sweetness from the molasses, creating a balance that quenches thirst and provides energy. Switchel was also valued for its medicinal properties, as ginger is believed to aid digestion and vinegar is thought to help maintain good health and reduce inflammation. This is the recipe that I make for my family during the summer months in So Cal, and for my doula clients after they deliver their babies to aid in their hydration with the added benefits of being rich in minerals and vitamin C.'

1. In a large pan, combine the chopped ginger, hibiscus flowers, vanilla pods and cinnamon sticks with the measured water. Bring the mixture to the boil over a high heat. Once boiling, reduce the heat and allow it to simmer for 30 minutes. Remove the pan from heat and let the mixture cool. Strain the cooled liquid into a large jug, discarding the solids.

2. Add the remaining ingredients to the jug and stir or whisk thoroughly to ensure everything is well combined.

3. Pour the mixture into three 1 litre (1¾ pint) swing-top bottles, leaving some space at the top. Close the lids, but do not secure them tightly. Store the bottles in a cool, dry place for 24 hours.

4. After 24 hours, secure the lids tightly and transfer the bottles to the refrigerator to chill. This will keep in the refrigerator for up to 1 month.

5. When ready to serve, mix the chilled beverage with sparkling or still water in a 50/50 ratio, or adjust to taste.

Rhubarb, Raspberry & Peppermint Shrub

rhubarb | peppermint

MAKES 600ML (20FL OZ)

300g (10½oz) bright pink rhubarb, cleaned trimmed and chopped
150g (5½oz) raspberries fresh or frozen
400g (14oz) caster sugar
400ml (14fl oz) rice wine vinegar
Tiny bunch (about 2g) of fresh peppermint leaves, plus a sprig, to serve (optional)
small pinch of sea salt flakes
pink Prosecco or hibiscus syrup (optional, to serve)

1. Add the ingredients to a 1 litre (1¾ pint) glass pitcher or non-reactive bowl. Cover with a cloth and stand it on the kitchen counter, stirring every 15 minutes or so until the sugar is dissolved. When dissolved, place in the refrigerator, cover and infuse for 2–4 days, stirring occasionally. Using cheesecloth, or a fine screen chinois, strain the liquid into a clean dry 1 litre (1¾ pint) jar and seal tightly. Refrigerate until needed.

2. To serve, add 4 tablespoons of shrub to an ice-filled glass and top with sparkling water. Or, for a pink sparkle mimosa, add 4 tablespoons of shrub to a coupe glass. Top with pink Prosecco and a teaspoon of hibiscus syrup, if you like, garnish with a mint sprig and serve.

Natasha MacAller

Sea Buckthorn & Champagne Gelée

sea buckthorn | rose hip | citrus

This sparkly, light and refreshing gelée, with a hint of aromatic rose petals and tangy sea buckthorn, was inspired by a recipe from American Pastry Chef Gesine Bullock-Prado. It is both a pretty and simple celebration of summer berries mixed with sweet, tart citrus and a few tiny fragrant bites of peach. For a fall celebration substitute the summer berries with peeled persimmon, pomegranate seeds or fresh cooked and chilled halved cranberries, a handful of diced pear or apple, or even tiny slivers of firm fresh figs or plum.

SERVES 6

480ml (17fl oz) Champagne, chilled
100g (3½oz) caster sugar
1 teaspoon mild runny honey
1 tablespoon dried rose hip petals
1½ teaspoon sea buckthorn powder
7g (⅛oz) packet gelatine granules
1 teaspoon vanilla bean paste
2 tangerines, segmented and dried on kitchen paper

To serve
wild or tiny strawberries, hulled and quartered
blackberries, raspberries or blueberries
strawberry flowers, small viola or other seasonal edible flower petals
mascarpone cheese, thickened cream or yogurt (optional)
mint sprigs (optional)

1. Add 360ml (12fl oz) of the Champagne, the sugar and honey to a medium saucepan over a low heat, stirring gently until the sugar has dissolved. Fold in the rose hip petals, remove from the heat and leave to infuse.

2. In a small bowl or measuring jug, add the remaining cold Champagne and sea buckthorn powder, stirring well. Sprinkle the gelatine powder over the surface, it will get spongy in about a minute. Pour the spongy liquid into the warm rose hip liquid and stir gently until dissolved.

3. Pour the liquid gelée into 6 clean small glasses or Champagne coupes until half-full. Set the remaining gelée aside. Decorate the glasses with a few strawberries and blackberries or blueberries, plus some edible flower petals. Add 3 small drops of vanilla bean paste to each glass. Tap the glasses gently to release any air bubbles, then place in the refrigerator for about 1 hour to cool and set.

4. Remove from the refrigerator and garnish with more fruit and flower petals, then carefully pour over the remaining gelée. (If the jug of gelée has solidified, gently rewarm to melt, allow to cool and stir then pour into the glasses.) Return to the refrigerator to chill for at least 1 hour.

5. To serve, remove the glasses from the refrigerator and serve as they are, or top with a spoonful of mascarpone, thickened cream or yogurt and garnish with mint sprigs and more edible flower petals.

*You can subsitiute the Champagne for a dry prosecco or a good quality alcohol-removed dry Champagne or prosecco.

BENEFICIAL EDIBLE PLANTS

In the cold, dark and rainy days of winter, a garlic grower's joy emerges, and the kale and carrot season gatherers pick and snip their freshly harvested veg. Then, the first sights, sounds and scents of spring: little leaves, then a handful of blossoms, then hundreds appear on once empty branches to the welcoming sounds of buzzing bees and birdsong, as you discover a tiny green curl emerging from the garden bed that will soon become a broccoli forest...Suddenly, summer's breathtaking explosion of basil, tomato, lavender and plum aromas amongst a rainbow of colours reaching to the sun. And, just as fast, autumnal harvests burst forth a cornucopia of sweet potatoes, artichokes, persimmons and figs as you gaze into long-shadowed sunsets. This is the time for putting by, hanging the mustard and dill stalks to dry for spring seed planting, and spreading the pea straw over the beds for next season's garden gifts.

Here is our bounty of edible plants, herbs, and a few honourable mentions, all with beneficial merits for health. Welcome to the world of the Apothecary Chef.

OTHER HEROES

Honey
APIS MELLIFERA

Whilst honey is a sugar, it contains health-promoting plant compounds called polyphenols, which have been shown to help improve health, especially in those with chronic disease[1] such as heart disease, diabetes and cancer[2]. Honey is known for its antioxidant benefits, and the darker the honey the higher the antioxidant potential, as well as antibacterial activity – especially in Manuka honey – and important anti-inflammatory and immunomodulatory benefits. One of the more extensively studied benefits of honey is its wound healing ability because of its powerful bioactive compounds, as it can activate an immune response to infection and has also been used topically to treat ulcers and burns[3].

Maple Syrup
ACER SACCHARUM

Maple Syrup comes from the sap of sugar maple trees and, despite being a sugar, is a good source of minerals including manganese, which plays an important role in digestion, bone health, brain health and neurotransmitter synthesis[4]. The active compounds found in maple syrup have been identified to potentially slow down the release of carbohydrates, which could offer benefits to those with diabetes[5]. These same compounds may also have potential in preventing colon cancer[6]. Maple syrup also has anti-inflammatory benefits[7], and potential neuroprotective effects[8].

Pine Tips & Nuts:
PINUS

Pine needles have natural antioxidant and antimicrobial benefits, which may offer potential benefits in human health[9]. The oils found in pine nuts have been researched for their anti-inflammatory benefits which may help those suffering with an inflammatory disease such as rheumatoid arthritis. Pine nuts are actually cholesterol-free, and studies have demonstrated that they may help reduce blood pressure and cholesterol[10]. This may be due to pinolenic acid which is a polyunsaturated acid found in pine nut oil[11] that may help lower LDL cholesterol levels in the blood[12].

HERBS

Dill
ANETHUM GRAVEOLENS

Dill's soft, feathery leaves and distinctive, soothing scent bring calm; its strongly flavoured seeds and delicate fronds were historically infused in baby gripe water to soothe tummies and stave off colic. Indigenous to Western Asia, North Africa and Iran, this annual herb grows plentifully in North America and most of Europe and is also cultivated from China to New Zealand.

If you would like to grow your own, sow in early summer, in well-drained soil and full sun, sheltered from strong winds. Alternatively, grow indoors in pots on a sunny windowsill. You can also allow a few seed globes to blossom, leave whole to dry on the plant, then pick and store the seeds. Or nip fronds off and dry flat on a baking tray. When fronts are dried and brittle, crumble and store in an airtight jar in a dark cupboard.

CULINARY USES

Dill's distinctive flavour is a must-include seasoning for many traditional Scandinavian and Eastern European dishes, such as gravalax, or egg and potato salad. It is also an essential ingredient in the beloved Ukranian dish, Borsch (see page 12). The bright yellow dill flowers make a dramatic and delicious finish to pickled beetroot and the seeds are a brilliant addition to Sherry Yard's Energize Flatbreads (see page 44).

MEDICINAL USES

Dill has been used in traditional medicine for thousands of years, in particular for pain relief, indigestion and anxiety. Both the seeds and leaves of dill are rich in plant compounds called flavonoids, which have been associated with a reduced risk of heart disease and some forms of cancer.[1] More recently, dill has shown positive benefits in helping to lower both total cholesterol and LDL ('bad') cholesterol, as well as helping to improve blood glucose levels in those with diabetes.[2]

BENEFICIAL EDIBLE PLANTS

Angelica
ANGELICA ARCHANGELICA

Known also as garden angelica or wild celery, angelica is an edible herb that can grow up to 2.5m (8ft) tall and loves damp soil. Its leaves are very similar in appearance to those of a celery plant, but when it blooms in summer it produces large, allium-type flower heads made up of clusters of tiny, yellow-green flowers.

CULINARY USES

All parts of the plant can be consumed, including the young shoots and unopened flower buds, as well as the leaves, seeds and flowers, with different parts of the plant having different tastes. The unopened flower buds can be used in a similar way to courgette (zucchini) flowers and are delicious when dipped in batter, fried and served with nutritious manuka honey.

The stems themselves have a floral yet anise-like flavour and can be pickled, making a great pairing with cheese, made into a jam or retro cocktail, or used as a feature decoration for cakes – you can often find whole candied stalks in old-fashioned, creaky, wooden-floored sweet shops and historic department stores such as London's Fortnum & Mason or KaDeWe in Berlin. You can replace rhubarb with angelica stems in recipes like rhubarb and custard tart! As for the seeds, they are an excellent substitute for herbs like fennel (*Foeniculum vulgare*) and anise (*Pimpinella anisum*) and can be used in pickles and sauces. The leaves are a little more bitter but can be added to salads and stir-fries, so pick the smaller, more tender leaves if you wish to eat them raw.

MEDICINAL USES

With a long history of use in both traditional and herbal medicine (its close relative *Angelica sinensis* is used in *dong quai*, the respected women's tonic in traditional Chinese medicine), angelica is also known as an 'angel plant' due to its healing properties. These include as a possible remedy for reducing anxiety,[3] as well as improving mild cognitive impairment, thanks to a compound called ferulic acid, which is found in the cell wall of the plants.[4] There is also some promising research that angelica contains important phytochemicals that may help in the treatment of breast cancer.[5]

Tarragon
ARTEMISIA DRACUNCULUS

Tarragon, beloved in France where it is known as l'estragon, has slender, sword-like, smooth, dark green leaves with an anise-liquorice fragrance and flavour. It prefers a slightly alkaline-rich soil. Originating from wide parts of the Northern hemisphere including North America, Eastern Europe, Russia, Siberia and the Middle East, tarragon germinates surprisingly rarely and instead depends on propagation by division or stem or root cuttings.

When tarragon takes in the summer's warmth and sunshine, it can develop into a small tarragon tree or sit stubbornly growing just a few spindly leaves – temperamental tarragon. But the fragrance and taste are worth the work and the benefits. Grow in full sun in well-drained soil and allow mature plants to dry out between waterings.

CULINARY USES

Used in classic French dishes and sauces, tarragon, like its sister basil, is best used fresh, as it loses much of its flavour when dried. You can create a herb vinegar, oil or syrup, as well as compound butters and pesto, with fresh tarragon leaves – a must-make when your plant is flourishing. Its aromatic fragrance pairs perfectly in softly scrambled eggs, custards, chicken salad, tomatoes and chocolate gelato. Tarragon's liquorice-like flavour is a winner with oranges, grapefruit and tangerines, in particular. It is also an essential part of the infamous blend *herbes de Provence* – I love a generous sprinkle of this on a simple leafy green salad with cucumber, onion and tomato.

MEDICINAL USES

Tarragon is a great source of the trace mineral manganese. We need manganese to help the body form healthy connective tissue and bones and also for its blood-clotting effects.[6] It is also essential for our neuronal health and may help protect against Parkinson's disease and Huntington's disease.[7] Other benefits of tarragon include helping to improve poor sleep,[8] pain management[9] and appetite,[10] which can occur with age, in depression or in those undergoing chemotherapy.

Old Man Saltbush
ATRIPLEX NUMMULARIA

Old man saltbush is a large woody shrub that flourishes in areas of saline-rich, low-lying flood plain. Its ability to adapt to other saline soils has allowed this hardy plant to thrive in subtropical regions, from Taiwan to New Zealand to North America, as well as in sandy soils in Europe and Northern Africa.

Saltbush (*Atriplex*) research has been an enlightening discovery; so much so, I now have an old man saltbush thriving in my New Zealand garden. The seeds and leaves of this astonishing plant have been used for centuries by First Nation cultures of Australia as a nutritious and medicinal native ingredient. This shrub has fleshy, blue-grey leaves with a salty, herb-like flavour, making it a resourceful, versatile plant.

CULINARY USES

Add fresh leaves to a salad, throw them into a stir-fry or use them alongside meat and fish. The fresh leaves can also be boiled or steamed, a bit like spinach, and these work brilliantly with lamb. Dried saltbush leaves can be used as a substitute for salt. Saltbush seeds need to be cooked before eating, but they too can be ground down and used to thicken soups and stews.

MEDICINAL USES

Old man saltbush and other species of Atriplex such as tree purslane (*A. halimus*) are not extensively researched yet, but they have been documented so far for their antioxidant, antibacterial, antiviral and antifungal potential, as they contain a number of valuable biochemicals, including flavonoids and phenolics.[11] Saltbush is also a rich source of vitamin A, which is needed for healthy vision and immune function,[12] and vitamin C, which has been linked to multiple health benefits, including healthy ageing, reduced cardiovascular disease and reduced risk of certain cancers like cervical and lung cancer.[13]

Chamomile

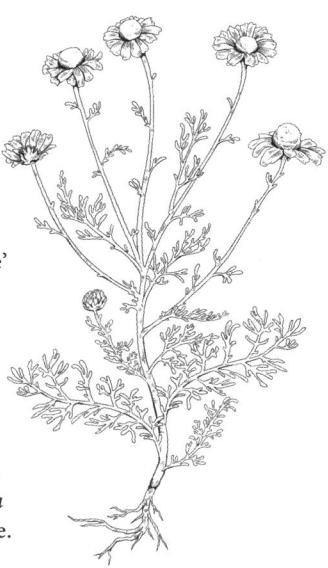

Chamomile, with its pretty, delicate flowers, has been used for centuries, and was notably discovered in the ancient Egyptian pyramids. The word 'chamomile' comes from the Greek word *chamaimelon*, which means 'apple on the ground' because the flowers of the perennial English/Roman chamomile (*Chamaemelum nobile*) smell exactly like that, an apple, while German chamomile (*Matricaria recutita*) has a sweet, grassy taste.

CULINARY USES

When cooking chamomile, note that the flowers have a sweet, mild taste. They can be used fresh or dried and have a wide range of uses outside of a nice cup of chamomile tea! They can be included in sweet dishes such as vanilla cheesecake with strawberries, chamomile and pink pepper syrup, chamomile-sugared shortbread biscuits, wispy meringues and ice cream. Whisk up a dressing with olive oil, lime, honey and chamomile flowers to dress salads, fruit or fish, or try gently poaching fish such as sustainable salmon, cod or

BENEFICIAL EDIBLE PLANTS

scallops in chamomile tea for added flavour. Try Lee Westcott's Isle of Wight Tomatoes with Chamomile, Ricotta, Cherries & Green Almonds (see page 166) – a true stunner.

MEDICINAL USES

Chamomile is in the Asteraceae family, like the daisy and sunflower, and is probably one of the most ancient medicinal herbs. It is perhaps best known as a tea, but can also be used as a salve to help treat wounds, soothe skin irritations and reduce bruises. As a food, chamomile flowers contain flavonoids, which may help reduce the risk of heart disease and provide anti-cancer benefits. Chamomile can also offer several digestive health benefits, including helping to calm an upset stomach, ease cramps and dispel flatulence. It is especially effective in soothing the stomach and relaxing the muscles, so food can move more easily through the digestive tract.[14]

Coriander
CORIANDRUM SATIVUM

Often called Chinese parsley, I find there are two camps when it comes to coriander: you either love it or hate it! Coriander has a very distinctive, floral yet citrus taste. You can eat fresh coriander (cilantro) leaves and stems, as well as the sweet seeds, which are dried and then used either whole or ground in cooking.

CULINARY USES

Fresh coriander can lose its flavour quite quickly when cooked, so it is best in a raw dish or thrown in at the last minute to soups and stir-fries. Also called cilantro, it is a star ingredient in Thai soup and a must-have for Latin American fresh salsas made with tomatoes, onion, lime and chilli. Ground coriander has a milder taste and can be used in dishes that take longer to cook, like stews or curries, allowing time for it to infuse into the dish. Or try ground coriander in a rub, pairing it with ground ginger, cumin and cinnamon. Whole coriander seeds can then be used in pickling or even a festive glass of mulled wine!

MEDICINAL USES

Coriander seed, and to a lesser extent the leaf, is an antioxidant-rich herb that helps to protect our body's cells from the damage caused by free radicals and to reduce inflammation, which can contribute to chronic diseases.[15] These antioxidants, including quercetin and tocopherols, also help support a healthy immune system, as well as offering neuroprotective benefits against dementia[16] and Alzheimer's disease.[17] Other benefits of coriander include helping to lower blood sugar[18] and blood pressure[19] and supporting healthy digestion. One study using coriander found that it helped to significantly reduce digestive symptoms such as abdominal pain, bloating and discomfort.[20]

Fennel
FOENICULUM VULGAREM

Fennel is a Mediterranean herb of which all parts can be eaten, from the white bulbs with their feathery, green leaves to the yellow flowers and subsequent fruits, or seeds. It loves to live in dry soil near the sea or on river banks but is also a common plant for the keen gardener or allotment owner.

CULINARY USES

Fennel is such a versatile vegetable as it can be eaten raw, roasted or sautéed, although the bulb is used most often in recipes. When eaten raw or quick-pickled, it has more

of a liquorice-type taste and makes a great addition to a salad or as a side for pork, chicken or fish. To prepare, choose a younger, smaller bulb, peel off the outer covering (save for scrap stock), slice thinly with a sharp knife or mandolin, then marinate in lemon juice, olive oil and salt. Roasting or grilling fennel adds a delicious caramelization, which enhances any meat or fish, and thinly sliced fennel can even be tossed into a pasta dish.

Those feathery fronds, while often discarded, are easily used as a delicious garnish for soups and dressings, or as a substitute for dill. Use the sweet, anise-scented, little yellow flowers not only for garnishing dishes but also to flavour foods like goat's cheese, or swirl into yogurt with cracked pepper, orange zest and a squeeze of orange juice for a twist on a dip!

Then, finally, the fennel seeds, which appear on the plant after the flowers fade. Try lightly toasting and using them in hummus, salads, or sprinkled on sea-salted popcorn, as well as in breads, pickles and chutneys.

MEDICINAL USES

All parts of fennel are rich in plant compounds that have valuable health benefits, but the seeds are more potent as they contain essential oils which have higher concentrations of these health-supporting compounds. Fennel is a rich source of the antioxidant vitamin C, which is vital to the health of the immune system[21] but may also help in reducing stress and anxiety.[22] The essential oil found in fennel contains over 85 active compounds, including polyphenols, which are known for their strong anti-inflammatory effect, and there are many studies that demonstrate the links between anti-inflammatory diets and a lower risk of chronic health conditions[23] such as heart disease, cancer and dementia. Fennel also contains the nutrients magnesium, potassium and calcium, all of which are important for heart health, too.[24]

Lovage
LEVISTICUM OFFICINALE

Lovely lovage, related to parsley, is a tall perennial native to the Mediterranean (though the Romans introduced lovage to Britain and Northern Europe) where it still grows wild today. In Roman times lovage was particularly abundant in the province of Liguria in Italy from where the old name for lovage *'Ligusticum'* originated. Considered an 'old-fashioned herb', the name is derived from 'love-ache', ache being the medieval name for parsley. I have found several mentions in medieval cookery books calling for the use of this beneficial herb.

When grown, lovage looks very much like a giant celery plant with long, green stems and giant, parsley-like leaves. It dies back in the winter but come spring rushes back, reaching for the sun. Lovage can be cultivated from seed or you can grow a small plant in a large container. It does have a deep taproot, however, so be prepared to transfer your lovage to a garden bed in a few years.

CULINARY USES

Lovage tastes stronger than celery, with hints of parsley and anise, and the entire plant is edible: the root as a vegetable, the leaves as a herb, and the seeds as a spice. The comforting, old-fashioned lovage lemon and potato soup is a delicious classic – all that is needed is some garlic bread to clean the bowl and that's lunch! You can also use lovage in stronger-flavoured oily fish and meat dishes that can hold their own against it. I prefer lovage when briefly pickled; if using it raw, the flavour can be quite intense. The seeds can be included in recipes such as curries or stews where you would use fennel, dill or celery seeds. Lightly toasted, lovage seeds can flavour salad or potato dressings or in place of celery salt on hard-boiled eggs.

MEDICINAL USES

Lovage is known for its high levels of phenolic compounds, which can act as antioxidants to protect various tissues in the human body from oxidative stress.[25] It may also offer some symptomatic relief from urinary tract infections,[26] but one of its biggest benefits is the high concentration of a polyphenol called quercetin, which is known for its ability to cross the blood brain barrier (BBB) and offer protection in neurodegenerative disease and to protect against age-related disorders.[27] Lovage, and its quercetin content, also offers heart health benefits by helping to lower blood pressure, reduce cholesterol and improve endothelial function,[28] which plays a key role in keeping your blood moving smoothly through your body.

Lemony Herbs

This 'alternative family' of beneficial, lemon-scented herbs has origins all over the globe. They include lemon balm, lemon verbena, lemon myrtle and common sorrel, which all have a range of culinary and medicinal uses.

LEMON VERBENA
ALOYSIA CITRODORAS

Lemon Verbena hails from South America, yet is commonly used in France, where it grows prolifically. The captvating scent of its yellow-green leaves pairs especially well with summer's fruit and veg.

Culinary uses: The leaves can be simmered in cream to make a sauce for a summer peach dumpling (see page 34). They are also delicious in a sauce with halibut and freshly shelled spring peas.

Medicinal uses: For centuries, lemon verbena has been used to treat several health complaints, including respiratory conditions and digestive issues. Like other herbs, it is rich in plant compounds that have anti-inflammatory and antioxidant health benefits, including verbascoside, which may have a protective effect on the liver[29] and eyesight.[30] Inflammation is one of the main contributing factors to conditions such as multiple sclerosis (MS), and lemon verbena has been shown to help reduce inflammation in MS patients, even better than a placebo.[31] Studies have also demonstrated its benefits in helping to reduce muscle damage and soreness post-exercise[32] due to its antioxidative and anti-inflammatory properties.

LEMON MYRTLE
BACKHOUSIA CITRIODORA

The scented leaves of lemon myrtle, a tree or shrub native to Australia, have an almost creamy, lemony scent and when dried they are said to be 'lemonier than lemon'.

Culinary uses: Grind dried leaves and use to season a marinade for roast chicken, infuse in butter to create a lemon myrtle hollandaise or add to your favourite baking recipes, try the Lemon Myrtle Cheesecake on page 37.

Medicinal uses: Lemon myrtle has powerful anti-inflammatory and antioxidative properties. These have been researched for their ability to reduce proinflammatory cytokines, which are released by the body's immune system, and may be of benefit to those struggling with irritable bowel disease.[33] This is largely due to a compound called citral, which is found in lemon myrtle and involved in the synthesis of vitamin A, but which also offers antimicrobial benefits and may be used to help treat skin infections.[34] Lemon myrtle's natural oils may also protect against various gut infections because it has shown significant antimicrobial activity against certain organisms,[35] which can help support a healthy gut microbiome. It may also benefit eye health, as it contains essential eye-supporting nutrients, including lutein, magnesium and calcium.[36]

LEMON BALM
MELISSA OFFICINALIS

Gently scented lemon balm rhymes with calm, its properties lift one's spirits from head to heart, and it's also known as the soothing 'bee herb' plant. Originating in ancient Ephesus (Turkey), lemon balm (the genus name of which is derived from the Greek word for bee) is a prolific grower and attractive to bees. Easy and quick to grow in a pot or a bed and tolerant of moist soil, use its fresh leaves any time, or dry it out in a dark space to retain the leaves' lemony yellow flavour.

Culinary uses: Luxuriate in a lemon balm tisane made with rose hips, mint and honey or use in a creamy sauce for salmon on shaved poached fennel with crispy shallots.

Medicinal uses: Traditionally, lemon balm has been used to reduce stress and anxiety by promoting a greater sense of calm,[37] but it may also help in reducing symptoms of nervousness and excitability, too. This is due to a compound called rosmarinic acid (also found in rosemary and sage), which has also been found to help improve memory, concentration and cognition when consumed.[38] Lemon balm's calming effects may benefit the digestive system, too, as consuming it might reduce the symptoms of indigestion[39] and also nausea.[40] Another study found that lemon balm may help ease menstrual cramps and the severity of premenstrual syndrome (PMS).[41]

COMMON SORREL
RUMEX ACETOSA

The phrase 'pucker up' immediately brings lemony common sorrel to mind. Tart as ever, so refreshing in a salad. Native to Eurasia, sorrel is perennial, easy to plant and quick to grow – it literally grows like a weed. Be sure to select the smaller, tender, less astringent leaves. The sourness comes from oxalic acid, an active component also found in rhubarb, so eat and enjoy sorrel sparingly and avoid cooking in aluminium or cast-iron pans.

Culinary uses: Classic French lemon sorrel sauce on salmon is divine, as is sorrel sabayon (zabaglione) and soup. Try the Four Fish and Herb Stew on page 110.

Medicinal uses: Lemon sorrel is rich in vitamin A, needed for healthy vision,[42] and vitamin C, which helps support a healthy immune system and reduces the risk of infection.[43] Its potent plant extracts may also offer anti-cancer benefits by helping to prevent cell growth and cell proliferation in certain cancers.[44] Helicobacter pylori (H. pylori) is a bacterium that often causes digestive issues and lemon sorrel has been shown to be a possible natural remedy[45] for this. It also has benefits for the cardiovascular system, having the potential to prevent high blood pressure by helping to dilate blood vessels[46] and prevent blood clot formation.[47]

melissa officinalis   *aloysia citrodoras*   *backhousia citriodora*   *rumex acetosa*

BENEFICIAL EDIBLE PLANTS

Magnolia

There are hundreds of species in the *Magnolia* genus, which are found worldwide. The delicately scented flowers range in colour from the palest creamy white to a shocking pink. Most magnolia flowers are edible (although some taste much better than others), with the fresh blooms tasting distinctively of cardamon and ginger. A garden favourite is *Magnolia grandiflora*, but highly recommended edible species include *M. glauca* and *M. liliiflora*.

CULINARY USES

An easy but exciting ingredient to forage when magnolias are in flower, pick the blooms while they are still firm and the petals are unwrinkled and include a few unopened blooms in the mix, too. The petals can be poached or pickled, or you can use a freshly picked, rinsed and dried large petal as a wrap for sweet or savoury ingredients such as sliced pears, olive oil and a few toasted sliced salted almonds. Or tempura the petals along with some freshwater peeled prawns (shrimp), root vegetables, like parsnip or carrot and courgette (zucchini) with a light soy-based dipping sauce.

MEDICINAL USES

The active compound in magnolias is known as HNK (honokiol), which is found in the leaves and bark. It has traditionally been used to treat inflammatory conditions. Research has demonstrated its ability to cross the blood brain barrier (BBB) and it therefore has the potential to offer neuroprotective benefits, which could be of benefit for conditions such as dementia and Alzheimer's disease.[48] Magnolia flowers, on the other hand, could be used to treat headaches, toothache and nasal congestion,[49] due to their essential oil compounds. Some research has also indicated that the polyphenols in magnolia flowers may help protect the body against Advanced Glycation End Products (AGEs). AGEs are harmful compounds that can form when sugar interacts with protein or fat in the bloodstream, which can have a negative impact on our metabolic health.[50]

Peppermint
MENTHA × PIPERITA

Peppermint is a cross between water mint (*Mentha aquatica*) and spearmint (*M. spicata*), and although there are around 25 different types of mint plants, peppermint is one of the most common and contains the most concentrated levels of the compound menthol, which has beneficial properties. Peppermint is quite distinctive from other mint plants because the leaves are a dark green with reddish veins.

CULINARY USES

Peppermint complements so many dishes and can be used alongside both vegetables and fruits. Watermelon and lime garnished with a spray of mint, or a simple but stunning mint salsa verde, mint tabbouleh or raita are enough to make your mouth water. You can also use peppermint in classics such as rack of lamb with homemade mint sauce or mint jelly and pea and mint soup, or a Greek mezze platter with tzatziki will never grow old. Simply add chopped leaves to a fruit salad or a rice or pasta dish, too. Peppermint also produces lovely little clusters of purple flowers which are also edible and have a similar but milder taste to the leaves. They can be used to infuse syrups and sorbets. Or try out-of-this-world French-style Peppermint Panna Cotta with Dark Chocolate Tuile Shards by Alan Bartos (see page 66).

MEDICINAL USES

Peppermint, and its natural oils, have long been used as a treatment for many gastrointestinal ailments. It has been shown to help relax stomach muscles, reduce visceral sensitivity and ease digestive issues caused by social stress.[51] Peppermint is known for its effectiveness in offering short-term relief in conditions such as irritable bowel syndrome (IBS).[52] It not only helps to relax the muscles of the digestive system but can also help relieve headaches and migraines,[53] while its natural menthol content may help reduce associated pain.[54] Some research has also demonstrated that peppermint, and its high menthol content, can help improve cognitive performance[55] and reduce fatigue.[56]

Holy Basil
OCIMUM TENUIFLORUM

Holy basil, or tulsi as it is sometimes called, is a member of the mint family (Lamiaceae). 'Tulsi' is the Hindu word for holy basil. It is primarily native to tropical areas across Asia and India and thrives in humid climates. You'll find it growing as a small shrub with hairy stems and green or purple leaves, depending on the variety.

Holy basil, like other prolific varieties of basil, such as Thai basil (*Ocimum basilicum* var. *thyrsiflora*), Greek basil (*O. minimum*), sweet basil (*O. basilicum*) and dark opal basil (*O. basilicum* 'Dark Opal'), enjoys warm, moist conditions. Easy to grow from seed, basil thrives in full sun in moist, well-drained soil – avoid sitting in areas with strong breezes until well-established. Basil can also be grown on a sunny windowsill, but be careful not to overwater. Frequent picking of the leaves of this fast-growing herb encourages growth.

CULINARY USES

You can eat the leaves, flowers and seeds of holy basil, as with other varieties, but its taste is peppery and floral, sometimes with astringent or bitter notes, unlike other varieties. Used frequently in Indian and Malaysian dishes, from curries to chutneys, dahl and vegetable dishes, plus numerous Thai dishes, in which holy basil is added to stir-fries, noodles and curries.

Try adding freshly picked leaves, together with garlic, fresh chillies and fish sauce, and you've got the perfect partner to any Asian meat or seafood dish. Holy basil, with its cortisol-lowering free radicals, is also a popular option for a cup of tea. The softer and sweeter varieties of basil contain many of the heartier holy basil compounds, but are just not as concentrated. All types of basil can be used in all types of dishes, but when purchasing or picking basil, only choose what you need for a few days as it bruises and blackens quickly.

MEDICINAL USES

Known in Ayurvedic medicine as 'The Queen of Herbs', holy basil is an adaptogen, which has been shown to help counter the impact of stress on the body by helping to regulate blood sugar levels, blood pressure and cholesterol. It also has psychological benefits for the brain, supporting memory and cognition due to its antidepressant and anti-anxiety effects. The benefits of holy basil can be attributed to the high content of plant compounds and antioxidants. It is also being researched for its antibacterial, antiviral and antifungal activity, which helps to support the body against infection and enhance the immune system.[57]

Oregano
ORIGANUM VULGARE

The genus of this herb, a member of the Lamiaceae family like mint and sage, means 'Ornament of the Mountains'. The scent of oregano is familiar and unforgettable, whether wafting from US city sidewalk pizza joints, faraway Mediterranean and Middle Eastern mountainsides, homegrown hedges or windowsill red clay pots. Oregano, a woody, hardy, perennial, temperate herb thrives in climates worldwide.

The Origanum genus is widespread, with oregano (*Origanum vulgare*) being indigenous to Europe and *O. syriacum* – which is also known as za'atar or Middle Eastern hyssop and mentioned in the Bible – to the Middle East. Additional beneficial varieties include Mexican oregano (*Lippia graveolens*) and Greek oregano (*O. vulgare* subsp. *hirtum*).

BENEFICIAL EDIBLE PLANTS 193

Oregano is a well-travelled, pungent, super-power herb with small, sturdy, oval-shaped, dark green leaves and tiny, white or purple blossom clusters in spring. Its fuzzy leaves and stems are packed with the potent and beneficial compounds thymol and carvacrol.

Easy to grow from seed or cuttings and preferring mildly acidic soil, hardy oregano thrives in sunshine and will take root on a steep hill or in a windowbox. Check your local garden shop, farmers' market or green-thumbed neighbour to see which variety grows best in your neighbourhood and make sure it is culinary and not ornamental oregano. And take note, the less expensive, stronger flavoured Mexican oregano is not true oregano but related to lemon verbena. If drying your own, use a food air dryer or sun dry as the low heat of an oven will lessen the strength of its beneficial oils.

CULINARY USES

Often referred to as 'the pizza herb', Oregano's pungent leaves are added fresh or dried to numerous Mediterranean-based dishes, sauces and dressings. It pairs well with tomatoes, pungent Parmesan cheese, lemon roast chicken, slow-cooked lamb shoulder, rustic soups and My Garden Ratatouille (see page 10), plus it is a great foil to a dark chocolate mousse, drizzled with oregano leaf and and orange-zest-infused virgin olive oil.

MEDICINAL USES

Oregano contains compounds that provide antioxidant and antimicrobial benefits which support health. In fact, over 60 compounds,[58] including thymol and carvacrol, have been identified so far, and on a weight-for-weight basis, fresh oregano has a three to twenty times higher antioxidant capacity than other herbs such as dill and sage. It may also be effective at preventing cardiovascular disease.[59] Oregano's medicinal uses, and its essential oil, which comes from the leaves, can be traced all the way back to the ancient Greek and Roman empires.[60]

ZA'ATAR : Known by many names, including Palestinian oregano, za'atar grows in the warm, dry climates of the Middle East. It is a component of the world-trending za'atar mix, which is made from air-dried za'atar leaves and flowers, sumac berries, seeds and salt. Traditionally, bread is dipped in olive oil, then into za'atar mix, is delicious, comforting and beneficial. Even better with hummus.

Parsley
PETROSELINUM CRISPUM

There are two main types of parsley in the genus: curly leaf parsley (*Petroselinum crispum*) and flat leaf parsley (*P. crispum var. neapolitanum*). Native to the Mediterranean, flat leaf parsley is the most popular and widely used herb in professional and home kitchens worldwide. Best grown from seed, parsley of either variety enjoys full sun and moist, well-drained soil.

CULINARY USES

Used in an array of dishes, including meat, chicken, fish, vegetables, pulses and grains, and added into soups, stews, pestos and salads. As with many other herbs, the graceful, mildly aromatic flat leaf parsley and the curly, strongly scented variety are best used fresh. One of the traditional ways to use parsley is to tie it, stems and all, with other stemmed herbs to make a bouquet garni 'posy' and use this to add extra flavour to soups, sauces and stews. Use flat leaf parsley to make a simple parsley pesto with toasted walnuts, Pecorino Romano grated cheese and olive oil, or melt some salted butter, throw in lots of freshly chopped parsley, lemon juice or preserved lemon, a peeled smashed garlic clove or two, and cracked pepper or a chopped chilli pepper and you have an easy yet delicious sauce to pair with fish or prawns. Parsley is also a must for adding to green juice smoothies along with apple, pear, kale, lemon and spinach.

BENEFICIAL EDIBLE PLANTS

MEDICINAL USES

Parsley is rich in iron and antioxidants, in particular flavonoids, carotenoids and vitamin C. Diets rich in flavonoids have been shown to lower the risk of several health conditions, including type 2 diabetes[61] and heart disease,[62] whereas carotenoids have been linked with the reduction of certain cancers, namely lung and colon cancer, and eye-related disorders such as age-related macular degeneration and cataracts.[63] Parsley has potential antimicrobial benefits, too, helping to protect against *Staphylococcus aureus*[64] (*S. aureus*), which can cause skin infections. It is also an excellent source of vitamin K, which helps support bone health and may play a role in preventing bone fractures.[65]

Rosemary
SALVIA ROSMARINUS

One of those herbs that has the most wonderful fragrance, I love to see rosemary growing wild on the side of the road or in people's gardens where it can develop into a large, evergreen bush. When summer comes, it bursts into bloom with tiny, purple-blue flowers that the bees just love!

The stems are quite woody, so mainly the needle-shaped leaves are used, fresh or dried, in cooking. You can also eat the flowers and use the thick, woody branches as fragrant barbecue skewers.

CULINARY USES

Rosemary is a very versatile herb, used in both sweet and savoury dishes, and has quite a distinctive taste – a combination of woodiness and aromatics such as citrus, sage, pepper and pine. Think delicious Italian focaccia bread straight out of the oven or a roast leg of lamb studded with fresh garlic and rosemary. It also works well in soups and casseroles or a homemade stuffing, or you can simply add some sprigs to a tray of root vegetables and roast in the oven. I love to make a rosemary-infused olive oil too, by dropping some rosemary sprigs into a bottle of extra virgin olive oil (adding a thin piece of lemon peel, if you like) and letting it infuse for a minimum of a week. Then drizzle the oil over pasta, roasted vegetables or an orange panna cotta, or just enjoy as a dip for warm fresh bread.

MEDICINAL USES

Rosemary has long been studied for its many health benefits, including alleviating headaches, insomnia and digestion. More recently, it has shown positive benefits in improving mood, memory, pain and anxiety, including helping to reduce feeling of stress and burnout.[66] Studies have shown that rosemary can help improve cognition, which may offer real benefits for conditions such as dementia and Alzheimer's disease. Even the smell of rosemary has been shown to have a positive impact on mood and cognitive performance in exam students. Rosemary also appears to be beneficial in maintaining healthy blood sugar levels,[67] while also supporting a healthy gut microbiome and helping to mitigate symptoms of diabetes.[68]

Sage
SALVIA OFFICINALIS

Sage is such a distinctive herb, both in taste and texture. With almost one thousand types, this drought tolerant herb of Mediterranean origin is now naturalized on most continents. The common sage has green-grey leaves with a downy-like texture, a bit like the skin of a peach, and then when in bloom it produces wonderful, tiny, mauve flowers, which are edible, too. It is an aromatic herb that has a peppery taste with hints of lemon and mint, and it loves to grow in warm, sunny spots in the garden.

CULINARY USES

Versatile sage works superbly with poultry, pork or game, but it's a really understated herb in the kitchen. You'll commonly see it together with butternut squash soup topped with flash-fried sage leaves, but it also adds flavour minced and mixed into sweet potato mash, and in traditional stuffing recipes. Its earthy flavour balances heavier dishes containing cream or butter, such as a savoury scones, risotto, or infuse honey with dried sage leaves, which can then be used for cooking or drizzled over a cheese plate.

MEDICINAL USES

Sage contains over 160 plant-based compounds, known as polyphenols, which act as antioxidants and help protect the body, and its cells, from damage and ill health.[69] It has also been shown to offer improved cognitive function and mood in both young healthy participants and those with Alzheimer's disease.[70] Sage also has oral health benefits, acting as both a natural antibacterial and reducing dental plaque,[71] and may help reduce pain in conditions like pharyngitis.[72] One of sage's more popular benefits is its ability to reduce some of the symptoms of menopause, including hot flashes.[73]

Calendula
CALENDULA OFFICINALIS

The colours of sunshine orange, ruby red and lemon-drop yellow adorning a pot marigold bring smiles to young and old alike. Easy-to-grow marigolds thrive in pots and keep pests away when planted as a bright colour border in garden beds.

Look for rich, green, oblong leaves to distinguish beneficial calendula from French and African marigolds (*Tagetes*), an unrelated genus. Plant pot marigolds in spring and summer in well-drained planting beds warmed by the sun.

Native to the Mediterranean, in many cultures the marigold is often referred to as 'the herb of the sun' as the bold hues of the petals inspire feelings of warmth, happiness, joy, exuberance and positivity. Yet there is a sombre side too, as the pot marigold is also linked to darker emotions such as unexplained anger, jealousy, grief and mourning, with many cultures associating the plant with resurrection, remembrance and honouring the dead – most famously celebrated yearly in Mexico as *Dia de los Muertos* (Day of the Dead). Calendula is also widely used in religious services celebrating the Virgin Mary.

CULINARY USES

Enjoy fresh calendula petals in salads, soft cheeses, quiche, biscuits and infused into sauces for chicken or fish, chutneys and dressings. Try Palmiro Campo's magical Green Pea and Calendula Soup (see page 130).

MEDICINAL USES

The petals of the calendula flower have been used medicinally for centuries to treat symptoms such as stomach cramps or used topically to soothe the skin. Calendulas are rich in antioxidants,[74] which help protect the body's cells from oxidative stress and may offer protection against certain cancers.[75] Calendula is also a cleansing and detoxifying herb,[76] containing powerful anti-inflammatory compounds[77] that have been linked with a reduction in inflammation in certain health conditions such as obesity, metabolic syndrome and type 2 diabetes.

NOTE: From the ancient civilizations of Greece, Egypt and India, through the Middle Ages, Christianity and Buddhism, to the official Zodiac flower of Sagittarius, 'Calendula officinalis' is not only rich in symbolism, but also heals and supports human and animal alike with its bounty of beneficial attributes.

Ashwagandha
WITHANIA SOMNIFERA

Also known as winter cherry or Indian ginseng, ashwagandha is an ancient, respected super herb that is part of the nightshade family (Solanaceae), along with potatoes, tomatoes and aubergines (eggplants). This evergreen shrub is native to Asia and Africa but rarely found outside Nepal and India.

Drought-tolerant ashwaganda thrives in the warmth of summer but is very forgiving. If you are lucky enough to have one in your garden, make sure you bring it inside when the nights get frosty. Check seed companies that sell medicinal herb seeds for the best outcome when growing.

CULINARY USES

Ashwagandha has been well-known in herbal medicine for centuries as a functional food and in Ayurvedic medicine for its health benefits. It is usually consumed as a powder made from the root.

If you are lucky enough to grow ashwaganda, you can also nibble on its beautiful, red, pea-sized berries when they are ripe. The berries are contained within lovely, orange, lantern-like seedpods. You can either eat the berries raw – they have a slightly bitter, tart-like taste – or use them in cooking by adding to a rice dish. The root is more versatile, especially as it is usually bought in powdered form, and it is typically used for its health benefits rather than its slightly bitter, earthy taste. Simply add a teaspoon to a mug of hot milk with other spices like turmeric and cinnamon for a wonderful nightcap, or add to recipes such as homemade granola, nut butter or overnight oats.

MEDICINAL USES

In Sanskrit ashwagandha means 'smell of the horse' in reference to its scent, as well as its potential to improve physical strength. It is traditionally used as an adaptogen, assisting the body in countering both the physical and mental effects of stress, as well as to improve mental well-being by helping to reduce symptoms of anxiety and depression.[78] Ashwagandha may also promote a more restful night's sleep, including for those who struggle with insomnia, helping not only to improve sleep quality but also to make people feel more alert when they wake up.[79]

Sea Greens

Sea greens are typically found in rock pools, on rocks, in sand dunes or on water edges around the world. Each has its own individual look and salty taste. They have grown in popularity, not just because they are easy to forage and for their salty complementary flavours, but also because of the many health benefits they offer.

AMERICAN SEA PURSLANE
SESUVIUM PORTULACASTRUM

This evergreen perennial loves to grow in coastal and mangrove areas worldwide, especially where there are sand or salt marshes, and can easily be identified due to its sprawling habit and small, oval-shaped, succulent leaves with their light grey-green colour.

Culinary uses: Native American tribes in Florida eat this salty crunchy delicacy raw. When blanched or steamed it also makes a delicious pairing for fish, shellfish and fire-roasted vegetables. Simple is best.

ROCK SAMPHIRE
CRITHMUM MARITIMUM

There are many different types and shapes of samphire, which are salt-tolerant, succulent plants with finger-like leaves. One of my foraging favourites, rock samphire is a small, bushy, green-grey plant typically found within a few yards of the sea.

Culinary uses: Rock samphire has quite a strong flavour, which is like a blend of salt, parsley and carrots, but is not to everyone's taste. It can be eaten raw, but is very salty, so I like to cook it for a few minutes with a little oil, garlic and shallots.

MARSH SAMPHIRE
SALICORNIA EUROPAEA

Also known as glasswort, marsh samphire is very similar to rock samphire, but it has a milder taste and is usually more widely available. It grows, as the name suggests, in salt marshes and estuaries and on mud flats.

Culinary uses: The best samphire eaten raw is marsh, which can also be cooked in the same way as rock samphire. You can also try pickling it with vinegar and spices and using it to accompany fish dishes, or I love it alongside new potatoes when they are in season.

KELP

Kelp, which is in the order Laminariales, is a seaweed but is often referred to as a sea vegetable because of its versatility. It can be found growing in cold, shallow waters across the globe as it needs light to grow.

Culinary uses: Kelp can be eaten raw or cooked, hot or cold. It has a delicious salty, umami flavour that works brilliantly in a coleslaw alongside shredded cabbage and carrots, or in a pasta dish with some lemon and garlic. The other benefit of kelp is that it is environmentally friendly, 100 per cent sustainable and helps to keep our oceans less acidic.

SEA BUCKTHORN *HIPPOPHAE RHAMNOIDES*

Sea Buckthorn, the bright orange powerhouse berry of Vitamin C[80], thrives in colder climates throughout winter, growing wild, or planted, near the sea from Canada to Denmark, China, the UK and Japan. It has become trendy of late as it has beneficial properties, being not only high in anti-oxidants[81], that are good for skin and hair health[82], and it has also indicated improvements in women's postmenopausal health.[83]

Culinary uses: The juicy berries are extremely acidic due to their high malic acid content[84], so best enjoyed combined with other ingredients. Add to yoghurt or try it with creamy mascarpone (see page 172).

SEA GREENS MEDICINAL USES

Seaweed (kelp) and sea vegetables (sea purslane and samphire) are nutrient powerhouses. They are packed with minerals and antioxidants, including iodine which is vital for healthy thyroid function. One of the main functions of the thyroid is to help regulate the body's metabolism, as well as growth and development.[85] Seaweed and sea vegetables have also been shown to have several biological benefits, including anti-cancer activity in colorectal and breast cancer.[86] These antioxidants also have the potential for neuroprotective benefits,[87] as well as immunomodulatory activity.[88]

crithmum maritimum   *salicornia europaea*   *sesuvium portulacastrum*

BENEFICIAL EDIBLE PLANTS

ROOTS

Alliums

'Alliumland' is my happy place. How many times does one begin when creating a recipe or simply making dinner by saying or thinking, 'first you take an onion…'

Growing them is a delight, too. Pressing the cloves of last season's seed garlic (*Allium sativum*) into rich, moist earth on the shortest day of the year, then sprinkling the seeds of onions (*A. cepa*) in garden beds, planting the new shoots of leeks (*A. porrum*), spring onions/scallions (*A. fistulosum*), flowering chives (*A. schoenoprasum*) and shallots (*A. cepa Aggregatum* Group) in springtime is nearly as exciting as harvesting and drying them out in the autumnal sun. And then there are the alliums you can forage, such as wild garlic/ramsons (*A. ursinum*), onion shoots, wild chives and leeks, and ramps (*A. tricoccum*).

Culinary uses: Whether raw, cooked or caramelized, you can enjoy the multiple flavours of alliums. Their versatility and medicinal benefits also make them ideal for so many dishes and so many pairings – I do draw the line at chocolate, but as you may know, I gladly welcome and celebrate all alliums with vanilla. Foraged alliums can all be cleaned up, then made into soups, savoury soufflés, sofrito or scones; the possibilities are endless!

Medicinal uses: All alliums contain flavonoids, which have been shown to have anti-cancer, antioxidant, antidiabetic, cardioprotective, neuroprotective and antimicrobial benefits. These dietary flavonoids, such as quercetin, help not only to lower cancer-related mortality but may also play a role in delaying cancer development and progression. Alliums have also been found to promote a healthier post-meal blood sugar response, lower blood pressure and reduce the risk of cardiovascular disease risks.[1] As for gut health, the gut microbiome is involved in numerous activities needed for good health, and alliums are known prebiotics which are necessary for healthy gut flora and growth. Prebiotics have been shown to increase the metabolic activity of the beneficial bacteria in the gut, which has a positive impact on digestion, nutrient absorption and the immune system.[2]

Horseradish
ARMORACIA RUSTICANA

Horseradish in the little jar on the shelf is actually the root of the horseradish plant, which has been growing in the English countryside since the 15th century. Pale brown on the outside, the inner carrot-like core is white-fire, nose-running hot. And so good…

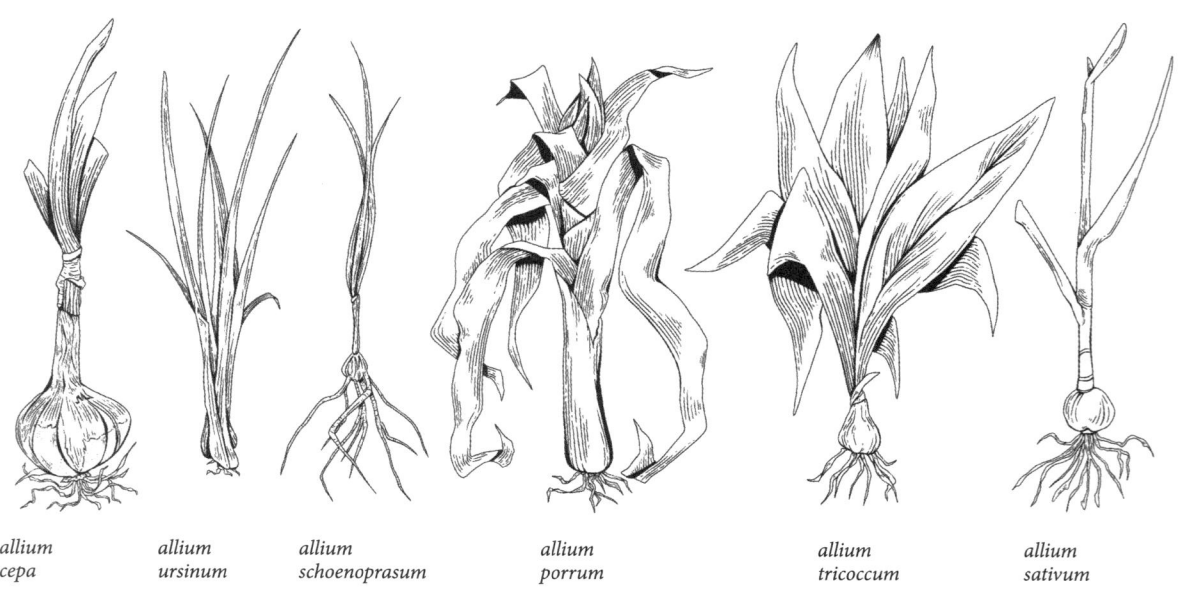

allium cepa *allium ursinum* *allium schoenoprasum* *allium porrum* *allium tricoccum* *allium sativum*

Horseradish is not to be confused with true Japanese horseradish (*Eutrema japonicum*), also known as wasabi, a bright green root grown in fresh running mountainside streams and popular in Asian cuisine.

I recommend growing horseradish in a large container, otherwise it will take over your garden. An easy-to-grow, slow-growing hardy perennial, horseradish only develops a taproot in cold weather. Plant in early spring for a late autumn harvest and get grating.

CULINARY USES

Horseradish is traditionally used as a condiment because of the 'kick' it can give to food. Making it from scratch using a kitchen countertop blender not only clears your sinuses but also the occupants of the entire house. Freshly made, grated horseradish needs to be used immediately or added to a jar with white vinegar, sealed and refrigerated to preserve it. You can use horseradish as a base – the sauces are endless. For example, try stirring in tomato ketchup and lemon juice for an instant cocktail sauce for prawns (shrimp) or adding to mayo, German grainy mustard and dill for a potato salad dressing. Or top a baked potato, prime rib of beef or poached salmon with horseradish crème fraîche, fresh herbs and a pinch of salt. Try pairing with eggs, on a tomato herb salad, with mackerel and capers or in a Bloody Mary to add zing to your dishes and medicinal benefit to your health.

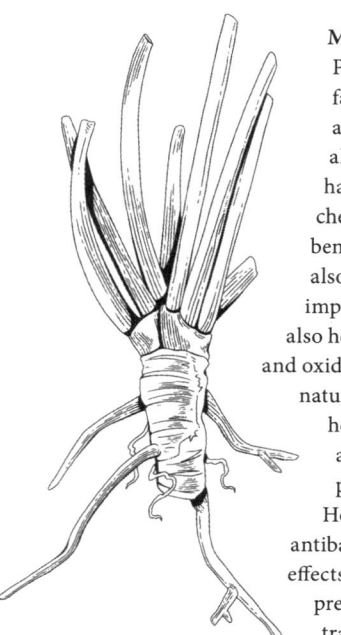

MEDICINAL USES

Part of the Brassicaceae family, horseradish contains a bioactive compound called allyl isothiocyanate, which has the potential for both chemoprotective and anti-cancer benefits.[3] This same compound has also been studied for its positive impact on diabetes and it may also help in reducing inflammation and oxidative stress.[4] Horseradish is naturally antibacterial and may help support healthy digestion[5] and oral health,[6] as well as prevent fungal nail infections.[7] Horseradish's combined antibacterial and antioxidant effects may also have potential for preventing or treating urinary tract infections.[8]

Beetroot
BETA VULGARIS CULTIVAR

What a rich, versatile and unctuous vegetable is beetroot (beet) and also one of the easiest garden plants to grow and watch grow – and every part of the plant is edible.

You can grow beetroot in full sun or partial shade and your crop will be ready for harvesting in about six to nine weeks. Beetroot likes low-nitrogen fertilizer, so add only aged manure to the soil; fresh manures are high in nitrogen and can cause your beetroot to fork, twist or become 'hairy'.

CULINARY USES

The leaves and stalks are super in salads, while the beetroot itself can be quickly pickled or grated. Or peel and slice a large beetroot into large circles, then pickle and bottle with spices, red wine vinegar, garlic and herbs to be opened months later to reveal your home-growing at a feast. Serve with platters of cheese and charcuterie.

You can also add beetroot freshly picked from your garden to vegetable smoothies for an extra antioxidant boost. Plus, whipped beetroot hummus is superb in a vegetable, avocado and feta grain bowl. And the moistest and darkest chocolate vegan brownies can be made with grated beetroot and cocoa (unsweetened chocolate) powder, all from your beetroot veggie bed.

MEDICINAL USES

Beetroot is ranked as one of the top ten most potent antioxidant vegetables,[9] and it has the potential to help support healthy cholesterol levels as well as offer cancer-protective benefits.[10] These antioxidants, known as betalains, may also help reduce inflammation and improve joint function, facilitating functional movement.[11] Beetroot is also known as a source of dietary nitrate, which helps the body's blood vessels to dilate, reducing stress on the body and heart by improving blood flow.[12] There is also evidence of the role that beetroot, and its nitrate content, can play in enhancing sport performance.[13]

Chicory
CICHORIUM INTYBUS

The dainty, purple flowers that adorn the chicory plant belie the massive herbaceous root network in the soil. Related to the dandelion family (Asteraceae), chicory can be dried, broken into small chips and added to coffee beans for a flavourful coffee, or substituted for coffee as an ever-popular daily beverage in New Orleans.

Inulin, extracted from the dried chicory root and ground to a powder, is considered a 'functional food' when added to food or drink, and is one of the best and tastiest ways to up that daily fibre. This root can help ease digestive complaints and support our gut microbiome with its rich probiotic and bifidogenic properties. Current health studies indicate that it may also help to increase calcium absorption and bone mineral density – in athletes, weekend warriors, those suffering from chronic skeletal complaints and an ageing population. Indeed, chicory's blue cornflower petals that last only a day, only to be replaced by another flower grouping the next day, have been used in German folk medicine tonics for centuries.

CULINARY USES

Roasted chicory can be used in place of and ground like coffee but without the caffeine. Pairs well with any type of chocolate, corn recipes such as polenta with garlic-chicory sofrito, masa bread with roasted tomatoes and haricot (navy) beans or stews.

MEDICINAL USES

Chicory root contains inulin,[14] a type of soluble fibre that acts as a prebiotic when consumed. Prebiotics help to feed the good bacteria in the gut. Some research indicates that this may also offer positive benefits in blood glucose control and antioxidant status in those with type 2 diabetes.[15] Inulin has also been shown to be beneficial for weight loss, reducing inflammation and the risk of colon cancer, improving mineral absorption and even relieving depression.[16] The natural antioxidants found in chicory have also been found to have protective benefits for the liver.[17]

Turmeric
CURCUMA LONGA

Turmeric is a tropical plant that loves growing in full sun. While it is thought to originate from South and Southeast Asia, turmeric root can grow happily in pots in the summer in a sunny spot in your garden. It is related to ginger and is grown specifically for its edible roots. These have a brown, ribbed skin on the outside and are a deep orange-yellow inside.

CULINARY USES

The turmeric root is either eaten fresh or dried and ground into a powder, and it has an earthy, slightly spicy yet citrus taste. One word of warning with turmeric: its gorgeous, orange-yellow colour can permanently stain anything it touches, so use carefully!

If you're using fresh turmeric, peel off the brown skin, then simply grate into dishes like soups and stir-fries, add to a vinaigrette or blend into a smoothie to add a little zing. The powder is usually more readily available and easier to use, adding colour and flavour to curries, soups, rice dishes and vegetables. Also remember that turmeric is fat-soluble, which is why drinking those pricey turmeric juice shots or cooking with turmeric at home also calls for some sort of fat – even just a few drops – to activate the beneficial qualities in turmeric. Including some black pepper compounds the absorption of the turmeric, too.

Try a sprinkling of turmeric in your scrambled eggs, or before bed make a golden milk by gently warming some milk (or plant-based milk of your choice) with a little honey, a pinch of black pepper and a teaspoon each of turmeric and cinnamon. It's delicious and comforting at the same time.

MEDICINAL USES

The medicinal compounds in turmeric root are called curcuminoids, and the most important, and well known, is curcumin. Curcumin is poorly absorbed by the body, but adding black pepper, which contains piperine, and a small source of fat, significantly enhances absorption. Curcumin is a natural anti-inflammatory and antioxidant,[18] but it may also increase brain levels of brain-derived neurotrophic factor (BDNF), which plays an important role in memory and learning.[19] Curcumin has anti-cancer and cardioprotective properties, can improve blood glucose and help boost skin health and wound healing.[20] It may also have potential for protecting the brain from neurodegenerative disorders such as Alzheimer's disease.[21]

Echinacea
ECHINACEA PURPUREA, ECHINACEA ANGUSTIFOLIA

Native from Western Canada to Central USA, Echinacea was revered by the Native Americans who introduced its healing benefits to the colonists. It can be grown in temperate climates in a garden bed or pot. It will die down in winter but regenerate and bloom from late spring into early fall. Keep well-watered and you will be rewarded with glorious beneficial blooms.

CULINARY USES
The entire plant can be used to make a tea or tisane (see page 124) that is equally soothing and strengthening.

MEDICINAL USES
Also called the purple cornflower, the regal Echinacea Purpurea is probably the best-known of the seven varieties for its purported support of the immune system[22] against first symptoms of respiratory infections such as the common cold. Its anti-inflammatory prowess may reduce pain and shows a promising benefit in reducing anxiety and depression.[23]

Sweet Potato
IPOMOEA BATATAS

This tuber, only distantly related to the traditional starchy potato, is known and revered worldwide as a nutrient-rich meal. An herbaceous perennial vine, the sweet potato is known as kumara in New Zealand and to many people a daily staple. Due to centuries of vine transfer clippings, believed to have begun in Polynesia, it now grows in most warm climates worldwide. The easy-to-grow tubers mature in two to nine months and thrive best in warm temperate regions, surprisingly requiring little, if any, pesticides.

CULINARY USES
A satisfyingly filling ingredient, sweet potato is delicious grilled, fried or mashed and topped with herbs, a dollop of yogurt or butter, a pinch of salt, lemon juice and maybe a squeeze of chilli sauce – this gem of a plant is a joy to eat.

MEDICINAL USES
Sweet potato is one of the richest sources of beta carotene, a plant pigment that is converted into vitamin A. Beta carotene is what gives sweet potato its red/orange colour, and it has powerful antioxidant properties that are important in maintaining mental health and cognitive function, working in synergy with other nutrients.[24] Beta carotene intake is also important for healthy immune function[25] and reducing inflammation in the gut,[26] and may offer protection against skin damage from the sun, as well as contributing to the maintenance of skin health and appearance.[27]

Liquorice
GLYCYRRHIZA GLABRA

Liquorice root, dark and alluring, is a woody underground rhizome with a yellow centre and brownish bark, while the straight, rigid stems of the plant above ground bear purple flowers and seedpods with a few seeds. The liquorice plant grows best in warm temperate climates and is usually grafted and grown from pieces of the rhizome rather than the seeds.

Native to the Mediterranean, liquorice was used by the ancient Romans and Egyptians, but the most famous place for liquorice use was, and still is, Pontefract, in Yorkshire, in the UK, where Spanish monks created a liquorice monopoly in the coin-sized liquorice Pontefract cakes in the 16th century. The town of Pontefract manufactured the little liquorice cakes until the 1960s.

CULINARY USES
Liquorice adds an intensely sweet taste to food and yet it is not actually sweet, so can be enjoyed by people who are sensitive to sugar such as diabetics.

MEDICINAL USES
Liquorice root use dates back to the ancient Egyptians, and it contains almost 300 different compounds[28] which may offer health benefits, including improved skin health. Of these compounds glycyrrhizin is the main active constituent and this has been shown to have an anti-inflammatory effect in atopic dermatitis (eczema) as well as for acne.[29] A common use of liquorice root is to help support digestive health, especially gastroesophageal reflux disease (GERD) and gastric irritation,[30] as it has a soothing effect and helps to protect the gut mucosa that line the digestive tract. This may also extend to helping alleviate gastric ulcers by promoting mucus cell regeneration and supporting the gut microbiome.[31]

HEALTH WARNING: An excessive intake of liquorice root may raise blood pressure and is not recommended in pregnancy.

Ginger
ZINGIBER OFFICINALE

The rhizome of the flowering plant Zingiber officinale is the familiar ginger root. The plant most likely originated in Southern China or Northern India, has been grown from ancient times and used ever since to ease digestion and nausea. The pungent, spicy-hot taste of fresh ginger is due to gingerol, the dominant compound, which is converted to a gentler, sweeter essence, zingerone, when cooked.

Ginger is very easy to grow yourself – simply plant an unsprayed piece of ginger in moist, rich soil and it will root and grow. But be mindful because, as with other rhizomes, it will take over the yard, so a retired wine barrel might be a better option.

CULINARY USES
Dry ground ginger is more pungent than fresh because gingerol converts to the concentrated form, shogaol. Candied or crystallized ginger is made by simmering fresh ginger pieces in a sugar syrup, dredging them in granulated sugar and then drying them. Pink sushi ginger or nori, which is used as a sushi garnish, is thinly sliced ginger that is then pickled with sugar, rice wine vinegar and salt. Ginger is also bottled and fermented to make ginger beer and made into ginger oil to flavour food and drink or use as medicine. And I enjoy them all.

MEDICINAL USES
Gingerol is the main active ingredient in ginger and responsible for many of its health benefits in both traditional and alternative medicine, including helping to prevent neurodegenerative diseases such as Parkinson's and Alzheimer's disease.[33] Ginger has been found to have multiple biological effects, especially in terms of its antioxidant and anti-inflammatory capabilities.[34] It has also been shown that ginger can help reduce inflammation in conditions such as arthritis, lupus and psoriasis. It may offer, not only protection against cancer, but might also reduce some of the side effects of chemotherapy, such as nausea. In addition, ginger could also help in reducing both pain and disability in those with osteoarthritis,[35] as well as improving blood glucose levels in people with diabetes.[36]

LEAVES & SEEDS

Mustard
BRASSICA

The familiar condiment mustard is usually made from two plants in the Brassicaceae family: white, or yellow, mustard (*Sinapsis alba*), which originates in the Mediterranean, and brown mustard (*Brassica juncea*) from the Himalayas. Mustard plants are grown in temperate regions across the world and you may have seen large, yellow fields from horizon to horizon in the summer months – these are actually fields of mustard flowers. It is the flowers that produce the mustard seeds, of which there are over 40 different varieties.

It is brown mustard (*Brassica juncea*) – also known as Indian mustard, Chinese mustard or leaf mustard – that is commonly used in cooking, especially in Indian or Asian cooking and to make English mustard powder and my favourites, Dijon and grainy prepared condiment mustard.

CULINARY USES
The tiny, round seeds are often first cooked in hot oil until they pop and release their flavour, then added to other spices such as cumin, fennel seeds and coriander.

Mustard greens are the leaves of the mustard plant, which are edible and have grown in popularity. They have a strong, bitter yet spicy flavour and are best enjoyed cooked, whether steamed or blanched or in a stir-fry. Simply swap mustard greens into recipes where you usually reach for other greens like kale. You can also make a pesto, add a few small leaves to a green smoothie or throw a handful of leaves and mustard flowers into a pasta dish for an extra peppery zing.

MEDICINAL USES
Both the seeds and the leaves of the mustard plant have health benefits and a medicinal history dating back to the ancient Greek and Roman civilizations. Mustard leaves are a rich source of vitamins A, C and K, while the seeds are particularly good for their selenium content – essential for the proper functioning of the immune system and thyroid health.[1] Mustard contains important antioxidants, isothiocyanates and sinigrin, both of which are thought to help prevent the progression of cancer.[2,3] Other flavonoid antioxidants found in mustard have been linked to antidiabetic[4] effects and the reduction of inflammation in psoriasis.[5] The leaves of mustard have also been shown to have a positive impact on the gut microbiome by providing antimicrobial benefits.[6]

Cavolo Nero
BRASSICA OLERACEA VAR. PALMIFOLIA

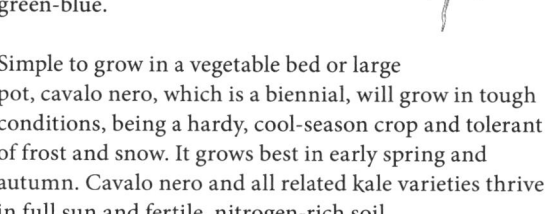

Cavolo nero has many names, including black or Tuscan kale, in a nod to its heritage, which is believed to date back to 600 BC, as well as dinosaur kale due to its bumpy, embossed-like leaves that look like dinosaur skin! Essentially, cavolo nero means 'black cabbage' because it has long, distinctive leaves that are a dark green-blue.

Simple to grow in a vegetable bed or large pot, cavolo nero, which is a biennial, will grow in tough conditions, being a hardy, cool-season crop and tolerant of frost and snow. It grows best in early spring and autumn. Cavolo nero and all related kale varieties thrive in full sun and fertile, nitrogen-rich soil.

BENEFICIAL EDIBLE PLANTS

As for taste, cavolo nero has an earthy, bitter flavour with a sweeter aftertaste, and is best eaten cooked – especially the stems, otherwise these can be quite tough and stringy. Some like to remove the stems and just consume the leaf, but that can be a waste, I think. Instead, just chop off the woody, thicker bottom part of the stem.

CULINARY USES

In Italy, cavolo nero is famously used in pasta or soups to add depth of flavour, and it pairs brilliantly with chilli and garlic in any dish. Essentially, you can do most things with it: boil, steam, stir-fry, sauté or braise. And don't forget those air fryer kale chips! Just make sure you don't overcook it, as it tastes best with a slight bite to it.

MEDICINAL USES

A member of the Brassicaceae family, cavolo nero has very similar benefits and nutritional profile to others in the group. In particular, the darker leaves of cavolo nero are rich in a compound called sulforaphane[7] which has been found to reduce inflammation and oxidative stress, helping to promote health span and longevity.[8] It may also help promote weight loss and reduce leptin resistance.[9] Leptin is a hormone that tells your brain when you are hungry or when you are satiated. Leptin resistance can block this signalling and drive obesity. Being part of the Brassicaceae family, cavolo nero is also a rich source of carotenoids, which are essential antioxidants and the precursor to vitamin A,[10] which we need for healthy eyesight and mental health, as well as playing a part in reducing the risk of cancer, type 2 diabetes and neurodegenerative disease.[11]

Miner's Lettuce
CLAYTONIA PERFOLIATA

Miner's lettuce is native to North America but can also now be found across Europe after it was allegedly introduced to Kew Gardens back in the Georgian period. Other names include winter purslane or Indian lettuce. It typically grows in mountain or coastal regions where it is cool and moist. History states that the common name of miner's lettuce comes from the Californian Gold Rush where miners ate the leaves to prevent scurvy, due to their high vitamin C content. The succulent green leaves are like little rosettes, and when the plant flowers it produces tiny, white flowers in the centre of the leaves. The best time to pick or forage for miner's lettuce in late winter or early spring following rainfall.

CULINARY USES

Miner's lettuce can be used raw in salads where it has a mild and slightly tangy taste, and works well dressed with a simple vinaigrette. When cooked it takes on a taste not dissimilar to that of spinach. Instead of using basil as a base, miner's lettuce can be subbed in to make a delicious pesto, too!

MEDICINAL USES

Miner's lettuce is best known for its high vitamin C content, with 100g (3½ oz) providing about a third of the daily recommended intake.[12] Vitamin C helps promote collagen formation and acts as a powerful antioxidant against environmental pollutants and UV radiation from the sun.[13] Miner's lettuce is also a great source of vitamin A.[14] Vitamin A is essential for wound healing, as well as good eye health and blood sugar balancing, which can help in the prevention of type 2 diabetes.[15]

Globe Artichoke
CYNARA CARDUNCULUS

Is it a vegetable? Is it a flower? The simple globe artichoke is surprisingly full of healthful ingredients and when you know how to use it becomes fun, exotic and elegant to eat. Not to be confused with the Jerusalem artichoke or sunchoke (*Helianthus tuberosus*), a tuberous vegetable unrelated to the leafy green globe artichoke, it is high in fibre and potassium and low in calories, but so satisfying to eat.

Globe artichokes are easy to grow in climates similar to the foggy, then sunny days of central California where 99 per cent of the US artichoke crop is grown in the farmlands of Castroville, CA. The countless varieties of artichokes grow on stalks with enormous, sword-like leaves protecting the flower bud thistle centre. It is the enchanting bud we eat – if allowed to grow for longer, by mid-summer the artichoke bud will blossom into a rich, but inedible, purple thistle flower.

CULINARY USES

Popular for centuries in the Mediterranean, globe artichokes are at their peak in mid- to late spring and make a wonderful starter to a meal, be they boiled, steamed or stuffed with garlic, shallots, herbs, a little anchovy and splash of wine or chicken stock and braised à la Julia Child.

MEDICINAL USES

Globe artichokes are particularly high in folate (vitamin B9), which is essential for healthy red blood cell formation and the making and repair of our DNA, as well as important brain chemicals such as serotonin and dopamine.[16] They are probably more well known for their positive impact on liver health, helping to increase the production of bile, which aids in the digestion and absorption of fat and fat-soluble vitamins,[17] as well as offering protective benefits.[18] Globe artichokes also contain a type of fibre called inulin, which acts as a prebiotic, helping to support a healthy gut microbiome.[19]

Sunflower
HELIANTHUS ANNUUS

I am in jaw-dropping awe of where a packet of unshelled sunflower seeds comes from. The seeds, and oil that is pressed from them, are part of this flower that you can't help but look up to and are used most often in food and medicine. There are about 70 species of Helianthus, both annuals and perennials, some presenting with small, daisy-like flowers, while others are 1.8m (6ft) tall and have bright flower faces up to 30cm (12 inches) across.

If you happen to be travelling past a field of sunshine-yellow sunflowers, take a moment to stop and look closely at the extraordinary beauty and wonder that they hold. The perfect concentric circle of the flower head of black and white seeds is created by nature! Then there is the sunflower's heliotropic movement, which follows the sun from dawn in the east to dusk in the west, then turns eastward again in the night to welcome the morning sun. An extraordinary delight to observe.

CULINARY USES

Sunflower oil provides a less expensive (although still healthy alternative) to olive oil, but like many seed oils may break down when exposed to the high heat used for frying. The smile-yellow petals make a delicious addition to herbal and flower teas, scattered in salads and used as garnishes for cakes and puddings. The peeled stem of the sunflower is also edible and high in protein, and the seeds, roasted in or out of the shell and lightly tossed with salt, make a quick nutritious after-school snack, or can be added to a muffin batter to kick up the protein.

MEDICINAL USES

Sunflower seeds are technically the fruit of the sunflower plant, and they are a good source of protein, which is needed for muscle and bone development as well as insulin production. The natural oils found in the seeds may also help reduce both total cholesterol and LDL ('bad') cholesterol, as well as offering antioxidant benefits – oleic acid, in particular, can lower the risk of heart attack and may be protective against breast cancer. Sunflower is also a rich source of vitamin E, which has been associated with both cardiovascular[20] and liver[21] health benefits, and of antioxidant and calming melatonin.

NOTE : To this day, the sunflower is still an important symbol and ingredient for indigenous North American native tribes and to the Aztecs and Incas of South America. Sunflowers were cultivated as a vital food source by native peoples for at least 3,000 years before the Spanish arrived at America's shore in 1514.

Moringa
MORINGA OLEIFERA

A tree native to India and Pakistan but widely introduced to warmer regions around the world, all parts of the moringa can be used in cooking, but it is mostly the fruit pods, leaves and flowers that are consumed. The fruit pods are shaped like drumsticks, hence the tree is often called the 'drumstick tree'.

CULINARY USES
The long, green pods need to be eaten young and tender, either fresh or cooked. To eat them, hold them between your teeth and pull out the flesh and seeds from the inside, as you would with an edamame pod. The nutritious leaves can be boiled, added to stews and soups as in Dr Agatep's Fillipino recipe Tinolang Manok (see page 16). And then there are the delicate white flowers, which are similar to those of jasmine. You can make moringa flower fritters, curry and even a recipe called sabzi, an Indian term for a vegetable stir-fry dish.

MEDICINAL USES
Moringa has many health benefits, and it is often called 'the miracle tree' as a result. Some of its uses date back to the 6th and 7th centuries, when the oils were used to ease ailments such as earache and insomnia, but more recent research has found that the flavonoid properties in the leaves may help protect against breast cancer, diabetes and heart disease, as well as offer antioxidant and anti-inflammatory benefits. The leaves also contain antifungal and antibacterial compounds which have been found to help prevent urinary tract infections, as well as having gastroprotective and neuroprotective benefits.[22] Maybe moringa is a miracle tree after all!

Water and land cress
NASTURTIUM OFFICINALE

Members of the mustard family, watercress and land (or winter) cress are superfoods when eaten raw. They were once consumed by sailors to stave off scurvy but have since waned in popularity with the introduction

of citrus. A hardy perennial, land cress has lobed leaves and yellow flowers and is happy to grow in a pot or garden bed, no freshwater stream necessary. Watercress, with dark green irregularly shaped leaves and tiny white flowers, thrives in fresh running streams and brooks. Both varieties share similar beneficial attributes. Note: wild harvested watercress is best avoided, as it can contain the parasitic eggs of a livestock fluke.

CULINARY USES
The bracing fresh taste of cress is a great balancer of rich and lush ingredients such as cheese, meat and eggs. Garnish a mushroom risotto or a hot-out-of-the-oven quiche Lorraine with a handful of cress. Add to a green smoothie for a quick get up and go or sip a spoonful of sorrel and watercress bisque (see page 98).

MEDICINAL USES
Water and land cress are both excellent sources of vitamin K, which is found in the green part of plants, and is traditionally known for its role in healthy blood clotting. More recent research has found that vitamin K may also play an important role in preventing soft tissue mineralization and providing anti-inflammatory effects on our mitochondria, the energy powerhouse of the body's cells. Plant compounds called isothiocyanates, found in water and land cress, have also been associated with helping protect against breast cancer[23] as well as colon and prostate cancers[24].

Alexanders
SMYRNIUM OLUSATRUM

Like miner's lettuce, this edible flowering plant can be found in and around hedges in the coastal regions of the United Kindgom and Europe, as well as parts of New Zealand and Australia. Related to the carrot family (Apiaceae), the whole of the plant can be eaten, with the taste a cross between celery and parsley.

CULINARY USES
Alexanders can be eaten raw in salads, or cooked similarly to spinach. The younger stems and leaves are a lot more tender than the larger ones – it is best to boil these to stop them becoming too fibrous, but they are, in fact, the sweetest part. Try swapping them for celery in a stock, or dry the seeds and use them as a peppery seasoning.

MEDICINAL USES
Alexanders, also known as orse parsley, looks similar to angelica and was used to stave off scurvy due to its high Vitamin C content. Today it is used to fend off colds and boost the immune system. Its high fibre content supports digestive health and also was believed by Medieval, Greek and Roman societies to have a diuretic effect on the system.[25]

Dandelion
TARAXACUM OFFICINALE

The humble yellow-flowered dandelion is so often discarded because it is seen as a weed, and yet you can eat the leaves, hearts (the base of the plant), flowers and even the roots.

CULINARY USES
When foraging for dandelions, also known as dandelion greens, look for young shoots and the smallest, most tender leaves in spring and then cook them low and slow until they become tender. Dandelion hearts, or crowns, sit at the base of the plant and have small, pearl-like buds with a light, bitter-sweet taste. They need to be harvested when young for the best flavour.

The bright yellow dandelion flowers, with their sweet, honey-like flavour, are eaten fresh in salads or used in cooking. Try frying them in batter, using them to bake dandelion bread or cookies, or making them into a delicious dandelion syrup with water, sugar and lemon juice. You can also make a tea by steeping dandelion flowers in water for ten minutes, adding a touch of honey if it tastes too bitter.

MEDICINAL USES
The leaves, root and flowers of dandelion may offer several health benefits, including helping to protect the liver against damage and disease, by having a protective, antioxidant effect, as well as reducing excess fat stored in the liver,[26] which can happen due to diets high in sugar and calories.[27] Dandelion may also be effective in regulating fat and sugar metabolism in the body,[28] which can help in the treatment of metabolic conditions such as type 2 diabetes, atherosclerosis, obesity and metabolic syndrome. There is also some evidence that dandelion has potential cardioprotective benefits due to being a rich source of health-supporting plant compounds.[29]

Nasturtium
TROPAEOLUM MAJUSE

A lovely companion creeper for the garden, nasturtiums are related to watercress and are also known as Indian cress. Not only are nearly all parts of the plant edible – the leaves, stems, bright orange flowers and little green pods – but they are also a great, beneficial and quick-growing plant for the beginner gardener.

High in vitamin C, the origins of this meandering ancient Inca food plant date back to the Andes of Peru. Easily propagated by sowing seed from the seedpods after the last spring frost, nasturtiums grow at a rapid rate and can be ready to eat in as little as four months.

CULINARY USES
The leaves and stems have a mild but peppery taste and combined with the flowers easily lend themselves to salads or an hors d'oeuvres platter. Sprinkle with the salty pickled flower buds known as Poor Man's Capers (see page 82) on salads, omelettes or pasta dishes.

MEDICINAL USES
Nasturtiums, both the flowers and the leaves, are a rich source of vitamin C, and can play a role in helping to reduce stress and improve stress tolerance.[30] What's most impressive about nasturtiums is that they are thought to contain one of the highest levels of lutein found in any edible herb or plant. Lutein[31] has been researched for its many benefits, including supporting eye and brain health, protecting against diabetes neuropathy, reducing the risk of certain cancers, and in helping to reduce inflammation and oxidative stress[32] in the body, which can lead to many chronic health conditions.

Nettles
URTICA DIOICA

This wild and commonly foraged herb is often overlooked because of the stinging hairs on the leaves and stems, but pick them carefully and they are delicious! Grab a pair of gloves when picking, then simply blanch them in a saucepan of boiling water, or steam them, to remove the sting.

CULINARY USES
You can use nettles in much the same way as any green leafy vegetable, and they have a taste that is like a cross between spinach and cucumber. They make a terrific side dish just wilted and buttered, but you must also try Root, Rice, Leek and Nettle Soup (see page 96). Blanch then shock fresh nettle leaves to immediately remove the stingers. You can then squeeze the nettles dry and blitz into a puree to freeze in ice cube trays for later use in cream sauces or broths, a savoury quiche or a nettle walnut pesto pasta

MEDICINAL USES
Nettles are a rich source of vitamin K, which is important for bone health and blood clotting,[33] and also play an important role in heart health by helping to regulate calcium and prevent plaques forming in the arteries (atherosclerosis).[34] Nettles have been researched specifically for their protective role in prostate health in men,[35] as well as their potential to help reduce pain in conditions such as arthritis.[36] Nettles contain bioactive compounds and are a rich source of flavonoids, making them beneficial for conditions such as diabetes, high blood pressure and metabolic syndrome.[37] They may also be of benefit to women with polycystic ovary syndrome (PCOS) by helping to improve hormone balance.[38]

FRUITS
Citrus Fruits

Not only is a little citrus zest often the secret ingredient in a salad dressing, a thick green pea and root soup or a citrusy herb sauce for fish, but citrus fruits also contain compounds called flavonoids that can help fight a number of complaints and diseases, from aching feet and clearing the sinuses to, according to new studies, certain types of cancer.

CULINARY USES
The range of citrus varieties and peel preparations is astonishing. The peel of sweet orange (*Citrus × sinensis*), mandarin (*C. reticulata*) and tangerine (*Citrus × tangerina*) is traditionally used in liqueurs, confectionery, pastries and cakes. Lemon (*C. × limon*) is the most popular citrus fruit, for both its juice and peel. Indeed, that citrus lift of lemon does much to raise the spirits, taste buds and flavour of our food and drink.

There are thousands of other citrus varieties found across the globe, including the trending Japanese citrus **yuzu** (*C. × junos*). With its addictive perfume and flowery flavour, it crossed boundaries around the world and is the new must-have citrus flavour along with that of **finger lime** (*C. australasia*). Now established in several countries, it is an experience to eat with its pop-pop caviar texture and alluring citrus scent. The finger lime is a fascinating plate addition, plus it's fun to figure out how exactly how to eat one.

MEDICINAL USES
While citrus fruits have many health benefits, their zest and leaves contain important bioactive compounds, including antibacterial properties that can protect against tooth decay[1] and support the immune system,[2] and may offer wound healing benefits (makrut).[3] Some research has also demonstrated the potential of yuzu in helping prevent osteoporosis[4] and its ability to help protect the brain from neurodegeneration.[5] All citrus fruits have a high flavonoid content, typically highest in the peel, which has powerful antioxidant and anti-inflammatory benefits. Many studies in recent years have demonstrated that diets high in these compounds can play a significant role in health and longevity by reducing the risk of many chronic diseases such as heart disease and cancer.[6]

Pineapple
ANANAS COMOSUS

I had never looked closely at a fresh pineapple with its spiky crown until I began writing this book. Taught to carve a pineapple into boats from an early age, I did not notice their complex intricacy until then. A stunning gift of nature's ingenuity with a layer of crocodile skin like tiles with spiky eyes, these pineapple 'eyes' are actually many small fruits fused together.

Native to Brazil and Paraguay, the pineapple is a compound and delicious fruit, pollinated by hummingbirds, and likes a warm tropical climate and full sun, but it can also be successfully grown indoors. Not a fan of frosts, pineapples crave high-nitrogen fertilizer and a rich, moist, but well-drained, soil.

When next you buy and carve an unsprayed pineapple, save the spiky crown, peel the bottom leaves then place on a plate for the cut area to dry out for a few days before planting in soil or water, then watch it reach out and take root. It is rather difficult to tell when a pineapple is ripe – look for the eyes/scales that run down the length of the pineapple turning a light pale green.

CULINARY USES

Due to its high bromelain content, pineapple makes a flavourful and effective marinade for tougher cuts of meat. The skin is also the base for the classic South American fermented beverage *Tepache* and is a refreshing and effective method for nutritional rehydration.

MEDICINAL USES

Pineapples are an excellent source of vitamin C, which is needed to help make important brain chemicals, support the immune system and skin health, as well as acting as an antioxidant and protecting the body from oxidative stress.[7] In particular, pineapple contains an enzyme called bromelain, which assists with protein digestion[8] and helps support the health of the small intestine and kidneys.[9] It also helps reduce inflammation in conditions such as osteoarthritis and inflammatory bowel disease.[10] The anti-inflammatory properties of bromelain may also offer some pain relief for arthritis sufferers, post-surgery[11] and after exercise.[12]

Peppers
CAPSICUM ANNUUM

Part of the larger nightshade family (Solanaceae) and originally cultivated around 6,000 years ago in Central and South America, chilli and bell peppers contain the lion's share of the heat-searing ingredient capsaicin, the active beneficial component that soothes a variety of complaints, from digestive issues to sore muscles.

Due to the endorphin rush of nose-running heat, then the exhilarating lift of blood coursing through one's body, chillies are included in nearly every cuisine worldwide – the rich and expansive dishes of Mexico being a nose-tingling, starring example of the deliciously memorable chilli pepper. Columbus is credited for having 'discovered' capsicums when he was introduced to the alluring vegetable by the Mayans who, I might add, created the original hot (and I mean spicy) hot chocolate. The Capsicum genus also includes peppers, which are packed with vitamin C, in varying grades of spiciness.

Chilli varieties number in the thousands and are available in almost as many colours. They are easy to grow on a suntrap windowsill or in a pot or garden bed. Chillies love the sun and a rich, moist but not soaked soil. They can be grown from seed in winter or as spring seedlings with great success.

CULINARY USES

The best reason for eating chillies is their flavour; they make everything – including chocolate – taste better. From a spicy Indian vindaloo to gentle butter chicken, a citrus-zesty Mexican guacamole scattered with quick-pickled jalapeños and a chilli leaf, garlic and prawn (shrimp) stir-fry from China, all taste finished with the addition of chillies.

MEDICINAL USES

Chillies are a common spice for adding flavour and heat to dishes, but are also known as one of the major sources of carotenoids, the precursor to vitamins A and C,[13] which help to support healthy immunity and skin health.[14] Consuming chillies may help promote longevity by reducing heart disease,[15] plus more recent studies have also found that chilli may have potential anti-tumour and anti-cancer benefits[16] too. Chillies contain a compound known as capsaicin, which is known for its ability to reduce pain,[17] especially neuropathic pain, but more recently has been found to potentially improve blood flow and regeneration of nerve fibres.[18]

Persimmon
DIOSPYROS

Persimmons are sweet edible fruits that are packed with vitamin C and beta carotene. They look a bit like a tomato, but the colour, shape and texture varies depending on the variety.

Persimmon trees can be grown in a pot or in an orchard garden in well-drained soil in warmer climates with a full day of sun. Be patient – it will be three to five years before the tree fruits, but this is well worth the wait.

First cultivated in China over 2000 years ago, persimmons are now generally identifed by two categories using Japanese names regardless of where they are grown: Hachiya and Fuyu. The Hachiya, which is acorn-shaped with a red-orange colour, is quite astringent until soft and ripe and tastes like honey with hints of apricot. The Fuyu is less astringent, squatter and flatter, yellow to rich orange in colour and typically eaten while still firm, sliced into triangular segments for salads. It has hints of cinnamon and pumpkin. Often known as the American persimmon, the common persimmon (*Diospyros virginiana*) bears round, orange-yellow fruit with a date-like texture and a caramel-tangerine taste. The flavour is stronger than that of the Asian varieties as the fruit have less water content.

CULINARY USES

Either variety of persimmon can be eaten fresh, including the skin, or used in cooking. Always a holiday favourite served with a soft moreish cookie with warming spices and an icing of maple syrup, persimmons also partner well with meats, including pork or saltier cuts, such as Parma ham.

MEDICINAL USES

For their size, persimmons pack in a lot of nutrient power, and are rich in plant antioxidants called carotenoids. These may lower the risk of diabetes in both men and women,[19] as well as reduce the risk of heart disease.[20] The antioxidant potential of persimmons may also be of benefit in reducing the risk of cancer, protecting our cells from DNA damage, and in reducing cholesterol.[21] Persimmon also contain compounds called tannins, which have been researched for their antiviral potential and positive impact on the immune system.[22]

Apple
MALUS DOMESTICA

The humble apple is a powerhouse in your hand, packed full of nutrients, flavour and fibre and a joy to cook. Or simply polish it up on your jeans, then take a bite and savour the crunch. Part of the rose family (*Rosaceae*), it is one of the most widely cultivated tree fruits.

The endless varieties of apples predominantly grown for sale include cookers to eaters to proper cider apples, plus varieties to feed livestock, but my hands-down favourites are Heirlooms, historic fruit tree stock of decades past. These old-fashioned apple cultivars,

Avocado

PERSEA AMERICANA

The avocado is an evergreen tree native to the Central America and bears an edible fruit. It grows prolifically in Mexico and Southern California. Beginning as a single avocado stone, my Nana's decades-old tree grew the best avocados. Its strong, gnarly branches shaded the patio with their large, shiny leaves and were a joy to climb.

There are hundreds of avocado varieties, but the most common is the Hass, which produces pear-shaped fruit with tough, dark green, pebbled skin and an edible, buttery, green-yellow flesh inside surrounding a round stone. Avocados have a subtle nutty but slightly sweet taste, are eaten raw, and have become a trending breakfast addition, although they can be enjoyed at any meal.

The key to a good avocado is knowing when it is ripe. Check that the colour is dark green or nearly black, the skin is firm but has a slight give and that the stem at the top comes off easily. Unripe avo? Simply place in a brown paper bag with apples or bananas and it will ripen magically in a day or two! If you want grow your own avocado tree, just make sure there is more than one other avocado growing nearby for cross-pollination or your lovely guacamole tree will not bear fruit.

CULINARY USES

Simply eaten on their own, with a few salt flakes and grinds of pepper, or a bit of chopped raw onion, smoked salmon and a dash of lemon or balsamic. Mashed, sliced or cubed, avocado can be eaten on toast, with eggs or a salad or in the classic guacamole. Try mashing avocado in a bowl with chopped onion, tomatoes, fresh coriander (cilantro), pickled or fresh jalapeños, lime juice, garlic (optional) and salt.

heritage and heirloom fruits that time almost forgot, provide a diverse and rich habitat for wildlife big and tiny. Vintage cultivars mainly from the 1700s will fill your garden not only with beneficial flora and fauna but also the infectious perfume of heirloom blossoms becoming apples to cherish and delight.

CULINARY USES

Once picked, apples should be stored in a cool shed or box and gently rotated weekly, so they don't bruise and become mouldy. If you happen to have a bumper crop and there's a mountain of rapidly ripening fruit, there are several 'putting by' options to make such as apple butter and syrup, cider, apple crumble and grilling sauce, or try fermenting apples to make apple cider vinegar. There's also always Dad's favourite apple and walnut pie (a family tradition) served with slices of mature Cheddar cheese.

MEDICINAL USES

Apples are a great source of fibre and polyphenols, which have been linked to healthier weight.[23] The skin of apples contains pectin, which is one of the richest sources of fibre, and this has been linked with several health benefits, including lower cholesterol[24] and improved blood sugar balance.[25] Pectin acts as a prebiotic, helping to support a healthy gut microbiome as well as inhibiting the growth of potentially harmful bacteria in the gut.[26] Research has also indicated that regular consumption of whole apples can help in preventing heart disease[27] and cancer.[28]

MEDICINAL USES

Avocados are rich in monosaturated fats and antioxidants, which together help to maintain healthy cholesterol levels and reduce the risk of heart disease.[29] While avocados are known as a good source of dietary fats, they are in truth a complete protein[30] and contain all nine of the essential amino acids that the body does not produce itself and must obtain from food. Avocado also helps to promote a healthier gut microbiome[31] and has one of the highest lutein contents compared to any other fruit.[32] Lutein is a carotenoid with antioxidant properties that may be of benefit for cognitive function, heart health and eye health.[33]

Pear
PYRUS COMMUNIS

The lovely, gentle pear (at least that is what your digestive system says). A gentle fruit for a traumatized digestive system is the pear, which offers calm respite. Easily digestible with high amounts of cholesterol-lowering pectin, pears are one of the world's oldest and most beloved cultivated fruits.

Young pear trees are very easy to grow and thrive in a warm, sunny, sheltered spot in fertile, free-draining soil. Pear trees need little maintenance once established, although it's beneficial to prune them annually to keep them in good shape and fruiting well. Harvest the fruit before it's ripe and bring indoors to complete the ripening process, which can take up to a month.

CULINARY USES

Choose firm pears that have smooth, unbruised skin and feel heavy in the hand. Stand the pear on its end and cut into quarters. Remove the stem and core, then cut into slices or chunks for pear on porridge (oatmeal). Or peel pears then poach them whole, with stem intact, in a mixture of spices, honey and rosewater or wine and serve with a dollop of thick Greek yogurt and dukkah or mixed toasted seeds. Homemade pear butter infused with sage, orange zest and ginger is a must for a cheese platter.

MEDICINAL USES

Pears contain many active compounds that are beneficial to health, and most of these are concentrated in the peel.[34] Chlorogenic acid, an abundant plant compound found in pears, has an anti-inflammatory and antioxidant effect, which helps protect our DNA from damage. Studies have shown that pears help with healthy blood sugar levels and healthy weight loss, as well as faster recovery from strenuous exercise. There is also some evidence that they may be of benefit to those with asthma, helping to reduce symptoms and downregulating inflammatory pathways.[35]

Rhubarb
RHEUM × HYBRIDUM

Rhubarb has always been mysterious to me and was rarely seen at home. I would watch without blinking as the Aunties made something that looked like stalks of pink celery into a rose-coloured, green-speckled, slimy, watery concoction and thought 'Hey, I like celery but this?' Not so sure.

Now I gleefully grow garden beds of unforced rhubarb stalks. I'm still not a fan of the watery, pink, slimy stuff, but roasted? With vanilla? Yes please.

Rhubarb is very easy to grow. Simply plant the rhubarb crowns (bare-root plants) in a sunny, sheltered spot in moist but well-drained soil. Avoid harvesting any stalks in the first year to allow the plants to get established. You can harvest a few stalks in the second year and then only a third of them from the third year. The green leaves and green-end tips where the stalk changes from green to red are poisonous and high in oxalic acid, which can have detrimental effects on health. Choose bright pink to red stalks that are as thick as your thumb, then gently twist the stalk at the base of the plant to snap off.

Well-kept rhubarb crowns will last several seasons. They do need thinning after the season finishes but will generally come racing back to show off their pink stalks, ready to be part of another delicious dish. When rhubarb was introduced in Europe, it was treated as a sour vegetable with the taste of sorrel. With the addition of honey and sugar and its pinkish hue, stewed rhubarb became all the rage.

CULINARY USES
My favourite flavour combination: rhubarb and ginger. Not a stodgy, batter-based dessert, but rhubarb, ginger and raspberry gazpacho with lime. Now go make that gazpacho.

MEDICINAL USES
Rhubarb is rich in antioxidants, including anthocyanins, which are what also gives it its red colour. Anthocyanins have anti-inflammatory and anti-cancer potential, as well as offering benefits such as healthy weight control and reducing the risk of diabetes.[36] Rhubarb also has the anti-inflammatory potential to support healthy endothelial function and therefore play an important role in cardioprotective health,[37] and is being studied for its ability to promote wound healing after surgery.[38]

Rose Hips

Rose hips are the fruit of certain types of rose bush, including *Rosa rugosa* and the dog rose (*R. canina*). They are round or oval berries (the hip) and typically red to orange in colour, although you can find some that are dark purple. Rose hips appear after the rose flowers have fallen, usually in late summer.

CULINARY USES
Rose hips can be eaten raw, but you need to cut off the stem and blossom end from the hip and remove the seeds from inside, as they have tiny little hairs that irritate when consumed. Then simply rinse and they are ready to be eaten or cooked.

Rose hips have a sweet, perfumey yet sour, floral taste and can be used to make rose hip syrup, jam or jelly, which are classic recipes. I enjoy them added to chilled summer fruit soups, creamy sauces and custards, vinaigrettes and baked goods. Another favourite is to make rose hip and lemon balm tea by steeping about ten rose hips and a small handful of lemon balm leaves and flowers (if in season) to 400–500ml (14–17 fl oz) of boiling water and leaving for ten minutes before straining.

MEDICINAL USES
Rose hips have long been known for their skin health benefits, often being used topically in lotions. As a food, they contain vitamin C, which plays an important role in collagen formation[39], wound healing and protecting the body from oxidative stress, which can contribute to ageing of the skin. One study found that rose hips may even help reduce wrinkles and improve skin hydration and elasticity.[40] They have also been found to help reduce pain,[41] specifically in osteoarthritis, and may aid in reducing cardiovascular risk by lowering blood pressure and improving cholesterol levels.[42]

BENEFICIAL EDIBLE PLANTS REFERENCES

OTHER HEROES
1. https://pubs.rsc.org/en/content/articlelanding/2023/fo/d2fo02715a
2. https://pubmed.ncbi.nlm.nih.gov/29128800/
3. https://www.ncbi.nlm.nih.gov/pmc/articles/PMC5424551/
4. https://pubmed.ncbi.nlm.nih.gov/30855111/
5. https://www.sciencedirect.com/science/article/abs/pii/S1756464611000296
6. https://onlinelibrary.wiley.com/doi/abs/10.1002/ptr.3677
7. https://pubmed.ncbi.nlm.nih.gov/26691759/
8. https://pubmed.ncbi.nlm.nih.gov/27418278/
9. https://pubmed.ncbi.nlm.nih.gov/38258063/
10. https://www.ncbi.nlm.nih.gov/pmc/articles/PMC9861571/
11. https://pubmed.ncbi.nlm.nih.gov/30404957/
12. https://pubmed.ncbi.nlm.nih.gov/15357026/

HERBS
1. https://www.ncbi.nlm.nih.gov/pmc/articles/PMC6357032/
2. https://journals.lww.com/nutritiontodayonline/fulltext/2023/05000/Dill__Potential_Health_Benefits.9.aspx
3. https://pubmed.ncbi.nlm.nih.gov/22960104/
4. https://www.ncbi.nlm.nih.gov/pmc/articles/PMC7592837/
5. https://pubmed.ncbi.nlm.nih.gov/30799248/
6. https://ods.od.nih.gov/factsheets/Manganese-HealthProfessional/
7. https://pubmed.ncbi.nlm.nih.gov/25974698/
8. https://pubmed.ncbi.nlm.nih.gov/26119953/
9. https://www.healthline.com/nutrition/tarragon-benefits-uses#TOC_TITLE_HDR_5
10. https://pmc.ncbi.nlm.nih.gov/articles/PMC8076785/
11. https://www.researchgate.net/publication/354161687_The_Therapeutic_Properties_Ethno_pharmacology_and_Phyto-_chemistry_of_Atriplex_Species_A_review
12. https://pubmed.ncbi.nlm.nih.gov/29493984/#:~:text=Vitamin%20A%20is%20a%20general,the%20diet%20in%20two%20forms.
13. https://pubmed.ncbi.nlm.nih.gov/35291895/#:~:text=Dose%2Dresponse%20analysis%20showed%20that,50%2D100%20mg%20per%20day.
14. https://www.ncbi.nlm.nih.gov/pmc/articles/PMC2995283/
15. https://www.ncbi.nlm.nih.gov/pmc/articles/PMC3249911/
16. https://www.ncbi.nlm.nih.gov/pmc/articles/PMC4808895/
17. https://www.ncbi.nlm.nih.gov/pmc/articles/PMC5451177/
18. https://pubmed.ncbi.nlm.nih.gov/19003941/
19. https://www.ncbi.nlm.nih.gov/pubmed/19146935
20. https://pubmed.ncbi.nlm.nih.gov/23281145
21. https://www.ncbi.nlm.nih.gov/pmc/articles/PMC4688356/
22. https://pubmed.ncbi.nlm.nih.gov/32745879/
23. https://pubmed.ncbi.nlm.nih.gov/26400429/
24. https://www.ncbi.nlm.nih.gov/pmc/articles/PMC3798927/
25. https://www.ncbi.nlm.nih.gov/pmc/articles/PMC8746501/#:~:text=Phenolic%20and%20polyphenolic%20products%2C%20either,fruit%20and%20vegetable%2Dbased%20diets.
26. https://www.ncbi.nlm.nih.gov/pmc/articles/PMC6963539/
27. https://www.ncbi.nlm.nih.gov/pmc/articles/PMC9032170/
28. https://www.ncbi.nlm.nih.gov/pmc/articles/PMC10384403/
29. https://pubmed.ncbi.nlm.nih.gov/26115272/
30. https://pubmed.ncbi.nlm.nih.gov/24059688/
31. https://pubmed.ncbi.nlm.nih.gov/25617561/
32. https://pubmed.ncbi.nlm.nih.gov/34104096/
33. https://www.ncbi.nlm.nih.gov/pmc/articles/PMC7011016/
34. https://www.mdpi.com/2304-8158/10/7/1596
35. https://www.mdpi.com/2304-8158/10/7/1596
36. https://www.mdpi.com/2304-8158/10/7/1596
37. https://www.ncbi.nlm.nih.gov/pubmed/15272110
38. https://www.mdpi.com/2072-6643/6/11/4805
39. https://pubmed.ncbi.nlm.nih.gov/20385075/
40. https://www.researchgate.net/publication/7144806_Lemon_balm_Melissa_officinalis_L_an_evidence-based_systematic_review_by_the_Natural_Standard_Research_Collaboration
41. https://www.ncbi.nlm.nih.gov/pmc/articles/PMC4557408/
42. https://pubmed.ncbi.nlm.nih.gov/30339818/
43. https://www.ncbi.nlm.nih.gov/pmc/articles/PMC5707683/
44. https://pubmed.ncbi.nlm.nih.gov/22473656/
45. https://pubmed.ncbi.nlm.nih.gov/38024697/
46. https://pubmed.ncbi.nlm.nih.gov/26769840/
47. https://www.ncbi.nlm.nih.gov/pmc/articles/PMC7092512/
48. https://pubmed.ncbi.nlm.nih.gov/28817221/
49. https://pubmed.ncbi.nlm.nih.gov/18673228/
50. https://pubmed.ncbi.nlm.nih.gov/28585905/
51. https://www.ncbi.nlm.nih.gov/pmc/articles/PMC5814329/
52. https://pubmed.ncbi.nlm.nih.gov/24100754/
53. https://journals.lww.com/ebp/citation/2023/01000/does_peppermint_essential_oil_relieve_headache.12.aspx
54. https://www.ncbi.nlm.nih.gov/pmc/articles/PMC9580369/
55. https://pubmed.ncbi.nlm.nih.gov/30087294/
56. https://www.ncbi.nlm.nih.gov/pmc/articles/PMC8457936/
57. https://www.ncbi.nlm.nih.gov/pmc/articles/PMC4296439/#:~:text=Tulsi%20has%20also%20been%20shown,anxiolytic%20and%20anti%2Ddepressant%20properties.
58. https://www.sciencedirect.com/topics/agricultural-and-biological-sciences/origanum-vulgare#:~:text=Oregano%20(Origanum%20vulgare%20L.),ones%20being%20thymol%20and%20carvacrol.
59. https://www.sciencedirect.com/science/article/abs/pii/B9781845690175500087
60. https://www.ncbi.nlm.nih.gov/pmc/articles/PMC8156404/
61. https://pubmed.ncbi.nlm.nih.gov/23591151/
62. https://pubmed.ncbi.nlm.nih.gov/23953879/
63. https://www.ncbi.nlm.nih.gov/pmc/articles/PMC3942711/
64. https://pubmed.ncbi.nlm.nih.gov/19919287/
65. https://pubmed.ncbi.nlm.nih.gov/28445289/
66. https://www.ncbi.nlm.nih.gov/pmc/articles/PMC4525344/
67. https://www.ncbi.nlm.nih.gov/pmc/articles/PMC5622728/
68. https://pubmed.ncbi.nlm.nih.gov/29372208/
69. https://www.ncbi.nlm.nih.gov/pmc/articles/PMC7347016/
70. https://www.ncbi.nlm.nih.gov/pmc/articles/PMC5634728/
71. https://www.healthline.com/nutrition/sage#TOC_TITLE_HDR_4
72. https://www.ncbi.nlm.nih.gov/pmc/articles/PMC5634728/
73. https://www.healthline.com/nutrition/sage#TOC_TITLE_HDR_5
74. https://www.ncbi.nlm.nih.gov/pmc/articles/PMC5937015/
75. https://pubmed.ncbi.nlm.nih.gov/22899374/
76. https://www.ncbi.nlm.nih.gov/pmc/articles/PMC3841996/#:~:text=A%20few%20species%20of%20this,%2C%20creams%2C%20lotions%2C%20shampoos.
77. https://pubmed.ncbi.nlm.nih.gov/19374166/
78. https://www.ncbi.nlm.nih.gov/pmc/articles/PMC8762185/
79. https://www.ncbi.nlm.nih.gov/pmc/articles/PMC8462692/
80. https://pmc.ncbi.nlm.nih.gov/articles/PMC8389226/#:~:text=2.1.&text=Other%20fruits%20commonly%20considered%20to,/100%20g%20%5B55%5D.
81. https://www.frontiersin.org/journals/nutrition/articles/10.3389/fnut.2022.1036295/full
82. https://pmc.ncbi.nlm.nih.gov/articles/PMC5438513/#:~:text=Sea%2Dbuckthorn%20oil%20in%20cosmetic,moreover%20collagen%20synthesis%20%5B81%5D.
83. https://pubmed.ncbi.nlm.nih.gov/25104582/
84. https://pmc.ncbi.nlm.nih.gov/articles/PMC8389226/
85. https://www.ncbi.nlm.nih.gov/books/NBK279388/
86. https://www.mdpi.com/1660-3397/12/9/4898
87. https://pubmed.ncbi.nlm.nih.gov/28146411/
88. https://pmc.ncbi.nlm.nih.gov/articles/PMC8232781/

ROOTS
1. https://www.ncbi.nlm.nih.gov/pmc/articles/PMC7555649/#:~:text=Flavonoids%2C%20particularly%20flavonols%20from%20alliums%2C%20neuroprotective%2C%20and%20antimicrobial%20activities.
2. https://www.researchgate.net/publication/366029251
3. https://www.ncbi.nlm.nih.gov/pmc/articles/PMC7448487/

4	https://www.ncbi.nlm.nih.gov/pmc/articles/PMC9457932/		31	https://www.ncbi.nlm.nih.gov/pmc/articles/PMC8535525/
5	https://www.ncbi.nlm.nih.gov/pubmed/19346022		32	https://www.ncbi.nlm.nih.gov/pmc/articles/PMC8535525/#B184-ijms-22-10910
6	https://www.ncbi.nlm.nih.gov/pubmed/24077540		33	https://pubmed.ncbi.nlm.nih.gov/28403946/
7	https://www.ncbi.nlm.nih.gov/pmc/articles/PMC6049573/		34	https://pubmed.ncbi.nlm.nih.gov/34785587/
8	https://www.ncbi.nlm.nih.gov/pmc/articles/PMC6630587/		35	https://www.ncbi.nlm.nih.gov/pmc/articles/PMC3589769/
9	https://pubmed.ncbi.nlm.nih.gov/28620796/		36	https://www.thelancet.com/journals/lancet/article/PIIS0140-6736(05)72915-9/abstract
10	https://www.ncbi.nlm.nih.gov/pmc/articles/PMC8565237/		37	https://www.ncbi.nlm.nih.gov/pmc/articles/PMC9282742/
11	https://www.dovepress.com/betalain-rich-red-beet-concentrate-improves-reduced-knee-discomfort-an-peer-reviewed-fulltext-article-NDS#:~:text=It%20is%20conceivable%20that%20a,and%20of%20improved%20functional%20activity		38	https://www.semanticscholar.org/paper/Therapeutic-effects-of-stinging-nettle-(Urtica-in-Najafipour-Rahimi/25b7fc18d3ecf5afe2d592275aedad8ba455751e
12	https://pubmed.ncbi.nlm.nih.gov/18167491			
13	https://pubmed.ncbi.nlm.nih.gov/32292042/		**FRUITS**	
14	https://pubmed.ncbi.nlm.nih.gov/11497328/		1	https://www.ncbi.nlm.nih.gov/pmc/articles/PMC3551112/
15	https://www.ncbi.nlm.nih.gov/pmc/articles/PMC3638225/		2	https://pubmed.ncbi.nlm.nih.gov/27510009/
16	https://pubmed.ncbi.nlm.nih.gov/36876591/		3	https://pubmed.ncbi.nlm.nih.gov/36747533/
17	https://pubmed.ncbi.nlm.nih.gov/25807561/		4	https://pubmed.ncbi.nlm.nih.gov/27506630/
18	https://www.ncbi.nlm.nih.gov/pmc/articles/PMC6720683/		5	https://pubmed.ncbi.nlm.nih.gov/25522543/
19	https://www.ncbi.nlm.nih.gov/31279955/		6	https://www.mdpi.com/2076-3417/12/1/29#:~:text=The%20main%20flavonoids%20found%20in,%2C%20narirutin%2C%20naringin%20and%20eriocitrin.
20	https://www.ncbi.nlm.nih.gov/pmc/articles/PMC6770633/		7	https://ods.od.nih.gov/factsheets/VitaminC-HealthProfessional/
21	https://www.ncbi.nlm.nih.gov/pmc/articles/PMC5796761/		8	https://www.ncbi.nlm.nih.gov/pmc/articles/PMC8198275/
22	https://pubmed.ncbi.nlm.nih.gov/31876052/		9	https://www.researchgate.net/profile/Arvind-Singh-21/post/PINEAPPLE_What_are_the_health_benefits_of_pineapple/attachment/5ab8dd32b53d2f0bba5a56a4/AS%3A608397560909829%401522064690221/download/10.11648.j.ijnfs.20150401.22.pdf
23	https://www.sciencedirect.com/science/article/abs/pii/S0165032721006406?via%3Dihub			
24	https://pubmed.ncbi.nlm.nih.gov/37891835/			
25	https://www.ncbi.nlm.nih.gov/pmc/articles/PMC6162863/			
26	https://www.ncbi.nlm.nih.gov/pmc/articles/PMC6164597/			
27	https://pubmed.ncbi.nlm.nih.gov/23053552/		10	https://www.ncbi.nlm.nih.gov/pmc/articles/PMC8366142/
28	https://www.ncbi.nlm.nih.gov/pmc/articles/PMC6836258/		11	https://pubmed.ncbi.nlm.nih.gov/28065968/
29	https://www.ncbi.nlm.nih.gov/pmc/articles/PMC7168306/		12	https://www.ncbi.nlm.nih.gov/pmc/articles/PMC8534447/
30	https://search.informit.org/doi/10.3316/INFORMIT.950298610899394		13	https://www.ncbi.nlm.nih.gov/pmc/articles/PMC8839052/#:~:text=Recent%20studies%20on%20chili%20peppers,and%20oxidative%20stress%20%5B9%5D.
31	https://pubmed.ncbi.nlm.nih.gov/37952360/			
32	https://pubmed.ncbi.nlm.nih.gov/11494093/			
33	https://www.ncbi.nlm.nih.gov/pmc/articles/PMC8971783/		14	https://www.nhs.uk/conditions/vitamins-and-minerals/vitamin-a/
34	https://www.ncbi.nlm.nih.gov/pmc/articles/PMC9654013/		15	https://www.sciencedaily.com/releases/2020/11/201109074114.htm
35	https://www.sciencedirect.com/science/article/pii/S106345841401276X		16	https://pubmed.ncbi.nlm.nih.gov/17295509
36	https://pubmed.ncbi.nlm.nih.gov/35031435/		17	https://www.ncbi.nlm.nih.gov/pmc/articles/PMC6273101/
			18	https://pubmed.ncbi.nlm.nih.gov/35857438/
LEAVES & SEEDS			19	https://pubmed.ncbi.nlm.nih.gov/25716098/
1	https://pubmed.ncbi.nlm.nih.gov/10963212/		20	https://www.ncbi.nlm.nih.gov/pmc/articles/PMC3260072/
2	https://www.ncbi.nlm.nih.gov/pubmed/23978168		21	https://www.ncbi.nlm.nih.gov/pmc/articles/PMC4817420/
3	https://www.ncbi.nlm.nih.gov/pubmed/27043505		22	https://pubmed.ncbi.nlm.nih.gov/34880383/
4	https://www.ncbi.nlm.nih.gov/pmc/articles/PMC5618098/		23	https://pubmed.ncbi.nlm.nih.gov/29630462/
5	https://pubmed.ncbi.nlm.nih.gov/24067228/		24	https://www.ncbi.nlm.nih.gov/pubmed/24864109
6	https://pubmed.ncbi.nlm.nih.gov/37120197/		25	https://www.ncbi.nlm.nih.gov/pmc/articles/PMC3183591/
7	https://pubmed.ncbi.nlm.nih.gov/22857862/		26	https://www.ncbi.nlm.nih.gov/pubmed/12174091/
8	https://pubmed.ncbi.nlm.nih.gov/33471780/		27	https://pubmed.ncbi.nlm.nih.gov/31928209/
9	https://pubmed.ncbi.nlm.nih.gov/35323110/		28	https://pubmed.ncbi.nlm.nih.gov/26787402/
10	https://pubmed.ncbi.nlm.nih.gov/36903976/		29	https://www.ncbi.nlm.nih.gov/pmc/articles/PMC7373821/
11	https://pubmed.ncbi.nlm.nih.gov/35453480/		30	https://fdc.nal.usda.gov/fdc-app.html#/food-details/171705/nutrients
12	https://pubmed.ncbi.nlm.nih.gov/7391485/		31	https://www.ncbi.nlm.nih.gov/pmc/articles/PMC8030699/
13	https://www.ncbi.nlm.nih.gov/pmc/articles/PMC5579659/		32	https://www.mdpi.com/2076-3921/8/10/426#B65-antioxidants-08-00426
14	https://pubmed.ncbi.nlm.nih.gov/7391485/		33	https://pubmed.ncbi.nlm.nih.gov/29885291/
15	https://pubmed.ncbi.nlm.nih.gov/31697447/		34	https://www.ncbi.nlm.nih.gov/pmc/articles/PMC8409479/
16	https://www.psychiatrist.com/jcp/folate-depression-efficacy-safety-differences-formulations/		35	https://www.ncbi.nlm.nih.gov/pmc/articles/PMC8409479/
17	https://www.ncbi.nlm.nih.gov/books/NBK542254/		36	https://pubmed.ncbi.nlm.nih.gov/22129334/
18	https://www.ncbi.nlm.nih.gov/31739724/		37	https://pubmed.ncbi.nlm.nih.gov/36839307/
19	https://www.ncbi.nlm.nih.gov/pmc/articles/PMC6778948/		38	https://pubmed.ncbi.nlm.nih.gov/27592494/
20	https://pubmed.ncbi.nlm.nih.gov/30779288/		39	https://www.ncbi.nlm.nih.gov/pmc/articles/PMC5579659/
21	https://pubmed.ncbi.nlm.nih.gov/32810309/		40	https://www.ncbi.nlm.nih.gov/pmc/articles/PMC4655903/
22	https://www.ncbi.nlm.nih.gov/pmc/articles/PMC9916933/		41	https://pubmed.ncbi.nlm.nih.gov/18407528/
23	https://pubmed.ncbi.nlm.nih.gov/15953625/		42	https://pubmed.ncbi.nlm.nih.gov/22166897/
24	https://pubmed.ncbi.nlm.nih.gov/28394276/ and https://pubmed.ncbi.nlm.nih.gov/25712054/			
25	https://pmc.ncbi.nlm.nih.gov/articles/PMC8069533/			
26	https://www.ncbi.nlm.nih.gov/pmc/articles/PMC5553762/			
27	https://www.ncbi.nlm.nih.gov/pmc/articles/PMC7810416/			
28	https://www.ncbi.nlm.nih.gov/pmc/articles/PMC9498421/			
29	https://www.ncbi.nlm.nih.gov/pmc/articles/PMC9002813/			
30	https://pubmed.ncbi.nlm.nih.gov/27507778/			

GLOSSARY

UK	US	UK	US
Aubergine	Eggplant	Golden syrup	Light corn syrup
Baby onion	Pearl onion	Greaseproof paper	Wax paper
Baking beans	Pie weights	Ground almonds	Almond meal
Baking paper	Parchment paper	Hob	Stove
Beetroot	Beet	Icing sugar	Confectioners' sugar
Bicarbonate of soda	Baking soda	Jug/Measuring jug	Pitcher/Liquid measuring cup
Brine	Pickling solution	Kitchen paper	Paper towels
Butter beans	Lima beans	Mangetout	Snow peas
Cavolo nero	Tuscan or black-leaf kale	Minced (poultry/meat)	Ground (poultry/meat)
Caster sugar	Superfine sugar	Muslin	Cheesecloth
Chickpeas	Garbanzo beans	Natural yogurt	Plain yogurt
Chilli flakes	Red pepper flakes	Onion, brown	Onion, yellow
Chinese cabbage	Napa cabbage	Pak choi	Boy choy
Clingfilm	Plastic wrap	Pepper, red/yellow/green	Bell pepper, red/yellow/green
Coarse salt	Kosher salt	Plain flour	All-purpose flour
Cocktail stick	Toothpick	Polenta	Cornmeal
Coriander (fresh)	Cilantro	Prawns	Shrimp
Cornflour	Cornstarch	Rapeseed oil	Canola oil
Courgette	Zucchini	Shin of beef	Beef shank
Desiccated coconut	Dried shredded coconut	Soda water	Club soda
Double cream	Heavy cream	Spring onions	Scallions
Egg, large	Egg, extra-large	Stock cube	Bouillon cube
Electric hand whisk	Electric hand mixer	Tart case	Tart shell
Flaxseeds	Linseeds	Tea towel	Cloth dish towel
Frying pan	Skillet	Tin, e.g. baking/cake/loaf/tart	Pan, e.g. baking/cake/loaf/tart
Full fat	Whole/regular	Wholemeal (flour)	Wholewheat (flour)
Gelatine leaves	Gelatin sheets	Vanilla pod	Vanilla bean

THE CHEFS & EXPERTS

NATASHA MACALLER

NATASHA MACALLER spent 30 years as a professional ballerina performing with New York's prestigious Joffrey Ballet and Boston Ballet, finishing her stage career in the Broadway and Los Angeles productions of *The Phantom of The Opera*. Turning her artistic spirit to the kitchen, she channels the same passion, diligence and precision that made her a successful dancer into her love of creative cooking. She divides her time between Los Angeles, London and New Zealand, where she consults for restaurants and wineries, volunteers at fundraiser food and wine events, teaches cookery courses and writes.

She is married to actor and singer Michael Crawford.

The Apothecary Chef, her third international cookbook, bloomed from Natasha's passion for the distinctive, varied culinary medicinal herbs and plants, homegrown or foraged, that she cooks with while travelling and consulting. Joining her are 40 award-winning international chefs and culinary medical doctors and nutritional experts and the book includes over 65 herbs and plants.

Her second book, *Spice Health Heroes* (Jacqui Small, UK 2016) and first book, *Vanilla Table: The Essence of Exquisite Cooking from the World's Best Chefs* (Bateman, NZ 2013 & Jacqui Small, UK 2014) are all stunningly photographed by Manja Wachsmuth.
IG: @dancingchefnatasha
www.dancingchef.net

ELMO AGATEP, MD

Elmo is board-certified in family medicine and sports medicine. He is physician for the USA Women's Water Polo Team and the USA Beach Volleyball Team at the Rio, Tokyo and Paris Olympic Games.

Apart from extolling the virtues of active and healthy lifestyles, Elmo avidly advocates for wholesome nutritional habits with his patients. He firmly believes in the wisdom of what Hippocrates said about the healing effects of good food, 'Let food be thy medicine, and let thy medicine be food.'
IG: @dragatep

ALLAN ALTSCHUL

Allan is Chef Manager at The Farmyard at The Newt in Somerset. He is passionate about local ingredients, different cooking techniques, seasonality and working with the great people that produce amazing things in Somerset. He has been a chef for more than 14 years and has worked in different countries and experienced many different cultures. He is originally from Brazil, but left in 2012 to travel and learn more about kitchen life and cooking techniques. He lives in Somerset.
FB: allan.altschul
IG: @allan_altschul

DR. ALLEN ARNETTE

Dr. Arnette believes that food, home cooking and kitchen skills are the foundational bedrock for health. He believes that herbs gathered from the garden or local farmers' markets have wild/unprocessed compounds that make a big difference in taste and effect over the processed versions available in supermarkets.

Dr. Arnette encourages his patients to learn and love fostering and nourishing health through self-care. Influenced by his studies in Chinese medicine in particular, his desire is to bring ancient-inspired herbal traditions to life for the modern culture. It is his hope that these recipes (and this book in general) inspire more of his views and beliefs around the globe. Dr. Arnette has a wellness-based clinic in Long Beach, California, where he focuses on the treatment of difficult conditions using a variety of natural and holistic approaches.

ALAN BARTOS

Alan is a renowned French-born pastry chef celebrated for his artistry and commitment to flavour. Now based in Kerikeri, New Zealand, Alan is dedicated to using local ingredients in his creations. A finalist in the Cuisine Good Food Awards 2021/2022 in the Best Pastry Chef category, he is always seeking to innovate and perfect his craft. Alan's latest recipe features a softer-set French-style panna cotta infused with chocolate mint, showcasing his ability to blend unique flavours into classic desserts. His work continues to delight and inspire, reflecting his passion for pastry in his adopted community.
IG: @alan.bartos

APRIL BLOOMFIELD

April is originally from Birmingham, England. The Michelin-starred chef has been cooking for over 30 years in London, New York and Los Angeles. She is currently the executive chef at Sailor, located in Brooklyn, New York.
IG: @aprilbloomfield

MECCA BOS

Mecca Bos is a culinary storyteller who has been working as a food writer and chef for more than 25 years. In the past five years, she has expanded her work into audio journalism with *The Godfather of Black Space in Minneapolis* and she is a regular contributor to Minnesota Public Radio. In 2022, she founded BIPOC Foodways Alliance, a nonprofit uplifting the stories of women of colour through home cooking.

She has worked as a chef, sous chef, and cook in many professional kitchens from casual to fine, including Platform by the James Beard Foundation in New York City, and has been published in many publications including *The New York Times*.

She is a devoted auntie to three of the cutest kids in the world, an avid cyclist and a world traveller. Mecca lives in Minneapolis with her partner Sean.
IG: @meccabos

ADAM BRYDON

Adam started his culinary journey aged 15 as a supermarket baker's assistant. It led him to take catering as a serious subject at school, after which he completed a diploma in Culinary Arts at Christchurch Polytechnic.

At 25, he bought a one-way ticket to Europe, where he worked in his first Michelin-starred restaurant under Michael Caines in Bath and spent a year at Petrus in London, working for Gordon Ramsay. He returned to Australia to be chef de cuisine on Hayman Island, then head chef at Harrisons, a one-hat restaurant, for two years.

He is now a senior sous-chef on a yacht based in the Middle East. His main focus is running a large-scale galley operation with 12 other chefs. He continues to gain experience through special training academies and world-class one-on-one tutors.

CHRIS COSENTINO

Chris began his career in Washington and the Bay Area, including as executive chef at Incanto, where he drew critical acclaim for whole-animal cooking.

Since 2014, he has opened his own restaurants: Cockscomb in San Francisco, Jackrabbit in Portland, Acacia House in the Napa Valley and Rosalie Italian Soul in Downtown Houston and Koast, a celebration of local ingredients and coastal cuisine, on the island of Maui in Hawaii.

Chris wrote a James Beard Award-nominated cookbook, *Offal Good: Cooking from the Heart with Guts* (2017), the seminal cookbook on offal. He won BRAVO's Top Chef Masters, earning over $140,000 for The Michael J. Fox Foundation.
FB: chefchriscosentino /
IG: @chefchriscosentino /
www.chefchriscosentino.com

JIM DODGE

Jim is a sixth-generation hotelier from the Lakes and White Mountains Regions of New Hampshire. His early training included a two-year Swiss pastry apprenticeship with pastry chef Fritz Albicker. In 1978 he became executive pastry chef at the Stanford Court Hotel in San Francisco, pioneering a new pastry focussing on building flavour using California's seasonal ripe fruits, minimally processed cream and less sugar.

In 1991, he opened The American Pie Pastry Shop, named finest pastry shop in Hong Kong for seven years running. He is the author of *The American Baker* and *Baking with Jim Dodge*. He has taught for over 35 years in the USA, Japan, Korea, Mexico and Panama. Jim is an advisor to the Julia Child Foundation and jury chair for the Julia Child Award.
IG: chefjimdodge / www.chefjimdodge.com

ELIZABETH FALKNER

Elizabeth is an award-winning chef who has owned restaurants in San Francisco and New York. She continues to cook at food and wine festivals, fundraisers and other events, and has cooked for countless celebrities.

Elizabeth also works as a consultant on projects and brands for companies such as Barilla, Starbucks, Hershey, Pepsi and Nestlé. She has appeared on many cooking competition shows over 20 years and serves on the board of trustees of the James Beard Foundation, and on the culinary councils of City Harvest, NYC and Forever Oceans. She was previously on the board and then president of Women Chefs & Restaurateurs.

In 2020 she produced and hosted a documentary called *Sorry We're Closed*, streaming on Apple TV and Amazon Prime.
IG: @cheffalkner
www.elizabethfalkner.com

PETER GORDON

Born in Whanganui, New Zealand, and of Māori and Scottish descent, Peter collated his first cookbook aged just four. Following a four-year chef's apprenticeship in Melbourne, he backpacked through SE Asia, India and Nepal for a year before returning to set up The Sugar Club kitchen in his home country in Wellington. This year of travel cemented in him the flavours and textures of Asia, which he utilized in his fusion style of cooking.

Peter returned to London in 1989, where he lived for 31 years, owning restaurants in the UK and New Zealand, alongside consultancies in Istanbul and New York, and authoring nine cookbooks. Peter now lives in Auckland.
FB: ChefPeterGordon
IG: @chefpetergordon
www.peter-gordon.com

NYESHA ARRINGTON

Nyesha is the co-star of FOX's hit culinary competition show *Next Level Chef*, as well as host and producer of the digital series *Plateworthy* on Eater. She started her culinary career at Michelin-starred restaurants Mélisse in Santa Monica, and L'Atelier and The Mansion, both in Las Vegas. She then opened restaurants Leona and Native in Los Angeles, where she was celebrated for using farm-fresh, locally and responsibly sourced ingredients. She was named in Zagat's '30 Under 30' chefs list as well as Eater's LA Chef of the Year. Her credits include FOX's *MasterChef* and *Hell's Kitchen*.

Nyesha draws inspiration from cooking through the seasons, travelling around the world and contemporary art. She lives in Los Angeles with her French bulldog, Bleu-Ginger, and cat, Mr. Robert Marley.
FB: ChefNyeshaArrington / IG: @nyeshajoyce / www.nyeshaarrington.com/

METTE FLORA HELBÆK

Mette is a self-taught chef, restauranteur and entrepreneur originally from Denmark. Author of four cookbooks, Mette has worked with healing plants as food as medicine for two decades, and has studied both herbalism, nutrition and shamanism in her quest to better understand the connection between plants and humans. Based in the breathtaking coastal town of San Pedro, Guatemala, she and her husband, Flemming, run a small hotel and cook side-by-side in their bespoke restaurant 'La Cocina Bonita' near the beach using the best ingredients from local farms and seasoning their delicious dishes from a multitude of organic herbs from their clifftop garden presented in a sort of nordic way-but super relaxed.
IG: @metteflorahelbak
www.thebeautifulsolution.com

credit: Joe Woodhouse

OLIA HERCULES

Olia was born in Ukraine, and at the age of twelve moved to Cyprus, then later to the UK to study. In 2008, she quit her journalism job to follow her dream of cooking for a living. She trained at Leiths School of Food and Wine, then worked as a chef de partie at Ottolenghi and as a recipe developer before publishing *Mamushka*, a cookbook celebrating traditional recipes from Ukraine, Moldova, Azerbaijan and Uzbekistan, which won the 2016 Fortnum & Mason Award for best debut cookbook. She has since released three other cookbooks: *Kaukasis: A culinary journey through Georgia, Azerbaijan & beyond*; *Summer Kitchens*; and *Home Food*. Olia also runs an online cookery school and hosts regular workshops at her home. She lives in London with her husband, food writer and photographer Joe Woodhouse, and their two sons.
IG: @oliahercules / www.oliahercules.com

HENRIETTA INMAN

Henrietta is an agroecological baker, cook, pastry chef and author. After working in professional kitchens in London for 10 years and writing two books, she moved home to Suffolk. There she founded a 100% wholegrain bakery on Europe's most diverse agroforestry site, Wakelyns, using produce directly from the farm. At the end of 2024, she moved on to found Heart Bakery based at Hodmedod, Britain's pulse and grain pioneers, where she uses their diverse and beautiful, directly traded ingredients in her wholegrain baking for local events, shops and their online shop. She believes that everyone has the right to nourishing food grown using methods that nourish our Earth also.
IG: @heart__bakery
IG: @henrietta__inman
www.hodmedods.co.uk/collections/bakery

SARAH JOHNSON

Sarah trained under the legendary Alice Waters at Chez Panisse in California. She is the author of *Fruitful: Sweet and Savory Recipes Inspired by Farms, Orchards and Gardens*. She currently divides her time between cooking professionally and food writing.
IG: @sarahjohnsoncooks

MARIA KALENSKA

Maria is a food writer born in Odessa, Ukraine. In 2011, she opened Odessa's first cookery school, and five years later relocated to the UK. In 2019, Maria contributed to the EU Geographical Indications project that established 'The First Ukrainian food and wine road in Ukrainian Bessarabia'. During the pandemic, she volunteered as a chef with the Carousel restaurant for London's hospitals. In collaboration with a Ukrainian team of wine experts, Maria established The Best Riedel Glass for Odessa Black variety to promote Ukrainian local wine. She moved to Berlin in 2021, where after the full-scale Russian invasion of Ukraine she launched Bake for Ukraine. She lives between Ukraine, Germany and the UK and is currently writing a cookbook on the cuisine of Odessa.
FB: mkalenska / IG: mkalenska / www.myodessacuisine.com/my-odessa/about-odessa-cuisine

credit: Laura Edwards

PIERRE KOFFMANN

Pierre has been at the heart of fine cuisine in Britain for over fifty years. After working in Strasbourg and Toulon, Pierre arrived in London in 1970 to work under Michel and Albert Roux at Le Gavroche. In 1972, he became first head chef of the Roux brothers' Waterside Inn at Bray. Pierre and his late wife Annie opened La Tante Claire in 1977. Within six years of opening, La Tante Claire had its third Michelin star, setting new standards for cooking, while also serving as an academy for many of today's culinary superstars.

After a short-lived retirement, Pierre returned to the kitchen at Koffmann's at The Berkeley, with a more informal style and classic provincial French cooking – the food that first inspired him to become a chef, introduced to him from a young age at his grandparents' farmhouse kitchen in Gascony.
IG: @pierre.koffmann

ANNE KRATZ

Anne is a passionate chef, having grown up and lived on her family's farm, which brought a love of local products and a closeness to nature.

She is captain of the national culinary team of Germany and has cooked for over five years in competitions around the world.

She was awarded 'Pastry Chef of the Year' in 2024 for her work, which is healthy, heartful and full of culinary innovation. Her motto is 'bringing the flavours of the world home'.

She works closely with her mentor and friend chef Julia Komp and together they bring a host of creativity and ideas to the plates of Michelin starred Sahila – The Restaurant, which she describes as 'a culinary stage, to reach and convince people with your ideas and thoughts'.
IG: @anne_kern_
www.kahnshof.de

JULIA KOMP

Julia is Germany's youngest female Michelin-starred chef and a world traveller, having visited more than 45 countries from Morocco to Japan, and cooked in small kitchens as well as Michelin-starred restaurants worldwide. She loves exploring spices from local markets and incorporating them into her cuisine. As a chef, she takes her guests on a journey to remote places with sustainable, organic ingredients of the highest quality.

In 2023, Julia became Chef of the Year, one of the highest distinctions in Germany. She opened Sahila – The Restaurant, which received a Michelin star after one year, and Yulia Mezze Bar in the heart of Cologne. She is also a regular guest on German television and has her own brand, selling the highest quality olive oil, spices and her own blend of coffee beans. Her book *My World Trip in Recipes* was published in 2021.
IG: @juliakompcuisine

KATHY KORDALIS

Kathy was born into a Greek family in Sydney, but currently resides in London with her English husband. She has over ten years' experience in the food industry and works as a food stylist, recipe writer and tester, and is the author of ten cookbooks. She previously managed the Divertimenti Cookery School, where she was inspired to embark on a cooking career and undertook the Leiths Diploma of Food and Wine, where she qualified as a chef. Her food style is light, relaxed and accessible, and she draws her inspiration from her formal training at Leiths, as well as her Australian and Mediterranean heritages, and years of food-industry experience. Her next endeavour is the world of olive oil, its health benefits, rich history, healing properties and importance in modern and ancient society.
IG: @kordalisk

DAVID LEBOVITZ

David spent thirteen years at Chez Panisse in California, the pioneering farm-to-table restaurant, beginning as a line cook in the café before moving to the pastry section. He was named one of the top five pastry chefs in the Bay Area by the *San Francisco Chronicle*.

In 1999, David left the restaurant business to write cookery books and launch a website and blog. His blog went on to become one of the most widely read food blogs in the world.

He is the author of nine books, including *Room for Dessert, My Paris Kitchen*, with stories and recipes about baking and cooking in Paris, and *Drinking French*, named the best new cocktail book by the Tales of the Cocktail Foundation. Other books include *The Great Book of Chocolate*, T*he Perfect Scoop*, *Ready for Dessert*, *L'Appart* and *The Sweet Life in Paris* – with the latter two in development for a TV series.

IG: @davidlebovitz

JOHN LA PUMA, MD, FACP

John is board-certified in internal medicine, a professionally trained chef and a regenerative organic farmer. Along with Dr. Michael Roizen, Dr. La Puma co-taught the first culinary medicine course for medical students in America. It is now taught in two-thirds of US medical schools and worldwide. A *New York Times* best-selling author twice, his seven books have sold over a million copies and have been translated into eight languages. He has spoken at Harvard, TEDMED, Stanford and aboard the privately owned residential yacht, *The World*, on longevity, food as medicine, and nature-based approaches. He is based in Santa Barbara, California.

IG: @johnlapuma
www.drjohnlapuma.com

CHRISTINE MANFIELD

Christine is one of Australia's most celebrated chefs – a perfectionist inspired by a culinary melting pot of global flavours and native ingredients. She is also a prolific food writer, publishing *Indian Cooking Class, Tasting India, A Personal Guide to India and Bhutan, Dessert Divas, Fire, Spice, Stir, Paramount Cooking* and *Paramount Desserts*.

Her professional life as a restaurateur culminated in three award-winning restaurants: Paramount in Sydney (1993 to 2000), East@West in London (2003 to 2005), and Universal in Sydney (2007 to 2013).

Christine has also hosted bespoke culinary adventures to exotic destinations for many years. Recently, she has focused on regional Australian destinations for meaningful, sustainable and immersive experiences highlighting First Nations indigenous culture.

IG: @christinemanfieldchef
www.christinemanfield.com

SEQUANNA MANZENITA

Sequanna's love of cooking began in childhood. Now, she pairs deep intention with nourishing, wholefood dishes that enliven both body and soul.

Sequanna is a longtime student of herbalism and Ayurveda, and has spent over 20 years as a birth and postpartum doula. She is also a professionally trained dancer, certified herbalist, yoga instructor and bodywork practitioner. She integrates movement, mindfulness and holistic nutrition to cultivate a multifaceted approach to well-being.

Based in Southern California, her passion for coastal living shines through in her appreciation for food, music and community. When she's not cooking or supporting others through her holistic wellness practices, you'll likely find her roller skating by the ocean, moving in rhythm with the waves.

www.studioair.space

PALMIRO OCAMPO GREY

Palmiro understood early on that his profession transcended the kitchen. He also realized that his years of experience and touring the best culinary places in Peru and the world would allow him to contribute his talent for a better economy. Food sustainability is his obsession, and reducing poor nutrition is his mission. He is a consultant chef for the development of sustainable gastronomy proposals. In 2014, he founded Ccori Cocina Óptima with his life partner, an organization dedicated to the research and development of educational programs in food optimization for community kitchens.

IG: palmiroocampo
www.palmiroocampo.com/en

ROGER PIZEY

Roger trained for two years at Le Gavroche under Albert Roux, then joined Marco Pierre White at Harvey's as Chef Patissier. His innovative desserts became an integral part of the shifting perception in British cooking and he has worked at some of the most exclusive restaurants in London. Following a period as Head Chef of The Criterion, Roger set up the bakery for Peyton & Byrne, then as Head Chef and Executive Chef of Marco's in Stamford Bridge. In 2017 Roger moved to Chelsea's Bluebird as Executive Head of Pastry and Baking. He is currently Executive Pastry Chef at Fortnum & Mason in London.

Roger has published two cookery books: *Small Cakes* in 2008, and *World's Best Cakes* in 2013. He has appeared in *Hell's Kitchen*, *Willie's Wonky Chocolate Factory* and on *MasterChef* Ireland.

IG: @rogerpizey

SEAN SHERMAN

A member of the Oglala Lakota tribe, Sean was born and raised on the Pine Ridge Indian Reservation in South Dakota. Sean's goal is to make indigenous foods accessible to as many communities as possible through the non-profit North American Traditional Indigenous Food Systems (NATIFS) and its Indigenous Food Lab.

In 2017, Sean published *The Sioux Chef's Indigenous Kitchen* with Beth Dooley, which received a James Beard Award in 2018. In 2021, he opened Owamni, Minnesota's first full-service indigenous restaurant, which received the James Beard Award for Best New Restaurant in America for 2022. Most recently, he was honoured as *TIME* magazine's 100 Most Influential People of 2023, and received the Julia Child Award for culinary activism, innovation.
IG: @the_sioux_chef
www.seansherman.com

BEN SHEWRY

Ben Shewry was born in Waitara in rural New Zealand. The son of artistic and open-minded farming parents, Ben grew up in a household where making a little go a long way was not only the rule but a necessity. Ben decided he wanted to be a chef at the age of five. He first set foot in a commercial kitchen at age 10, had his first paid restaurant job at 14 and began full-time chef studies at 16. After qualifying as a chef two years later, he worked in the New Zealand cities of New Plymouth and Wellington. He moved to Melbourne in 2002 to expand his culinary horizons, and became head chef at Attica in 2005, before taking ownership ten years later. He has dedicated the past 19 years to Attica, discovering what it means to be a chef in Australia from a cultural, community, creative and committed perspective (the 4 Cs). IG: @benshewry

LINDA SHIUE, MD

Linda is an internal medicine physician, chef and the Director of Culinary Medicine and Lifestyle Medicine at Kaiser Permanente in San Francisco, where she founded Thrive Kitchen, a teaching kitchen for patients.

She believes that the best medicine is prevention. Her cooking classes showcase seasonal produce, lavishly flavoured with spices and fresh herbs. Her first cookbook, Spicebox Kitchen, was a 2022 Gold Award Winner in the Nautilus Book Awards and a Finalist in the 2022 IACP Awards. Dr. Shiue is Associate Clinical Professor of Medicine at the Kaiser Permanente School of Medicine and serves on the boards of the San Francisco-Marin Food Bank, Meals on Wheels of San Francisco and the Teaching Kitchen Collaborative.
FB: thedoctorsspicebox
IG: @spiceboxtravels

NICOLA SHUBROOK

Nicola is a nutritional therapist and certified functional medicine practitioner with the Institute for Functional Medicine, specializing in mental health and our relationship with food. She runs an online clinic called Urban Wellness, where she and her team work across a wide variety of health challenges. She is also part of the team behind the British Network for Functional Medicine, and a member of the Professional Practice Panel of British Association for Nutrition & Lifestyle Medicine. Nicola is also a health journalist and regularly contributes to press, magazine and radio content, working with authors and appearing on podcasts. She loves to show others how they can take control of their own health through nutrition, making the science behind it simple and practical.
IG: @urbanwellnessuk
www.urbanwellness.co.uk

NANCY SILVERTON

Nancy Silverton is the co-owner of the Mozza Restaurant Group which consists of nine locations worldwide, with flagship locations in California: Michelin-starred Osteria Mozza, Pizzeria Mozza, chi SPACCA and Mozza2Go in LA. Her international restaurant locations include Los Cabos, London, and Singapore as well as a residency on the island of Lanai in Hawaii. Her most recent restaurant, Osteria Mozza DC, opened in the fall of 2024.

In 2014 she received the highest honour given by the James Beard Foundation for Outstanding Chef and was also listed as one of the Most Innovative Women in Food and Drink by both *Fortune* and *Food & Wine* magazines. In 2017 Nancy was profiled in an episode of Netflix's award-winning docuseries *Chef's Table*. She has authored eleven cookbooks.
FB: chefnancysilverton / IG: @nancysilverton

HIRO SONE

Born into a rice-farming family in Miyagi Prefecture, Japan, Hiro moved to Osaka in his teens to become a chef. After graduating from Tsuji Culinary Institute, he trained in Tokyo restaurants, then moved to the USA to serve as head chef at Spago, Los Angeles.

In 1988, he opened Terra in Napa Valley with his wife Lissa Doumani, a pastry chef. Three years later, he won America's Best New Chef Award from *Food & Wine* magazine. In 2001, *TERRA: Cooking from the Heart of Napa Valley*, was nominated for Best American Cookbook by the James Beard Foundation. In 2003, he won the Best Chef of California Award by the James Beard Foundation and in 2005, he opened Ame in St. Regis Hotel in San Francisco. Terra and Ame each retained their Michelin star every year until they closed. Hiro is currently working as a consultant.
IG: @hiro_sone

credit: Patricia Niven

ITAMAR SRULOVICH & SARIT PACKER

Husband and wife duo Itamar and Sarit co-founded central London Middle Eastern restaurants Honey & Co. and Honey & Smoke Grill House, deli Honey & Spice: Food Store, café-bakery Honey & Co. Daily and the Honey & Co. Pop-up Bakery. The couple have written four cookbooks, and also write a recipe column in the *FT Weekend* magazine and host a podcast called *Honey & Co: The Food Sessions*, as well as regular events across their locations.
IG: @honeyandco

PIM TECHAMUANVIVIT

Born and raised in Bangkok, Pim took a circuitous route through the world of food – from blogging to making award-winning jams – before finding her way home to the food she grew up with. In 2014, Pim opened her first restaurant, Kin Khao, in San Francisco. It received its first Michelin star the following year, and is the only Thai restaurant with a Michelin star in the USA. In 2018, Pim joined Nahm at the Como Metropolitan Hotel, Bangkok as executive chef, retaining its Michelin star every year.

In 2019 Pim opened Nari, her second successful San Francisco restaurant. Named for the Sanskrit-derived Thai word for 'women', Nari is Pim's love letter to the generations of women who have been the heart and soul of Thai cuisine. Nari attained a Michelin star in 2023.
IG: @chezpim

credit: Zodee Media

CYRUS TODIWALA, OBE, DL, DBA

Cyrus Todiwala is one of the most prominent celebrity chefs in the UK. He is famous for being a regular on BBC's *Saturday Kitchen* and for his TV series *The Incredible Spice Men*. Café Spice Namasté, his signature restaurant in the heart of London's Docklands, is a name synonymous with Cyrus. Together with his wife, Pervin Todiwala, and his team, he has built a strong brand and reputation for educating people about Indian cuisine, bringing it to the forefront of Britain's culinary map.
FB: cyrus.todiwala
IG: @cyrustodi

LEE WESTCOTT

Originally from Hertfordshire, Lee began hist career working with the Galvin brothers, then honed his craft in restaurants such as Tom Aikens, Noma (Copenhagen) and Jason Atherton (Hong Kong). However, it was at The Typing Room restaurant in the Town Hall Hotel in Bethnal Green, London, that Lee cemented his reputation, winning rave reviews for his inventive dishes using the best of British produce. After four years, Lee opened Pensons at the Netherwood Estate, a magnificent field-to-fork restaurant awarded a Michelin star seven months after opening. Lee then went on to open Birch Selsdon Hotel in Croydon. Here, he and his team utilized the land available to them by foraging throughout the seasons and setting up a garden to grow and produce their own herbs and vegetables.
IG: @leewestcott
www.leewestcott.com

SHERRY YARD

From Brooklyn, Sherry went to the school of culinary hard knocks. She tried to make it as a fashion designer before flipping burgers at McDonalds in Coney Island. She attended the Master Baking College, then moved to San Francisco, where she landed her first pastry chef job at Campton Place. She moved to Calistoga in the Napa Valley, then to Catahoula, Louisiana, for her second chef job.

She found her niche in farmers' market-inspired à-la-minute desserts and breads. She did heavy lifting as Wolfgang Pucks' sweet right hand for 19 years. In 2003 she wrote an award-winning book called *The Secrets of Baking*, then became an international TV presenter/judge on *The Great American Baking Show*.
IG: @chefsherryyard
www.bakerybytheyard.com

RUDOLPH VAN VEEN

Born in Belgium, Rudolph grew up in the Netherlands, where he still lives. He studied at the Culinary School in Breda, Holland, where he won the Best Graduate Award in 1985. His curiosity and creative instinct propelled him to explore many countries and cultures and to meet with distinguished chefs the world over.

In 1995, at the age of 27, Rudolph obtained the highest Dutch qualification in his field: Certified Master Chef (SVH MasterChef). In 2010, he was the first of two chefs in the Netherlands to obtain the official title of Certified Master Pastry Chef. He is currently the only chef in the Netherlands boasting these two Master titles. In 1998 he co-founded the Dutch Pastry Team. Two years later, Rudolph launched his television career co-hosting the Dutch TV show *Life & Cooking* and in 2011 he co-founded the TV channel *24Kitchen*.
IG: @rudolphvanveen_official

THE CHEFS & EXPERTS

USEFUL RESOURCES

BOOKS

Culinary Herbs & Spices of the World by Ben-Erik Van Wyk (2014, Kew Publishing)

Fifty Plants That Changed the Course of History by Bill Laws (2010, David and Charles)

Food in History by Reay Tannahill (1989, Crown)

Herbarium: One Hundred Herbs – Grow Cook Heal by Caz Hildebrand (2016, Thames & Hudson)

Hiakai: Modern Maori Cuisine by Monique Fiso (2020, Godwit)

Kitchen Garden Companion: Dig, Plant, Water, Grow, Harvest, Chop, Cook by Stephanie Alexander (2010, Quadrille)

Ottolenghi: The Cookbook by Yotam Ottolenghi and Sami Tamimi (2016, Ebury)

Salt, Fat, Acid, Heat: Mastering the Elements of Good Cooking by Samin Nosrat (2017, Canongate)

Tender: A Cook and His Vegetable Patch by Nigel Slater (2009, Fourth Estate)

The Diet Myth: The Real Science Behind What We Eat by Tim Spector (2016, Weidenfeld & Nicholson)

The Encyclopedia of Herbs and Spices by Andi Cleveley, Sallie Morris and Lesley Mackie (1999, Hermes House)

The Flavour Thesaurus by Niki Segnit (2010, Bloomsbury)

The Herb and Spice Book by Sarah Garland (1979, Weidenfeld and Nicolson)

The Oxford Companion to Food by Alan Davidson (1999, Oxford University Press)

The Way We Eat Now: How the Food Revolution Has Transformed Our Lives, Our Bodies, and Our World by Bee Wilson (2019, Basic Books)

Veg-Table: Recipes, Techniques and Plant Science for Big-Flavored, Vegetable-Focused Meals by Nic Sharma (2023, Chronicle)

OTHER RESOURCES

'The Artichoke', *The French Chef Season 7*, Julia Child

Chef Alan Bergo (www.foragerchef.com)

Chestnut School of Herbal Medicine (www.chestnutherbs.com)

Forks Over Knives (www.forksoverknives.com)

'Herbs and Spices in Cancer Prevention and Treatment' by Christine M Kaefer and John A Milner (www.ncbi.nlm.nih.gov/books/NBK92774/)

National Library of Medicine (pmc.ncbi.nlm.nih.gov)

Nicola Shubrook (@urbanwellnessuk)

INDEX

Alexanders 213
alliums 200
   allium & wild mushroom spinach galette 20–2
angelica 186
apples 219–21
   apple blossom 132
   old-fashioned plum, apple & rye buckle 32
artichokes 210–11
   the oak smoked artichoke with zesty mayonnaise 84
ashwagandha 196–8
asparagus: crispy asparagus with tarragon mayonnaise & crispy nettles 80
avocados 221–2
   overnight oat berries with avocado & maple syrup 8
   pan-seared scallops on silky avocado crema 140

bean sprouts: farro power bowl with dua gia, charred wild garlic & tahini fig vincotto dressing 102
beef: spring borsch with nettles 12
beetroot 202–3
bread: flaxseed, thyme & sunflower bread with smoked mackerel 78

cakes
   chocolate cake with liquorice espresso buttercream 64
   fennel seed & ginger gems 148
   pear, rosemary & walnut bundt cake 88–90
   rosemary calendula polenta cakes 46
   vegetable garden tea cakes 144
calendula 196
carrot & coconut sublime spice balls 68
cavolo nero 209–10
   New Zealand rack of lamb with goats' cheese parfait & cavolo nero pesto 164
   polenta with bitter greens & pan-fried sweet potato cubes 138
chakalaka: chicken chakalaka 58
chamomile 187–8
champagne: sea buckthorn & champagne gelée 180

cheese
   Dutch, Dutch baby with tangerine ricotta whip 174
   fattoush with charred lamb, pickled beetroot & whipped sumac feta 60
   Isle of Wight tomatoes with chamomile, ricotta, cherries & green almonds 166–8
   lemon myrtle cheesecake with Anzac wattleseed biscuit 37–8
   New Zealand rack of lamb with goats' cheese parfait & cavolo nero pesto 164
   pickled magnolia petal compote with mascarpone & triple lime sablés 172
   Reyes blue cheese caramelized onion tart with poached pears & pickled beetroot 23–4
   Swiss meringue pamplemousse Pavlova 169–70
   tomato and mozzarella salad 76
chia seeds: chocolate valencia balance balls 68
chicken
   chicken chakalaka 58
   sticky chicken meatballs & ketjap manis on steamed greens 86
   tinolang manok chicken tinola 16
chicory 203
   bittersweet chocolate chicory fandango 119–20
chocolate
   bittersweet chocolate chicory fandango 119–20
   chocolate cake with liquorice espresso buttercream 64
   chocolate valencia balance balls 68
   meadowsweet mousse globes 152
   peppermint panna cotta with chocolate tuile shards 66
citrus fruits 216
   Dutch, Dutch baby with tangerine ricotta whip 174
   fennel seed & ginger gems 148
   lemon buttermilk muhallebi puddings 150
   Santa Barbara date shake 154
   soothing summer switchel 178
   sunshine citrus salad with lemon balm vinaigrette 136

   Swiss meringue pamplemousse Pavlova 169–70
coconut
   carrot & coconut sublime spice balls 68
   curry leaf-crusted fish in a lemon myrtle coconut sauce with finger lime & sweet potato salad 114
   honey mango coconut paletas with chilli chamoy 62
   pineapple mint Hawaiian ceviche with blue coconut wafers 54
condiments
   fig, pear & cranberry mostarda for cheese 176
   patrani macchi 112
cookies, crackers & biscuits
   energize flatbreads 44
   lemon myrtle cheesecake with Anzac wattleseed biscuit 37–8
   mantulky honey cookies from Ukraine 122
   omakase nigiri with yuzu wasabi snow 142
   pickled magnolia petal compote with mascarpone & triple lime sablés 172
   sunflower seed cookies 132–5
coriander 188
   quick-pickled coriander 100

dandelions 213
   hanger steak, charred onions with dandelion green salsa 30
dates: PB & J balls 68
desserts
   bittersweet chocolate chicory fandango 119–20
   crispy peach amandine dumplings with pickled pink rhubarb & coconut yuzu whipped posset 34–6
   Dutch, Dutch baby with tangerine ricotta whip 174
   honey, pine nut & sage tart 160
   honey mango coconut paletas with chilli chamoy 62
   lemon buttermilk muhallebi puddings 150
   lemon myrtle cheesecake with Anzac wattleseed biscuit 37–8

INDEX   237

meadowsweet mousse globes 152
old-fashioned plum, apple & rye buckle 32
peppermint panna cotta with chocolate tuile shards 66
persimmon pudding 146
pickled magnolia petal compote with mascarpone & triple lime sablés 172
rødgrød med fløde 40
sea buckthorn & champagne gelée 180
Swiss meringue pamplemousse Pavlova 169–70
dill 185
dressings
　crispy asparagus with tarragon mayonnaise & crispy nettles 80
　farro power bowl with dua gia, charred wild garlic & tahini fig vincotto dressing 102
　the oak smoked artichoke with zesty mayonnaise 84
　rosemary & olive oil dressing 74
　sunshine citrus salad with lemon balm vinaigrette 136
　tarragon vinaigrette 76
drinks
　echinacea tisane 124
　rhubarb, raspberry & peppermint shrub 178
　Santa Barbara date shake 154
　soothing summer switchel 178

echinacea 204
　echinacea tisane 124

farro power bowl with dua gia, charred wild garlic & tahini fig vincotto dressing 102
fennel 188–9
fish
　allotment tomato, anchovy & Parmesan gratin 104
　aloha pineapple kimchi with teriyaki salmon 28
　curry leaf-crusted fish in a lemon myrtle coconut sauce with finger lime & sweet potato salad 114
　flaxseed, thyme & sunflower bread with smoked mackerel 78
　four fish & herb stew 110
　omakase nigiri with yuzu wasabi snow 142
　pan-grilled stargazer with rainbow relish 56
　pan-seared snapper, with nasturtium & poor man's 'capers' 82
　patrani macchi 112
　pineapple mint Hawaiian ceviche with blue coconut wafers 54

ginger 206
gremolata: corn, leek, cauli & chilli crisp chowder with preserved lemon gremolata 128

herbs 185–96
baby new potato, egg & herb salad with basil buttermilk horseradish cream 158
four fish & herb stew 110
salted herbs for winter 18
holy basil. see tulsi (holy basil)
honey 185
　honey, pine nut & sage tart 160
　mantulky honey cookies from Ukraine 122
horseradish 200–2

kelp 199
ketjap manis: sticky chicken meatballs & ketjap manis on steamed greens 86

lamb
　dushpra: cherries, lamb & sweet spice dumplings 14
　fattoush with charred lamb, pickled beetroot & whipped sumac feta 60
　New Zealand rack of lamb with goats' cheese parfait & cavolo nero pesto 164
lemon balm/myrtle/sorrel/verbena 190–1
liquorice 206
　chocolate cake with liquorice espresso buttercream 64
lovage 189

magnolia 192

mangoes: honey mango coconut paletas with chilli chamoy 62
maple syrup 185
meadowsweet mousse globes 152
miner's lettuce 210
　nasturtium & miner's lettuce pesto pasta with butter beans 108
moringa 212
mushrooms
　allium & wild mushroom spinach galette 20–2
　shiitake broth with aromatic herbs 72
mustard 209

nasturtiums 215
　nasturtium & miner's lettuce pesto pasta with butter beans 108
　pan-seared snapper, with nasturtium & poor man's 'capers' 82
nettles 215
　crispy asparagus with tarragon mayonnaise & crispy nettles 80
　root, rice, leek & nettle soup 96
　spring borsch with nettles 12
nuts: PB & J balls 68

oat berries: overnight oat berries with avocado & maple syrup 8
old man saltbush. see saltbush
olive oil: rosemary & olive oil dressing 74
oregano 193–4

parsley 194–5
pears 222
　fig, pear & cranberry mostarda for cheese 176
　fuyu persimmon & red pear wild greens salad with liquorice mint vinaigrette 26
　pear, rosemary & walnut bundt cake 88–90
　Reyes blue cheese caramelized onion tart with poached pears & pickled beetroot 23–4
peas: green pea & calendula soup with golden Peruvian potato shells 130
peppermint 192
peppers 218–20

pan-grilled stargazer with rainbow relish 56
persimmons 219
　fuyu persimmon & red pear wild greens salad with liquorice mint vinaigrette 26
　persimmon pudding 146
pesto
　nasturtium & miner's lettuce pesto pasta with butter beans 108
　New Zealand rack of lamb with goats' cheese parfait & cavolo nero pesto 164
pies, tarts & pastries
　allium & wild mushroom spinach galette 20–2
　honey, pine nut & sage tart 160
　Reyes blue cheese caramelized onion tart with poached pears & pickled beetroot 23–4
　tourte de pommes de terre à l'ail: potato & garlic pie 106
pineapple 216–18
　aloha pineapple kimchi with teriyaki salmon 28
　pineapple mint Hawaiian ceviche with blue coconut wafers 54
pine tips & nuts 185
plums: old-fashioned plum, apple & rye buckle 32
polenta
　polenta with bitter greens & pan-fried sweet potato cubes 138
　rosemary calendula polenta cakes 46
potatoes
　baby new potato, egg & herb salad with basil buttermilk horseradish cream 158
　green pea & calendula soup with golden Peruvian potato shells 130
　tourte de pommes de terre à l'ail: potato & garlic pie 106

raspberries: pickled magnolia petal compote with mascarpone & triple lime sablés 172
rhubarb 222–4
　crispy peach amandine dumplings with pickled pink rhubarb & coconut yuzu whipped posset 34–6

rhubarb, raspberry & peppermint shrub 178
rødgrød med fløde 40
rose hips 224
rosemary 195

sage 195–6
salads
　baby new potato, egg & herb salad with basil buttermilk horseradish cream 158
　fattoush with charred lamb, pickled beetroot & whipped sumac feta 60
　fuyu persimmon & red pear wild greens salad with liquorice mint vinaigrette 26
　sunshine citrus salad with lemon balm vinaigrette 136
　tomato and mozzarella salad 76
salsa
　hanger steak, charred onions with dandelion green salsa 30
　out-of-this-world vegan tacos with sweet potato, salsa macha & coconut yogurt 116–18
saltbush 187
　saltbush tempura 50
samphire 198
　suimono with samphire & shrimp shinjo 48
scallops
　pan-seared scallops on silky avocado crema 140
　seared sea scallops with buttered naam-jim & lemon basil 162
sea greens 198–9
　sea buckthorn & champagne gelée 180
seeds: energize flatbreads 44
shrimp: suimono with samphire & shrimp shinjo 48
sorrel & watercress bisque 98
soup
　green pea & calendula soup with golden Peruvian potato shells 130
　root, rice, leek & nettle soup 96
　shiitake broth with aromatic herbs 72
　sorrel & watercress bisque 98
　spring borsch with nettles 12

suimono with samphire & shrimp shinjo 48
steak: hanger steak, charred onions with dandelion green salsa 30
strawberries: rødgrød med fløde 40
sumac-egusi drizzle with charred sweet potatoes 52
summer fruits: summer's day 132–5
sunflowers 211
　summer's day 132–5
sweet potatoes 204
curry leaf-crusted fish in a lemon myrtle coconut sauce with finger lime & sweet potato salad 114
　out-of-this-world vegan tacos with sweet potato, salsa macha & coconut yogurt 116–18
　polenta with bitter greens & pan-fried sweet potato cubes 138
　sumac-egusi drizzle with charred sweet potatoes 52
sweets: herbal apothecary sweets jar 91–2

tarragon 186–7
tempura: saltbush tempura 50
tomatoes
　allotment tomato, anchovy & Parmesan gratin 104
　Isle of Wight tomatoes with chamomile, ricotta, cherries & green almonds 166–8
　tomato and mozzarella salad 76
tulsi (holy basil) 193
turmeric 203–4

vegetables
corn, leek, cauli & chilli crisp chowder with preserved lemon gremolata 128
　my garden ratatouille 10
　root, rice, leek & nettle soup 96
　spring borsch with nettles 12
　vegetable garden tea cakes 144

water and land cress 212
　sorrel & watercress bisque 98

za'atar 194

ACKNOWLEDGEMENTS

Thank you for your generous contributions:
Emily van Oosterom www.pantheon.apothecary.co.nz for your stunning apothecary equipment.
Anna and John Boulter for your antique apothecary cabinet.

Ingredients/equipment donated by (all handles for Instagram): @NZyuzu, @theyuzuco, @Ironcladpan, @heilalavanilla and Russ Wilkinson @newworldnz, Bri Dimattina, @iatemygarden, Good Gear Produce @goodgearproduce and Crawford Farms Garden! Additional props loaned by: Thea Ceramics (www.thea-ceramics.com), Lil Ceramics (www.lilceramics.co.nz), Hayley Bridgeford @hayleybridgfordceramics), The Iron Clad Pan (www.ironcladpan.com), Fiona Hugues (www.fionahugues.com), and Grant Allen @grantallencookltd.

To all of you tasters and testers with huge thanks for your support, help and humour: Pam Fischer, Kyra Strasberg, Kimberly Soanes, Wendy and Dr Graham Dobson, Sequanna Manzenita and an exceptional cast from Matt Miller's @KitchenLingoBooks including Matt, Vani Murthy, Kayla Gonzalez and the ever-patient Grant Bernstein.

Special thanks for your advice and assistance: Sherry Yard, Rochelle Huppin, Felicity Spector, Suzanne Trocme, Kathy Kordalis, Elizabeth Falkner, Chris Manfield, Anne Maree Desmond, Rosalinda Monroy, Sue Knight, Mary Margaret Chappell, Janice Wald Henderson, Jim Dodge, Jonathan Willows and my generous, talented and decades-long dear friend Peter Gordon. Thanks also to Pala Forest Farm, New Zealand.

Many thanks to John Kennett, plus Sandrine Masella and the Operational Space Medicine Nutritional Specialists Sam McCaig and Natalie Hirsch of the Canadian Space Agency, for your mind-expanding knowledge on growing gravity-free edible gardens in space and beyond.

To my food shoot assistants: Laughlan Simmons, BA Taylor, Maude Hughes, rockstar chef Nicole Turner and my forager/florist/runner/designer Rebecca T Alexander – thank you from the heart.

Finally, my grateful thanks to my patient *TAC* team: the lovely senior editor and scrutinizer Pauline Bache, super senior in-house designer Yasia Williams, freelance designer Rachel Cross for the gorgeous rethink design, Danica MacAller for her delicately detailed line drawings, Nicola Shubrook for plant vetting quoting and to Manja Wachsmuth for her stunning and visionary photographs.

To my former publisher, mentor and dearest friend Jacqui Small, thank you, I am so grateful for the introduction to my witty, clever and kind new publisher Joanna Copestick, who has steadfastly steered this project to the finish!

And lastly, thank you to each and every one of my inspiring contributing chefs and medical doctors; thank you for helping *The Apothecary Chef* come to life!

The Apothecary Chef was created, cooked and photographed in New Zealand.